The State and the Paradox of Customary Law in Africa

Customary law and traditional authorities continue to play highly complex and contested roles in contemporary African states. Reversing the common preoccupation with studying the impact of the post/colonial state on customary regimes, this volume analyses how the interactions between state and non-state normative orders have shaped the everyday practices of the state. It argues that, in their daily work, local officials are confronted with a paradox of customary law: operating under politico-legal pluralism and limited state capacity, bureaucrats must often, paradoxically, deal with custom – even though the form and logic of customary rule is not easily compatible and frequently incommensurable with the form and logic of the state – in order to do their work as a state. Given the self-contradictory nature of this endeavour, officials end up processing, rather than solving, this paradox in multiple, inconsistent and piecemeal ways. Assembling inventive case studies on state-driven land reforms in South Africa and Tanzania, the police in Mozambique, witchcraft in southern Sudan, constitutional reform in South Sudan, Guinea's *longue durée* of changing state engagements with custom, and hybrid political orders in Somaliland, this volume offers important insights into the divergent strategies used by African officials in handling this paradox of customary law and, somehow, getting their work done.

Olaf Zenker is professor of social anthropology at the University of Fribourg, Switzerland. He has published on modern statehood, rule of law, bureaucracy, justice, land reform as well as conflict and identity formations in South Africa and Northern Ireland. His book publications include the co-edited volumes *South African homelands as frontiers: apartheid's loose ends in the postcolonial era* (Routledge, 2017), *Transition and justice: negotiating the terms of new beginnings in Africa* (Wiley-Blackwell, 2015) and *Beyond writing culture: current intersections of epistemologies and representational practices* (Berghahn Books, 2010), as well as the monograph *Irish/ness is all around us: language revivalism and the culture of ethnic identity in Northern Ireland* (Berghahn Books, 2013).

Markus Virgil Hoehne is lecturer at the Institute of Social Anthropology at the University of Leipzig, Germany. He works on conflict, identity, state formation, borderlands, transitional justice and forensic anthropology in Somalia. He is the author of *Between Somaliland and Puntland: marginalization, militarization and conflicting political visions* (Rift Valley Institute, 2015), the editor of a special issue on 'The effects of "statelessness": Dynamics of Somali politics, economy and society since 1991' (*Journal of Eastern African Studies*, 2013), and co-editor of *Borders and borderlands as resources in the Horn of Africa* (James Currey, 2010) and *Milk and peace, drought and war: Somali culture, society and politics* (Hurst, 2010).

'A tour de force of the most profound kind – *The State and the Paradox of Customary Law in Africa* offers audacious insights into the dilemmas and paradoxes of "living customary law" that have emerged as key concerns of the twenty-first century. [...] It offers profound interventions into the desperately needed terrain for rethinking the modernity of customary law and its implications for Africa and beyond.'

Kamari M. Clarke, Professor of Global and International Studies, Anthropology and Law and Legal Studies, Carleton University, Canada

'Zenker and Hoehne and their contributors have done an admirable job of trying to bring intellectual order into the analysis of a very complex and fraught topic. [...] The originality of Zenker and Hoehne's approach is evident in their carefully reasoned Introduction in which they propose innovative theoretical criteria for sorting out the issues involved.'

Sally Falk Moore, Emerita Professor of Anthropology, Harvard University, USA

'Bringing together legal pluralism and the anthropology of the state, the authors offer a fresh and stimulating perspective on the various interactions between African states and local customs, much more complex and developed than has been said before. They brilliantly explore the modes of state engagement with customs and chiefs.'

Jean-Pierre Olivier de Sardan, Professor of Anthropology (Directeur d'études), Ecole des Hautes Etudes en Sciences Sociales (EHESS) and Emeritus Director of Research, Centre National de la Recherche Scientifique, France

'Zenker and Hoehne have given us a major contribution to the study of the realities of legal pluralism in the context of the day-to-day business of the state. This innovative volume stands out for its in-depth examination of how state agents in Africa creatively enact spatiotemporal legal hybridity as part of their official work.'

Bertram Turner, Senior Research Fellow at the Department of Law and Anthropology, Max Planck Institute for Social Anthropology, Germany

'Zenker and Hoehne's volume provides a fresh and revitalizing analysis of contemporary customary law in Africa. *The State and the Paradox of Customary Law in Africa* innovatively investigates how the state, enmeshed in complex national and transnational structures of law and governance, is transformed by the agency of local actors strategizing in the arena of customary law.'

Richard Ashby Wilson, Professor of Anthropology and Law, University of Connecticut, USA

Cultural Diversity and Law
Series Editor: Prakash Shah, School of Law,
Queen Mary University of London, UK

Around the world, most states are faced with difficult issues arising out of cultural diversity in their territories. Within the legal field, such issues span across matters of private law through to public and constitutional law. At international level too there is now considerable jurisprudence regarding ethnic, religious and cultural diversity. In addition, there are several layers of legal control – from communal and religious regulation to state and international regulation. This multiplicity of norm setting has been variously termed legal pluralism, inter-legality or internormativity and provides a fascinating lens for academic analysis that links up to cultural diversity in new and interesting ways. The umbrella of cultural diversity encompasses various population groups throughout the world ranging from national, ethnic, religious or indigenous groupings. This series particularly welcomes work that is of comparative interest, concerning various state jurisdictions as well as different population groups.

Also in the series:

Access to Justice and Human Security
Cultural Contradictions in Rural South Africa
Sindiso Mnisi Weeks
ISBN 978-1-1380-6077-7

The Challenge of Legal Pluralism
Local dispute settlement and the Indian-state relationship in Ecuador
Marc Simon Thomas
ISBN 978-1-4724-8057-6

Legal Pluralism in the Holy City
Competing Courts, Forum Shopping, and Institutional Dynamics in Jerusalem
Ido Shahar
ISBN 978-1-4094-1052-2

Muslim Families, Politics and the Law
A Legal Industry in Multicultural Britain
Ralph Grillo
ISBN 978-1-4724-5121-7

www.routledge.com/Cultural-Diversity-and-Law/book-series/CULTDIV

The State and the Paradox of Customary Law in Africa

Edited by Olaf Zenker and
Markus Virgil Hoehne

LONDON AND NEW YORK

First published 2018
by Routledge
2 Park Square, Milton Park, Abingdon, Oxon OX14 4RN

and by Routledge
711 Third Avenue, New York, NY 10017

Routledge is an imprint of the Taylor & Francis Group, an informa business

© 2018 selection and editorial matter, Olaf Zenker and Markus Virgil Hoehne; individual chapters, the contributors

The right of Olaf Zenker and Markus Virgil Hoehne to be identified as the authors of the editorial material, and of the authors for their individual chapters, has been asserted in accordance with sections 77 and 78 of the Copyright, Designs and Patents Act 1988.

All rights reserved. No part of this book may be reprinted or reproduced or utilized in any form or by any electronic, mechanical, or other means, now known or hereafter invented, including photocopying and recording, or in any information storage or retrieval system, without permission in writing from the publishers.

Trademark notice: Product or corporate names may be trademarks or registered trademarks, and are used only for identification and explanation without intent to infringe.

British Library Cataloguing-in-Publication Data
A catalogue record for this book is available from the British Library

Library of Congress Cataloging-in-Publication Data
Names: Zenker, Olaf, editor. | Hèohne, Markus Virgil, editor.
Title: The state and the paradox of customary law in Africa / edited by Olaf Zenker and Markus Virgil Hoehne.Description: Abingdon, Oxon ; New York, NY : Routledge, 2018. | Series: Cultural diversity and law | Includes bibliographical references and index.
Identifiers: LCCN 2017041704 | ISBN 9781409468639 (hardback)
Subjects: LCSH: Customary law--Africa, Sub-Saharan.Classification: LCC KQC105 .S73 2018 | DDC 340.50967--dc23LC record available at https://lccn.loc.gov/2017041704

ISBN: 978-1-4094-6863-9 (hbk)
ISBN: 978-1-315-55249-1 (ebk)

Typeset in Galliard
by Fish Books Ltd.

Contents

Notes on contributors   ix

1 Processing the paradox: when the state has to deal with customary law   1
OLAF ZENKER AND MARKUS VIRGIL HOEHNE

2 Bush-level bureaucrats in South African land restitution: implementing state law under chiefly rule   41
OLAF ZENKER

3 State police and tradition in post-war Mozambique: the dilemmas of claiming sovereignty in legal pluralistic contexts   64
HELENE MARIA KYED

4 Mixing oil and water? Colonial state justice and the challenge of witchcraft accusations in central Equatoria, southern Sudan   87
CHERRY LEONARDI

5 When the state is forced to deal with local law: approaches of and challenges for state actors in emerging South Sudan   109
KATRIN SEIDEL

6 Co-opted, abolished, democratized: the Guinean state's strategies to manage local elders   139
ANITA SCHROVEN

7 State-orchestrated access to land dispute settlement in Africa: land conflicts and new-wave land reform in Tanzania   163
RASMUS HUNDSBÆK PEDERSEN

8 One country, two systems: hybrid political orders and legal and political friction in Somaliland   184
MARKUS VIRGIL HOEHNE

9 The complexity of legal pluralist settings: an afterword   213
   JANINE UBINK

Index   227

Notes on contributors

Markus Virgil Hoehne is lecturer at the Institute of Social Anthropology at the University of Leipzig, Germany. He works on conflict, identity, state formation, borderlands, transitional justice and forensic anthropology in Somalia. He is the author of *Between Somaliland and Puntland: Marginalization, Militarization and Conflicting Political Visions* (Rift Valley Institute, 2015), the editor of a special issue on 'The effects of "statelesness": dynamics of Somali politics, economy and society since 1991' (*Journal of Eastern African Studies*, 2013), and co-editor of *Borders and borderlands as resources in the Horn of Africa* (James Currey, 2010) and *Milk and peace, drought and war: Somali culture, society and politics* (Hurst, 2010).

Helene Maria Kyed is a social anthropologist and senior researcher at the Danish Institute for International Studies (DIIS). She works on traditional authority, state formation, policing and justice provision in Southern Africa, and more recently in Myanmar, particularly interrogating the political dynamics of order-making in legally plural contexts. Among her publications are the books *Policing and the politics of order-making* (Routledge, 2015), *The dynamics of legal pluralism in Mozambique* (Kapicua, 2011) and *State recognition and democratization in Sub-Saharan Africa: a new dawn for traditional authorities?* (Palgrave, 2007).

Cherry Leonardi is associate professor in African history at Durham University in the UK. She works on the history of South Sudan and Uganda, with particular interests in traditional authority, witchcraft, conflict, local justice, state formation, boundaries and land governance. She is the author of *Dealing with government in South Sudan: histories of chiefship, community and state* (James Currey, 2013) and co-author of *Dividing communities in South Sudan and northern Uganda: boundary disputes and land governance* (Rift Valley Institute, 2016).

Rasmus Hundsbæk Pedersen is a post-doctoral researcher at the Danish Institute for International Studies (DIIS) and Roskilde University. His did his PhD on the implementation of Tanzania's 1999 land reform. Rasmus currently works on the political economy of land and extractive resource investments in sub-Saharan Africa with a focus on the role of policy-making and implementation. He is involved in two research projects, namely 'Hierarchies of rights, land and largescale natural resource investments in Africa' (2015–2018), focusing on investments into natural gas and energy, and 'Timber rush: private forestry on village land' (2016–2020), focusing on large-scale timber investments. Rasmus has mainly worked in East Africa.

Anita Schroven is researcher at the Max Planck Institute for Social Anthropology, Halle/Saale, Germany. She works on repeated conflicts and interventions, including the recent international intervention into the West African Ebola outbreak, especially the conceptualizations and practices with normalcy, exception and crisis in Sierra Leone and Guinea. She studies researchers' and interveners' practice of science, humanitarianism as well as knowledge production. She is the author of *Women after war: gender mainstreaming and the social construction of identity in contemporary Sierra Leone* (Lit Verlag, 2006) and a forthcoming book on *Identity politics at the margins of the state: the case of Guinea*.

Katrin Seidel is a post-doctoral research fellow at the Department of Law and Anthropology, Max Planck Institute for Social Anthropology, and was a fellow at Käte Hamburger Kolleg/Centre for Global Cooperation Research (2015/16). Based on her interdisciplinary background (law and African/Asian studies), her research is situated at the intersection of legal pluralism, heterogeneous statehood and governance. Her studies are concerned with interdependent relationships between plural normative and judicial orders at different levels of regulations and with intertwinements of respective social actors involved. She is the author of *Rechtspluralismus in Äthiopien: Interdependenzen zwischen Islamischem Recht und staatlichem Recht* (Koeppe, 2013). Her current research focus is on 'South Sudan's and Somaliland's constitutional geneses: a comparative analysis'.

Janine Ubink is a law professor/legal anthropologist at the University of California, Irvine (UCI) Law School. Her research focuses on legal pluralism, traditional authorities, land management, gender, transitional justice and rule of law reforms, with a focus on Ghana, Namibia, Malawi, Somalia, and South Africa. Janine is the President of the international Commission on Legal Pluralism. Among her publications are the books *In the land of the chiefs: customary law, land conflicts, and the role of the state in peri-urban Ghana* (Leiden, 2008), *Legalizing land rights: Local* *practices, state responses and tenure security in Africa, Asia and Latin America* (Leiden, 2009) and *Customary justice: perspectives on legal empowerment* (Leiden, 2011).

Olaf Zenker is professor of social anthropology at the University of Fribourg, Switzerland. He has published on modern statehood, rule of law, bureaucracy, justice, land reform as well as conflict and identity formations in South Africa and Northern Ireland. His book publications include the co-edited volumes *South African homelands as frontiers: apartheid's loose ends in the postcolonial era* (Routledge, 2017), *Transition and justice: negotiating the terms of new beginnings in Africa* (Wiley-Blackwell, 2015) and *Beyond writing culture: current intersections of epistemologies and representational practices* (Berghahn Books, 2010), as well as the monograph *Irish/ness is all around us: language revivalism and the culture of ethnic identity in Northern Ireland* (Berghahn Books, 2013).

1 Processing the paradox

When the state has to deal with customary law

Olaf Zenker and Markus Virgil Hoehne

Introduction

Customary law in Africa is not what it used to be. In a sense, this is a self-evident truth. Customary law is typically defined as a constantly evolving, usually unwritten and often partly uncertain normative order, observed as it is at any given moment in time within a population, that has been formed by regular social behaviour and the development of an accompanying sense of obligation (Woodman 2011: 10–18). As such, customary law in Africa and elsewhere is bound to change continuously. Customary law today should not be what it was in the past. Yet the historicity of 'customary law', both as an empirical and conceptual phenomenon, is less trivial when considered from another direction. Despite evoking, as the term 'custom' does, the image of an immemorial and immutable normative practice of unbroken antiquity, historical and anthropological research as well as legal practice have forcefully shown over the past decades that customary law is, indeed, dynamic, fluid, the outcome of multiple and contradictory interactions between various sets of actors (including the state), and generally hard to 'find' or ascertain in the lives of those said to follow it. No wonder that the quest for customary law has 'troubled researchers, administrators, lawyers, and judges alike, from the colonial period until the present' (Ubink 2011b: 85–86).

Customary law today surely is no longer what is used to be in the colonial imagination. Then it consisted of a set of officially recognized rules, procedures, institutions and office holders, identified on the basis of expert testimonies and preserved in commission reports, handbooks, academic texts (including ethnographies), restatements, codes or developing case law (also including expert witnessing) in order to ensure some legal certainty. *This* customary law was upheld by the state as valid on the condition that it did not challenge colonial overrule. As such, it had to be ensured that customary law was not contrary to legislation or public policy, nor repugnant to 'natural justice, equity and good conscience' – as the so-called repugnancy clause read, for instance, for colonial Ghana, Nigeria and Sierra Leone (Allott 1984: 59; Mamdani 1996: 115; Ubink 2011b: 84–85; Diala 2017: 4). Decades of careful historical and anthropological deconstruction have shown this version of customary law, now dismissively described as 'official customary law', to be a colonial invention that emerged from what June Starr and Jane Collier describe as 'historical struggles between native elites and their colonial or postcolonial overlords'. It is to be distinguished from 'indigenous law', 'precontact native law' (Starr and Collier 1989: 8–9). Multiple versions of 'official customary law' live on in postcolonial Africa, but the 'living customary law' – that is, what is actually observed with some sense of obligation and continuously adapted by people in their everyday life – has emerged as a matter of concern (and care) for social-scientific and legal scholarship and contemporary jurisprudence (Woodman 2012: 36). Many contemporary debates of customary law in South Africa, for example, now hinge on the notion of the 'living customary law': academic and policy-oriented publications (e.g. Claassens and Cousins 2008; Himonga 2011), introductory legal textbooks (e.g. Himonga and Nhlapo 2014), and even constitutional jurisprudence.[1] The difference between 'official' and 'living laws' is acknowledged, and only 'living customary law' is to be recognized as valid under South Africa's Constitution.[2]

The field of customary law – in Africa and beyond – has become ever more complex and unclear. It is a hodgepodge of multiplying perspectives, positions and practices, constituted by a plethora of documents, descriptions and (legal) decisions, all caught up in opaque dynamics between (post)colonial contaminations and current normative realities, between the official and the living. It is an assortment of uncertain sorts. 'What is customary law? Where can we find it? How to study it? How to bring it into the state realm?' (Ubink 2011b: 86). Academics who study customary law often enough get away with pointing out the problems and pitfalls of customary law, and with generating more questions than answers. This is a luxury that many practitioners, notably state officials in Africa, have not been able to afford. In their daily work, such public servants have had to deal with the reality of customary law in multiple settings and in numerous ways, both under colonialism and within their respective postcolonial realities. Whether or not they have liked it, whether they just wanted to get on with their business of 'doing the state', many local bureaucrats have found themselves in a position in which they could not really evade the realm or the rule of the 'customary'. Thus,

---

[1] See *Bhe and Others v. Khayelitsha Magistrate and Others* 2005 (1) SA 580 (CC), para 87. See also *Alexkor Ltd and Another v. Richtersveld Community and Others* 2004 (5) SA 460 (CC), paras 52–57. For discussions of this development, see Himonga (2011) and Zenker (forthcoming).

[2] In a recent article, however, Anthony Diala (2017) criticizes this conceptual distinction between official and living customary law, arguing that, as an adaptation to socio-economic changes (including state law), the living customary law can be as 'distorted' as official customary law. Diala's point is well taken: neither type of law is immune to adaptation. Nevertheless, the terminological distinction remains useful because it highlights the real difference between the two kinds of customary law that is introduced through what we describe below as the 'jurispathic' nature of state recognition.

states in Africa have often had to engage with customary law and somehow handle the contradictions emerging from this encounter – in short: the state had to process what appears from its perspective as a paradox of customary law, as we elaborate below – in order to, ultimately, get its own work done *as a state*. This focus on the everyday workings of 'the state' in its dealings with customary law constitutes the subject matter of this book.

The anthropology of the state has recently gained considerable momentum. There has been, of course, a longstanding interdisciplinary research tradition on various facets of statehood in Africa (Anders and Zenker 2015; Bayart 1993; Bayart et al. 1999; Bellagamba and Klute 2008; Chabal and Daloz 1999; Doornbos 2006; Hagmann and Hoehne 2009; Hagmann and Péclard 2010; Herbst 2000; Meagher 2012; Young 2012). We see our project in close alignment with the decidedly empirical (ideally, ethnographic) interest in 'states at work' (Bierschenk and Olivier de Sardan 2014; see also Blundo and Le Meur 2009; Anders 2010; De Herdt and Olivier de Sardan 2015b; Beek, Göpfert, Owen and Steinberg 2017). That is, we start from a curiosity in the daily functioning of state services through the mundane, day-to-day practices of public servants, bureaucrats and state officials – terms we use interchangeably to identify people officially acting in the name of the state and in orientation towards its image. We thereby draw on the state-in-society approach of Joel Migdal and Klaus Schlichte (2005), who propose a post-Weberian conception of the state, describing it as a field of power marked by the use and threat of violence and shaped by dialectics between its two key elements:

1 the image of a unitary, territorially bounded, supreme law-making organization with compulsive membership that claims the monopoly of legitimate violence and representation of the people; and
2 the enormously variable practices realized in ostensible orientation towards such an image. Actual practices are undertaken by, on the one hand, 'officials' who are formally empowered by the state's image and, on the other hand, the state's 'subjects' with whom the officials engage (see esp. Migdal and Schlichte 2005: 15).

As this characterization of the state emphasizes, the image of the state typically claims for itself supreme law-making powers. This claim has been identified and heavily criticized as 'the ideology of legal centralism' by legal pluralists since the 1980s (Griffiths 1986). Below, we discuss in more detail how this typical article of faith in the arsenal of statecraft importantly pre-structures the politico-legal field in which state officials engage with customary law, without predetermining the ultimate state practices on the ground.

Against this general background of focus and approach, we develop our argument in six steps. First, we briefly rehearse the arguments made since the 1980s in critical engagements with 'official customary law'. These were often phrased initially as 'inventions of tradition', and then gave way to a broader conceptualization of customary law as evolving through continuous (re)imaginations by multiple actors of their own pasts and the pasts of others. We argue that it has been crucially important to demonstrate how colonial constructions of custom facilitated and entrenched colonial rule and the advancement of capitalist interests. Indeed, this has been the dominant perspective on the matter advanced for some four decades. But it has arguably overshadowed another important facet of the complicated interrelation between statehood and the kingdom of custom which we take up here: the practical difficulties that emerge in any attempt to conjoin their different normative forms and logics.

Second, we then turn quickly to an exploration of the place of 'traditional authorities' within African political landscapes. We contrast Mahmood Mamdani's (1996) thesis of traditional authorities as persisting decentralized rural despots with other voices that have hailed them as representatives of African democracy. Representative perspectives from the latter camp see traditional authorities as accessible decentralized institutions within failing states and as actors with basic legitimacy, who, precisely because of their non-democratic nature, might further Africa's democratization locally. Here, we do not conclude that traditional authorities are either pro- or anti-democratic. Instead, we emphasize how such discussions about democratization, traditional authorities and customary law are very often normative in their approach and therefore unhelpful for analysing socio-political developments on the ground. Rather, we propose to take pluralism as the conceptual starting point for the analysis of complex normative systems, both political and legal (Benda-Beckmann 2002). Rendered this way, it no longer makes sense to ask *if* custom and tradition support or hinder democracy, as if they might only work in one direction: Instead, we must focus on the concrete entanglements of custom and tradition with states in their multifarious developments.

Third, we broker a discussion of legal pluralism. Legal pluralists have argued against the state ideology of legal centralism, demanding instead other non-state normative orders to be also given the full force of 'law' within a descriptive theory of strong legal pluralism as well as within the state. Broadening the focus beyond the classic legal pluralism of (post)-colonial states towards the general problem of how any legal order manages to engage with other normative orders (and taking inspiration from discussions pertaining to private international law), we highlight the 'jurispathic' nature of the state. That is, in defining law (jurisgenesis), the state inevitably kills off other normative orientations. In alignment with debates within the field of customary law, we argue that any attempt by the state to ascertain the 'living customary law' inevitably turns it into the next version of 'official customary law'. This forces state officials, when dealing with customary law, to manage awkward gaps regarding legitimacy, justice and historical authenticity.

On this basis, the fourth section sets out to characterize what we call 'the paradox of customary law'. This paradox emerges from the specific interrelation between the divergent forms and logics of custom and statehood. Yet from the perspective of the state, the 'problem' appears to emerge from inherent characteristics of 'the regime of custom', the state's Other. This paradox, we argue, materializes on three descending levels of abstraction:

1. as a paradox of liberal statecraft, where the choice for the state between acknowledging or ignoring customary orders remains indeterminate;
2. as a paradox of recognition by the jurispathic state (and one that weighs more heavily in postcolonies than in Euro-America) in which custom is killed even in the attempt to nurture it; and
3. as a paradox of policultural states at work, in that state officials operating under politico-legal pluralism in many local settings quite often must deal with the reign of custom simply to get their own work done.

The fifth section introduces a typology of common modes of state engagement – ignorance, awareness, recognition and rejection – which may characterize the state's attempt to process, in practice, the paradox of customary law. While state officials may draw on these modes as institutionalized official norms ('the rules of the game'), they may also use their discretion with regard to the practical norms guiding their actual practice ('the game of the rules') to deviate and transform official policies and prescriptions in order to manage their interactions with the world of custom. Using this typology of state engagements with customary law, the sixth section explores its usefulness through refocusing the chapters of this volume with regard to the question of how, in the different cases studies presented, the state in its many instantiations has to deal with customary law and thereby attempts to get its multiple jobs done.

From the invention of tradition to the custom of (re)imagination

Customary law in Africa has often been portrayed, and typically presented itself, as being in historical continuity with truly African cultures and traditions, appearing, in extreme renderings, as a relic of a timeless and static precolonial past. However, since the 1970s and especially the 1980s, a growing number of anthropological and historical publications have profoundly questioned this image of custom, highlighting instead its creation and invention during the colonial period through heterogeneous historical struggles between, and among, colonizers and the colonized.[3]

Important works – by now iconic for this revisionist historiography – include Francis Snyder's (1981a) analysis of the creation of customary law in

---

3   For an early and influential review of this literature see Merry (1991).

Senegal. Snyder argues that customary law in Senegal developed in close alignment with the locally transforming political economy (see also Snyder 1981b). Focusing on the Banjal Diola of the Casamance area in the southwest, Snyder demonstrates that their precolonial life centred on the recruitment of dependents through patrifiliation, fostering and capture, and the circulation of land and reproductive capacity between productive units for rice cultivation as part of the subsistence economy. However, since the late nineteenth century colonialism and the international market increasingly penetrated and radically changed the local setting: the colonial imposition of a cash payment for the head tax forced locals into wage labour, while the emerging international trade in rice, rubber, palm products and peanuts led to a drastic decline in Casamance rice production (as cheaper rice was imported from Asia) and the need to engage in migratory wage labour. Such changes produced new patterns of land use and ownership, and it was in this context that 'customary law' emerged in a body of court cases. For example, Snyder documents a court case from the 1950s, in which the 'rain priest' was established as 'the master of the land' with proprietary interests under 'customary law'. Historically, rain priests and other such office-holders had received 'total services' – that is, *prestation* in the Maussian sense (Mauss 1990 [1924]) – in exchange for ritually ensuring the well-being of the inhabitants in a delimited area; but the office holders did not 'own' the land area under their protection. Snyder argues that this creation of customary law was supported by powerful African elites (like court interpreters) with similar class interests to those of the rain priests. At the same time, such 'backward traditions' also legitimized the need for modernization, presented as depending 'necessarily and fundamentally upon foreign capital and the intervention of the state' (Snyder 1981a: 75).

Martin Chanock's (1985) *Law, Custom, and Social Order: The Colonial Experience in Malawi and Zambia* is another key text. Chanock argues that customary law – far from being an immutable precolonial survival – evolved from the late nineteenth century through the interactions of colonial administrators (who were seeking to understand and use African customs for colonial domination) and native Africans (typically male elders, who were presenting their versions of 'tradition' in a bid to manage profound social changes to their own advantage). During the early years of colonialism in Central Africa, customary regimes still operated according to fluid and shifting procedures and principles; this flexibility was taken as proof by British colonial administrators that such regimes were primitive, or certainly less developed than British laws. Accordingly, the colonizers resisted devolving authority to African chiefs and heard as many cases as possible before the colonial courts. Initially providing progressive judgments for people in subaltern positions (such as women seeking divorce), colonial jurisprudence challenged local systems of control of men over women, masters over slaves, and of witchfinders over witches. By the 1920s, colonial laws and policies had considerably undermined the power of traditional authorities, fomenting unrest and thereby threatening the stability of colonial rule. In the context of rapidly expanding market relations, an explosion in migratory wage labour and increasing Westernization, colonial officials decided to formally recognize African courts and customary law to shore up traditional authorities and thus to stabilize the situation. The increasingly rigid customary law that came to be implemented in African courts as 'an idealization of the past developed as an attempt to cope with social dislocation' (Chanock 1985: 4) began ruling in favour of preserving customary marriages and upholding the authority of husbands and male elders.[4]

While Chanock emphasizes the importance of African participation in the making of customary law, his book still contains more British than local African voices and does not fully address the internal diversities of the African population as shaped by ethnicity, class or region. A focus on the regional diversity of African contributions to the transformation of customary law is at the heart of another landmark study: Sally Falk Moore's (1986) *Social Facts and Fabrications: 'Customary' Law on Kilimanjaro, 1880–1980*. It focuses on the Chagga of Mount Kilimanjaro, who were cattle-herders and agriculturalists trading regionally in slaves and ivory before being drawn into the money economy and cash cropping under German colonial rule from 1886. Moore demonstrates how local law, initially flexible and negotiable, became institutionalized under British colonial rule after 1916, when customary courts came to exist alongside European courts, and grew increasingly rigid. In the context of the newly introduced cash economy (based on coffee), population growth and severe land shortage, Chagga chiefs emerged with a transformed level of executive and judicial authority. Through this process, which lasted into postcolonial times, the meanings of 'customary law' changed quite substantially: whereas in precolonial times it was closely related to local Chagga life and culture, it increasingly came to reflect the gap between official government versions and the living laws practised at the local level.

These and other works have highlighted the locally variable nature of 'law as the cutting edge of colonialism' (Chanock 1985: 4). As such, the historical creation of customary law has been revealed as advancing both the interests of colonial domination in its quest to co-opt local authorities for 'hegemony on a shoestring' (Berry 1992) and the ruling interests within an expansive capitalist world economy, especially with regard to the control of property (primarily land) and labour (Roberts and Mann 1991: 23–32; see also Snyder 1984). Studies like these have been perceived as following the contemporaneous paradigm of 'the invention of tradition' (Hobsbawm and Ranger 1983). That is, they build on Terence Ranger's assertion that '[w]hat

---

4   See Chanock (2001) for an illuminating analysis of South African legal culture in the early twentieth century, covering all areas of law, including state versions of customary law.

were called customary law, customary land-rights, customary political structure and so on, were in fact *all* invented by colonial codification' (Ranger 1983: 250, original emphasis).

Although influential, the term 'invention' rapidly also attracted criticism for its connotations of conscious projects of social and cultural construction. Worse, 'invention' was said to highlight the power and agency of colonial forces and local elites, while depicting ordinary locals under colonial rule as gullible subjects; and it downplayed continuous and multifarious historical processes of reinterpretation and reformulation against more singular events. Hence, only a decade after the publication of *The Invention of Tradition*, Terence Ranger (1993), self-critically declared his preference for the term 'imagination' – drawing on Benedict Anderson (1991) – over 'invention' because customary law was better described as having been '*imagined*, by many different people and over a long period of time. These multiple imaginations were in tension with each other and in constant contestation to define the meaning of what had been imagined – to imagine it further' (Ranger 1993: 81, original emphasis).

Moreover, as Thomas Spear (2003) argues, the room for inventing anew allegedly old traditions that were conveniently adjusted to the interests of colonial powers and African elites was severely limited by the lack of coercive power on the ground. For an 'invented' tradition to gain sufficient local legitimacy, it needed to use pre-existing local materials, traditions and customs. It is for this reason that the (re)production of customary law is thus typically characterized by transformations involving changes *and* continuities rather than by pure inventions of completely new forms (see Moore 1986: 316–317; Pels 1996; Hamilton 1998). For this reason, Günther Schlee (2004: 148) suggests speaking of 'constructions' rather than 'inventions' to highlight the frequent need to reuse 'old building materials'.

Mahmood Mamdani emphasizes a contested form of 'reproduction':

> The substantive customary law was neither a kind of historical and cultural residue carried like excess baggage by groups resistant to 'modernization' nor a pure colonial 'invention' or 'fabrication,' arbitrarily manufactured without regard to any historical backdrop and contemporary realities. Instead it was reproduced through an ongoing series of confrontations between claimants with a shared history but not always the same notion of it.
>
> (Mamdani 1996: 118)

For the sake of furthering this longstanding discussion, it is worth recalling that 'tradition', in comprising the realm of customary law, stems from the Latin verb *tradere*, which means 'to pass something [over]' or 'to hand something [over]'. Tradition, therefore, can be imagined as resulting from a process composed of actions that connect the present with the past. Such actions might well include 'strategic claims' to the past (see also Weber 1978

[1921]: 227; Dijk and Rouveroy van Nieuwaal 1999: 4). Customary law can thus be seen as continuously evolving through the complex and contested (re)imaginations, by multiple sets of actors, of their own past(s) and the past(s) of others at various scales of historical depth; such (re)imaginations are attempts to adjust to the present and provide for a future that remains in line with what can be claimed legitimately as 'the past'. As Helene Kyed and Lars Buur argue, in this way 'tradition' and 'custom' can be seen 'less as a question of simple continuity, and more as symbolic processes that take past equivalences for granted and produce them anew by reinterpreting them according to current requirements', while acknowledging that in emic definitions of tradition 'some form of reference to a "common past" – deeply united, benign, and unchanged – seems to be a constant' (Kyed and Buur 2007: 24).

As this brief recapitulation shows, research over several decades has demonstrated how 'customary law' – continuously (re)imagined and transformed under colonial rule in Africa – effectively 'consolidated the noncustomary power of chiefs in the colonial administration' (Mamdani 1996: 110) and thereby stabilized the colonial state, which was often rather weak on the ground. Moreover, this literature has also shown how this incessant (re)imagination of customary law simultaneously benefitted the economic (often capitalist) interests of metropolitan, colonial and African elites after the official abolition of slavery during the nineteenth century through the effective 'traditional' control of labour and access to land. Such control provided public work, migratory wage labour for farms, mines and emerging industries, and cash flows to be locally tapped and diverted (see Roberts and Mann 1991). There is no doubt that such instrumentalist arguments have been crucially important, offering a deeper understanding of why and how various sets of highly unequal and differently positioned actors in colonial and postcolonial Africa have engaged with customary law.

However, such instrumentalist readings of the (re)making of customary law have not exhausted fully the problem of the relation between the modern state and customary law in Africa. Put differently, the prevalence of instrumentalist arguments concerning the role of the kingdom of custom under colonial rule has overshadowed the potential analysis of the practical difficulties that follow from the attempt to conjoin their different normative forms and logics. Before dealing with this interrelation in more detail, we briefly engage the specific place of traditional authorities within the modern African state.

Traditional authorities between decentralized despotism and democratic political cultures

If the literature on customary law has focused on its continuous (re)imagination against the backdrop of colonial transformation, it can be said that much research on African chiefs has engaged a closely related question – the changing role played by 'traditional authorities' in African political cultures. The spectrum of positions has been quite broad, ranging from strong denunciations of chiefs as anti-democratic despots to celebrations of traditional authorities as either embodiments of a specifically African democracy or as paradoxically improving the responsiveness of democratic governments precisely because they themselves are unelected.

The denunciation of chiefs as decentralized despots, transformed beyond recognition under colonialism, is most prominently associated with Mahmood Mamdani's (1996) *Citizen and Subject: Contemporary Africa and the Legacy of Late Colonialism*. Mamdani argues that apartheid in South Africa, far from being exceptional to the African colonial experience, merely exhibited in extreme form the logic of indirect rule developed as British policy by Lord Lugard around 1900 and used more widely after World War I. This system, similarly implemented also in French, Belgian, Portuguese and Italian colonies, led to what Mamdani calls 'the bifurcated state' which distinguished firstly between non-native colonial rulers and native majority populations on the basis of race, and secondly between numerous tribal groupings within the native population, each to be ruled by their 'traditional leaders' under 'customary law'. With 'natives' in rural areas subordinated as the 'subjects' of tribalized, and thereby fragmented, traditional customary regimes, urban areas emerged as the realm of primarily non-native 'citizens' to be administered according to modern rule-of-law standards. This bifurcated legal system came to pervade the entire colonial state.

> Institutionally, civic power was organized along the principle of differentiation, the customary on the basis of the fusion of power. Ideologically, civic power claimed to defend rights, and customary power to enforce custom. [...] Yet civic and customary power were always joined under the same overall colonial authority. Without taking into account the backing of civic power, one cannot understand the stamina of customary power.
>
> (Mamdani 1996: 60)

Building on the decentralized exercise of precolonial African power, colonial powers fused legislative, executive and judicial, as well as administrative and fiscal, powers within the single authority of chiefs, thus creating a system of 'decentralized despotism' exempted from any proper rule-of-law checks and balances (ibid.: 37–61).

While lack of colonial personnel and limited resources made it necessary for colonial states to use local collaborators, Mamdani argues that this deeply anti-democratic system of indirect rule was not without alternatives. In fact, during the second half of the nineteenth century, some strata of Western-educated African elites emerged both in British and French colonies. Given the initially strong emphasis on Europe's 'civilizing mission', legitimizing the colonial project and leading to attempts to bypass and undermine African chiefs and their customary courts (see above), many of these educated Africans hoped for a partnership with colonial powers that would lead to independence (Mamdani 1996: 74–5). However, from around 1900 onwards, European powers profoundly shifted their policy orientations, moving from their 'civilizing mission' to an obsession with law-and-order, and from a concern with 'progress' to one of 'power' (ibid.: 50, 74). This shift, as Mamdani describes it, was motivated by the Europeans' growing realization that native cultural assimilation led to resurgence rather than to an effective subordination of the African population. As the problem of rule in the colonial context was hence accentuated rather than eased by alliance with educated African elites, local chiefs emerged as culturally more legitimate and more easily controllable allies, allowing European powers to divide and, thereby, to continuously rule. During the first half of the twentieth century, at the very time that African elites shifted from tribe to race as the organizing principle of oppositional politics (and thence to Pan-Africanist nationalism), colonial statecraft moved 'in an opposite direction, from race to tribe as the guiding point in adapting its strategy of native control to a new situation' (ibid.: 100).

It is one of Mamdani's key contentions that the deeply anti-democratic system of decentralized despotism survived independence, as the bifurcated state was merely deracialized but not truly democratized. Within 'conservative states' such as Nigeria and Côte d'Ivoire, the policy of the final colonial years was continued, reconciling traditional leaders and middle-class nationalists through some electoral reform, while the customary administration of chiefs effectively continued. In such conservative postcolonies, shifts between civilian and military regimes merely 'represented a change within a broader continuity: from a decentralized civilian despotism to a centralized military despotism' (Mamdani 1996: 107). In contrast, 'radical states' such as Guinea, Somalia, Tanzania and Mozambique attempted to erase the legacy of colonial indirect rule, often replacing chiefs with centrally-appointed party cadres (see the chapters in this volume by Anita Schroven, Markus Hoehne, Rasmus Pedersen and Helene Kyed). However, maintains Mamdani, these attempts to subordinate state administration to the will of a political party typically degenerated into state-party rule, in the course of which party cadre too came to exercise a fused power as both political representative and enforcement officer; the failed attempt to transform decentralized despotism merely produced centralized despotism (ibid.: 106–108).

Apart from some wholeheartedly supportive voices (e.g. Ntsebeza 2005), Mamdani's position has been subjected to extensive criticism. Mamdani's critics reject the sweeping generalizations of his argument for missing local complexities, including the numerous links between rural and urban constituencies and elites. His critics argue too that traditional authorities have not been just the willing agents of colonial and postcolonial states, but have also defended their communities against state intrusions (Leonardi

2013). More fundamentally, the different logics operating according to Mamdani, on (and for) citizens under modern law and those operating on (and against) subjects under customary law are suspected of having been less neatly separated in practice than in Mamdani's rendition. As Carolyn Logan (2009: 103) argues, traditional and state authorities are quite often 'two sides of the same coin'. Using survey data from 15 African countries she shows that 'Africans who live under these dual systems of authority do not draw a sharp distinction between hereditary chiefs and elected local government officials as most analysts would expect' (ibid.: 113). In her view 'Africans are thus creating for themselves, whether deliberately or by default, hybrid political systems that integrate the traditional systems with which they are deeply familiar and their newly minted electoral regimes' (ibid.: 123). Against Mamdani's view, there is evidence that state administration and local chiefs have accommodated each other and created a hybrid language that both sides can share – a process that Peter Pels (1996) describes for the Walunguru in colonial Tanzania as a 'pidginization of politics'. In a similar vein, Rijk van Dijk and Adriaan van Rouveroy van Nieuwaal (1999) characterize the 'mutational work' of chiefs as brokers as one of their key activities. However, the practical need for hybridization evidently presupposes (rather than refutes) the imagination of forms and logics as separate and different. Hence, we emphasize that such conversion work requires, in practice, the often creative transformation and alignment of such divergent forms and logics – something we explore below in terms of an interplay between 'official' and 'practical norms'.

The more general denunciation of African chiefs as intrinsically anti-democratic has also been criticized severely. Some authors argue that chiefs can supplement the frequently deficient states in Africa, allowing for a more authentic indigenous political expression (Ray and Rouveroy van Nieuwaal 1996); others celebrate traditional authorities as embodying specifically African forms of democracy based on non-violent consensus in contrast to the imported (and violence-based) modern state form (Skalník 1996). Such positive evaluations of chiefs' potentials to foster democracy also gained currency in the context of the democratization wave that has swept through sub-Saharan Africa since the 1990s. While multi-party democracy was (re)introduced in many states, Structural Adjustment Programmes and the neoliberal roll-back of the state simultaneously celebrated forms of (democratic) decentralization. The latter aimed at enhancing the participation of the local population in decision-making processes, thereby fostering transparency, accountability and responsiveness, and aiding efficient and effective policy implementation (Ribot 2002: 3). Especially in the context of weak or failed states, traditional authorities have been hailed by donor organizations, NGOs, and researchers as filling the gap of absent governments (Lutz and Lindner 2004). Under these conditions too, traditional authorities have experienced 'a new dawn' (Buur and Kyed 2007) in many African states since the 1990s, often leading to their formal recognition even by states that had attempted to abolish them in the initial years after independence (Rösel and Trotha 1999; Ubink 2008).

Looking at the contemporary situation of chiefs in Africa with a particular focus on Zambia, Kate Baldwin (2016) argues that traditional authorities can facilitate the democratic responsiveness of African states, not because they are in some way 'democratic' but, paradoxically, precisely because they are not. This is so because politicians also need to win rural votes, and thus have to respond to rural voters' demands which are often concerned with basic infrastructure and social services. Yet given the widespread weakness of African state bureaucracies on the ground, it is neither easy nor quick to improve local amenities. Politicians have difficulty responding to their rural constituencies, and turn for help to an established local institution: the chiefs. Given that traditional authorities often hold their positions permanently, and hence do not worry about being re-elected, they are uniquely positioned to organize local public goods provision in partnership with elected leaders and thereby facilitate these desired longer-term investments.[5] Hence, Baldwin argues 'democratic accountability in rural Africa operates better on the back of nondemocratic foundations. Politicians must work with traditional leaders if they are to provide the goods and services rural voters want' (ibid.: 17).

Looking at the literature, we see that traditional authorities in Africa have been defined quite inconsistently: as deeply democratic, paradoxically anti-democratic-and-thereby-democratic, and as deeply anti-democratic. However, numerous case studies have demonstrated the complexities of African political cultures on the ground, comprising traditional authorities and local governments in mutual entanglements that arguably defy easy categorization as either 'democratic' or 'anti-democratic' (Trotha 1996; Rösel and Trotha 1999; Buur and Kyed 2007; Ubink 2008). Moreover, irrespective of whether or not chiefs facilitate processes of democratization, many observers have pointed out that traditional authorities hold power *de facto* and enjoy considerable legitimacy in many African countries. In some contexts, they never ceased to be important; in others, they gained renewed influence in the light of state weakness, state collapse or state reconstruction after crisis (Rösel and Trotha 1999; Rouveroy van Nieuwaal and Dijk 1999; Bierschenk and Olivier de Sardan 2003; Buur and Kyed 2007; Bellagamba and Klute 2008).

As Mario Krämer argues with regard to traditional authorities in contemporary South Africa, chiefs are often 'neither despotic nor civil' (Krämer 2016). Building on Heinrich Popitz's (2017: 161) notion of 'basic legitimacy', he argues that traditional leaders often base their rule on various forms of legitimation situated between Max Weber's well-known ideal-types

---

5 There are, of course, chiefs and other kinds of traditional authorities who can be deposed if they do not satisfy the needs of their constituencies. Particularly in societies with no or weakly institutionalized positions of authority, as among the Nuer or the Somali, leaders 'must continually earn the support of their followers. If they fail, they are easily replaced' (Kurtz 2001: 49).

of legitimacy and a compliance that is based merely on habit, affect or interests. Locals acknowledge chiefly contributions to the establishment of political order. These contributions ensure a basic legitimacy for chiefs, even when people do not necessarily regard their customary regimes as truly justified or legitimate in the Weberian sense.

This suggests that African traditional authorities typically occupy an intermediary position 'betwixt and between' local citizens and the state (West and Kloeck-Jenson 1999), with variable room for manoeuvre. As a separation of powers with checks and balances that ensure accountability both down and up political hierarchies is usually missing in traditional institutions, chiefs are prone to power abuses; traditional rule often also compromises democratic promises of equity, human rights and gender equality. At the same time, in the light of the frequently bleak realities of local government, rural populations often benefit from the work of chiefs in terms of their accessibility, low costs and actual service delivery (Kyed and Buur 2007; Ubink 2008), which regularly gives their rule at least 'basic legitimacy' in the eyes of (some) locals.

The contributors to this volume thus insist that the precise nature of the interactions between traditional authorities, the state and the people (as citizen-subjects) needs to be investigated from an empirical perspective, scrutinizing overlapping politico-normative orders and their associated practices. As John and Jean Comaroff (forthcoming) put it in their interrogation of the increasingly assertive politics of custom in contemporary Africa, the enormous diversity among manifestations of the dialectics of chieftainship, capital and the state across the continent defies any attempt to develop a unified theory that explains it. From our discussion too, it is clear that diverse African traditional authorities, as well as their variable customary justice systems, are there to stay for the foreseeable future (see also Obarrio forthcoming). Legal pluralism is widespread in contemporary Africa and state officials, in their various capacities, somehow have to handle it one way or another in the course of their daily work.

Mind the gaps: legal pluralism and the jurispathic state

'Legal pluralism' is typically defined as a situation, in which two or more legal systems, or bodies of legal norms, operate within a single social field (Pospisil 1971: 125; Hooker 1975: 6; Griffiths 1986: 1, 38–39; Woodman 1996: 157–158). Alternatively, from the point of view of an individual, 'legal pluralism' prevails whenever a person is subject and has access to more than one body of legal norms (Vanderlinden 1989; Woodman 1996: 157–158). In modern Western history, the colonial context has constituted the classical case of such legal pluralism, where colonizing powers imposed certain versions of Western law on subordinated territories and groups with their own pre-existing normative orders, which were partly acknowledged and (mis)recognized as 'customary law' in the ways discussed above. This created the easily recognizable situation of legal pluralism in (post)colonies comprising what Hooker (1975: 4) calls the 'dominant' legal system of European ancestry as well as the 'servient' local law, which is typically labelled 'customary' or 'religious'. Since the 1970s, when 'legal pluralism' emerged as the term characterizing such situations of normative heterogeneity, this concept was increasingly extended to Western societies as well. According to Sally Engle Merry, many scholars who had worked on colonial legal pluralism started researching the complex mutual interactions between official and unofficial forms of ordering in Western contexts (e.g. Moore 1978), thereby initiating a shift from 'classical' to 'new' legal pluralism (Merry 1988: 872–874). Lauren Benton succinctly summarizes the rationale behind this move: '[c]olonies were not distinctive because they contained plural legal orders but because struggles within them made the structure of the plural legal order more explicit' (Benton 2002: 9). The new challenge consisted in revealing the normative heterogeneity hidden underneath the widespread misconception of Western societies as dominated exclusively and homogeneously by state law.

In broadening the analytic scope to include modern Western states, advocates of a descriptive social-scientific theory of legal pluralism strongly attacked what John Griffiths (1986) prominently rejects as 'the ideology of legal centralism'. According to this ideology,

> law is and should be the law of the state, uniform for all persons, exclusive of all other law, and administered by a single set of state institutions. To the extent that other, lesser normative orderings, such as the church, the family, the voluntary association and the economic organization exist, they ought to be and in fact are hierarchically subordinate to the law and institutions of the state.
>
> (Griffiths 1986: 3)

Against this backdrop, Griffiths (ibid.: 3–8) asserts that the classical case of the (post)colonies indeed constitutes a weak form of legal pluralism because it does not challenge the ideology of legal centralism. When the state recognizes other legal orders as subordinate and servient, it remains the sole source of validation for all orders and its own law remains supreme. When analysts adopt this perspective, Griffiths argues, they cannot pursue a truly empirical and descriptive approach to assessing the actual relations of the multiple normative orders within a social field. These orders, originating from different sources, do not necessarily recognize each other as valid and often lack integrative mechanisms to solve the norm conflicts that arise between them. From a 'strong' pluralistic perspective, state law is merely one order among the others. These really coexisting normative orders, Griffiths argues, should all be recognized as 'law' and, as 'strong legal pluralism', constitute the proper subject matter for a social scientific concept of legal pluralism (ibid.: 8).

Gordon Woodman echoes Griffiths's distinction between 'weak' and 'strong' versions of pluralism in his discussion of 'state law' versus 'deep legal' pluralisms (Woodman 1996: 156–159). Woodman, however, emphasizes that even the apparently hegemonic 'state law pluralism' is derived from multiple sources of validity and is potentially full of inconsistencies (ibid.: 158). In other words, 'weak' or 'state law pluralism' refers to the management of normative heterogeneity *from the perspective of the state*, which treats its own law as superior and all other normative orders as inferior to and dependent upon state law validation – irrespective of the origins of norms or potential inconsistencies within state law itself.

The strong pluralism paradigm, emerging within anthropological and sociological approaches to law, has been the subject of criticism. Legal scholar Brian Tamanaha (1993), for example, once prominently ridiculed 'the folly of the "social scientific" concept of legal pluralism'. But by the 2000s, it had reached into the realm of legal scholarship as well, with Gunther Teubner (1996), for instance, proposing a systems-theoretical approach to legal pluralism. Even Tamanaha (2000) now advocates a 'non-essentialist version of legal pluralism' and, in general, several international legal disciplines – in particular comparative law, private international law, public international law and European Union law – have begun adopting some ideas in the context of promoting a 'global legal pluralism' (Michaels 2009: 243, see also Berman 2007). However, as Ralf Michaels (2009: 246) points out, scholars of legal globalization still have been interested mostly in plural legal orders based directly or indirectly on the state, rather than in the specificities of non-state law.

Though 'legal pluralism' as such has a relatively brief intellectual history within socio-legal scholarship, the problem of how a legal system should deal with other normative orders is, of course, much older. In fact, as Marc Galanter (1981: 27) observes, '[e]very legal system has to address the problem of the autonomy and authority of the various other sorts of normative ordering with which it coexists in society.' In Western legal history, as Galanter (ibid.: 28) elaborates, the relationship between the state and the church (with its canon law) is the *locus classicus* for thinking about plural normative orders. Within modern state law, however, the discipline most explicitly dealing with this plurality of laws has been private international law, also aptly referred to as 'conflict of laws' (Ralser 2003; Boden 2005).

Under the three legal doctrines of jurisdiction, choice of law, and judgment recognition (Berman 2007: 1229), private international law determines – in cases which cross legal orders – which courts have jurisdiction, which law applies, and what force court decisions have outside the court's jurisdiction (Michaels 2009: 248). As the field's very existence makes clear, states rarely accept another's laws *in toto*. Instead, absent treaties, each state applies its own conflict-of-laws norms. In other words, from the point of view of a state dealing with a conflict of laws, the questions of jurisdiction, choice of law and judgment recognition (and execution) are not only answered according to the standards of the foreign law as (mis)understood by the enforcing court, but also based on its own legal standards (Michaels 2005: 1237–1240). Moreover, even if a state treats foreign laws as, in principle, applicable law or accepts the principal validity of a decision by a foreign court, it might still deny them actual applicability based on the exception of domestic public policy or the *ordre public* to avoid unacceptable effects in light of basic values of the enforcing forum (Gebauer 2007) – a legal device quite similar to the colonial 'repugnancy clause' (see above).

Against the same background of private international law, however, Michaels (2005: 1235–1244) argues that demands for strong legal pluralism – under which states should accept and enforce the decisions and laws of non-state communities just as they already enforce those of foreign states – miss a crucial point. A state does not, in fact, accept the laws of other states as such; it determines whether the laws of other states are compatible with, and therefore enforceable, as its own. For a state, the recognition of foreign law is not a question of 'legal theory, but rather one of construing the relevant conflict of laws rule' (ibid.: 1239). That is, 'enforcement does not follow automatically from the nature of "law," because what matters for choice of law is not an ontological definition of law, but rather, the determination of what is law from the perspective of the state and its choice of law norms' (ibid.: 1241). In other words, recognition is not a universal entitlement for foreign laws following from the objective fact of 'strong legal pluralism' but requires the consenting perspective of a recognizing actor (such as the state). Michaels hence proposes studying the ideology of legal centralism, as exhibited in 'weak legal pluralism', less as an adequate model of reality (as rightly criticized by legal pluralists) and more with regard to the multiple realities of this model in (state) actors' thoughts and practices:

> Recognition, so despised by early legal pluralism, reenters the analysis […], but the focus is now on recognition as a practice of the recognizing law rather than as a universal criterion of validity for the recognized law. Recognition, as a juridical category, is thus analyzed as a practice, an anthropological category.
>
> (Michaels 2009: 256)

As Michaels (2005: 1228) shows, in contemporary private international law, states accept only other states as potential equals, and do not normally recognize non-state law as 'law'. Yet the non-acceptance of non-state normative orders does not mean that states necessarily ignore them completely. Instead, a state may acknowledge non-state law in ways that Michaels (ibid.: 1231–1235) describes as deference, delegation and incorporation. We discuss these below as different registers within the mode of recognition. Still, in all these registers of acknowledgement, a state always asserts its own legal supremacy by appropriating and transforming its legal Other:

'normative orders are thus defined, by the state, with relation to the state. They are, in other words, "re-stated"' (ibid.: 1228).

Robert Cover (1983) refocuses this transformative 're-state-ment' of other legal orders by the state in even stronger terms by evoking the notion of a jurispathic state. States (and particularly judges), Cover (ibid.: 53) suggests, in continuously defining what the law *is* – itself an act of jurisgenesis – by necessity simultaneously *kill off* other normative orientations. Jurispathic acts are hence inevitable within the perspective (not only) of the state, whenever it defines what the law is. This does not only happen in instances of conflicts of law or 'weak legal pluralism' (when law is 'killed' for public policy or under the repugnancy exception). Instead, the jurispathic state is in perpetual operation as it attempts to apprehend another legal order *in its own terms* (the ambiguity of the possessive pronoun is intended): in 'seeing like a state' (Scott 1998), and in defining other normative orders in relation to itself, the state 're-states' all other legal orders, recreating them in its own image.

This observation harks back to old questions, posed during and after colonialism, regarding the ascertainment of customary law by the state. We have already referred to these questions in our discussion of 'official' and 'living customary law'. As various observers have noted, the mere (f)act of ascertaining the content of custom through state practices immediately freezes, ossifies and petrifies 'living customary law', and inevitably turns it into a distorted form of 'official customary law' (Woodman 1969, 2011; Bennett 2008). As Ubink aptly summarizes this jurispathic practice:

> Both the limited reliability of evidence by experts, witnesses, and assessors as well as the recording of customary law through codification, restatement, or case law, in effect changes the content and nature of customary law and creates a gap between what is locally practiced [i.e. living customary law] and what the state courts declare customary law, that is, judicial [official] customary law. In fact, recording customary law will always change its content and nature, independent of the way in which this is done. The manner of recording merely determines the size of the gap, depending on the extent to which the recordings freeze customary law and the space they allow, both *de jure* and *de facto*, for revision.
>
> (Ubink 2011b: 97–98)

Evidently, state officials can try to close the emerging gap between the actually living customary law and the jurispathically fixed official customary law through repeated ascertainment. Yet any attempt by the state to record the living law will inevitably generate an official, but distanced, version of 'custom'.[6]

---

6   Ubink (2011a) describes an interesting case of self-statement in Namibia, in which this gap seems to be mitigated. However, this is achieved by a bottom-up process at the grassroots level, in which the living customary law is voluntarily adapted to, and thereby *de facto* turned into, the newly created official standard.

In fact, there are three gaps that come to haunt any official dealings with customary law (see also Zenker forthcoming). First, is the above-discussed gap between the living and official customary laws. This gap points to the question at the heart of the debate over the very legitimacy of customary law – who has, and should have, the power to define and enforce custom? Second is the gap between 'traditional custom' and 'modern ideals'. Whether this gap appears around fundamental norms such as a Bill of Rights, exceptions of public policy or repugnancy (protecting basic values), or existing state law, it has to do, at its crux, with questions of justice. The third gap is between a customary past of proclaimed 'historical authenticity' and other histories that are claimed to be 'tainted' or 'misconstrued' according to (neo)colonial, capitalist, patriarchal (and similar) interests of 'evil' Others. This gap evolves, and is constantly repositioned, in the continuous (re)imagining of 'traditions' and 'customs' by variously entangled sets of actors, as previously discussed. In the very moment state officials address customary law, they begin to transform 'strong legal pluralism' into its 'weak' sibling, and are thus forced to manage the resulting gaps regarding legitimacy, justice and historical authenticity. At the same time, these officials cannot prevent strong pluralism from lingering on – thereby continuously producing a setting in which the paradox of customary law keeps unfolding.

The policultural state and the paradox of customary law

Many contemporary African postcolonies present themselves as adhering to the template of modern liberal statehood. African nation-states are, moreover, often described as 'multicultural' in recognition of the pluralities of all sorts with which they are riddled. John and Jean Comaroff (2004: 191) insist that a better descriptor for the postcolonial African nation-state is policultural. Unlike the more common 'multi-', '[t]he prefix, *poli-*, marks two things at once: plurality and its politicization.' Within the everyday realities of such policultural and ostensibly liberal states in Africa and beyond, public servants are frequently confronted with, as already noted, 'the paradox of customary law', a predicament which coalesces from questions, both abstract and concrete, of liberal statecraft, jurispathic state recognition, and policultural states at work.

The paradox of liberal statecraft emerges from two contradictory demands. On the one hand, the liberal state subscribes to the ideal that the rule of law should treat everyone as equal; on the other hand, the liberal state also attempts to accommodate specific forms of difference, especially under self-acknowledged conditions of multiculturalism. Thus, to varying degrees, the liberal state allows for special group or collective rights (Kymlicka 1995; Modood 2007). Thus, the liberal state potentially treats those within its jurisdiction as simultaneously similar and dissimilar, and can be accused of behaving unjustly on both counts. If it treats people equally, it denies the rights it has promised to acknowledge difference, and when it treats people as different, it violates their right to be treated as equals. As Thomas Hylland Eriksen describes 'the paradox of multiculturalism', 'both equal and differential treatment of minorities can be politically contentious' (Eriksen 2002: 145). Seen from within the logic of the liberal state, however, this problem emerges rather as a paradox of customary law in that such non-state normative orders may simultaneously be construed by different actors as demanding and as dismissing their accommodation by the state.

Second, we have already encountered *the paradox of jurispathic state recognition*. As discussed in the previous section, when a policultural state attempts to recognize the living customary law, the living law becomes ossified as the next version of official customary law. In private international law, such jurispathic effects are neither hidden nor seen as constituting a serious problem. This is so because a state, in dealing with foreign state laws, evidently takes it for granted that, unless regulated by treaties, it applies foreign law or recognizes and enforces foreign court decisions only according to its own domestic conflict-of-laws rules and under the condition of a possible public policy exception. But the state recognition of customary law in Africa and elsewhere is problematic because of the self-consciously postcolonial nature of the policultural state.

In Africa, doubt about the state's very legitimacy is widespread. This is because the state 'was imposed by force, by alien powers, and continues to seek to enforce norms which are different in principle and objective from the customary legal norms which receive popular acceptance' (Woodman 1996: 160). Accordingly, in the eyes of its subjects, the African liberal state oscillates between being an object of sympathy and an agent of aggression. It is perceived as a colonial (mis)transplant with which African normative realities have to engage, but it also succeeds in erasing its own sociocultural historicity, acting as if customary justice regimes were the Other in need of accommodation within its own universalistic legal supremacy. Against the backdrop of long and painful local histories of colonialism, with their consequential (mis)conceptions of customary law and traditional authorities, many people in Africa, officials and citizen-subjects alike, cannot so light-heartedly accept the jurispathic effect of (mis)recognizing African customs, as can practitioners of private international law. Hence, the painstaking attempts, for instance, in South African postcolonial jurisprudence to capture the truly 'living customary law' instead of contaminated colonial and postcolonial renderings of 'official customary law'. The former is seen as the true 'customary law' to be recognized as one of the laws of South Africa – even though, in principle, this endeavour ultimately also cannot escape the jurispathic force of its own 'violent appropriation' (Michaels 2005: 1258). This does not mean that because of this forceful constructional defect, all forms of state recognition (or lack thereof) are of equal value – far from it. This is merely to point out that state officials, even when they try to recognize the kingdom of custom as it really is, have to reckon with the paradox that recognizing custom within state law inevitably means transforming it. As we discuss below, this paradox cannot be solved, but merely be processed in different ways, with different practical consequences, potentials and pitfalls.

Finally, there remains *the paradox of policultural states at work*. As African history demonstrates, traditional authorities have played multiple, if varied and contested, roles before and after their respective states gained independence. The diversity of these roles contributes to the policultural nature of the 'African state' as a generic form. The omnipresence of traditional authorities means that public servants positioned at different levels of state hierarchies, often cannot easily ignore alternative political and legal orders. When focusing on the daily functioning of state services through the mundane practices of public servants in 'states at work' (Bierschenk and Olivier de Sardan 2014), it becomes obvious that even when officials do not want to engage with traditional authorities and customary law they must quite often, paradoxically, deal with them to get their own state work done. Sometimes traditional authorities and customary law constitute a reality that gets in the way of both law enforcement and the implementation of policies unless handled *en passant*. Sometimes the state – although neither 'weak' nor 'failed' in other respects – is not strong enough to implement politico-legal projects without enlisting the support of local non-state actors and their legal norms. Whether the state thus attempts to contain and exclude customary law or endeavours to include and enlist it for its own state project, as in the colonial policy of indirect rule and in Baldwin's (2016) argument about 'the paradox of traditional chiefs in democratic Africa', in both cases the *state*, paradoxically, has to deal with customary law in order to get on with its own business *as a state*.

What we have separated into three separate conundrums between the policultural liberal state and alternative politico-legal orders appear as a single 'paradox of customary law' in the daily work of state officials. We use the expression 'paradox' to highlight the self-contradictory nature of the foundational terms in this relationship and the lack of easy, unambiguous or permanent solutions for their reconciliation. Therefore, rather than expecting officials to solve the paradox of customary law, it seems more realistic to expect them to process the paradox in multiple, flexible, heterogeneous, inconsistent and piecemeal ways – that is, to find only temporary and contingent solutions to 'deparadoxify' the paradox (Luhmann 1991, 1995).

Processing the paradox: state officials between the rules of the game and the game of the rules

Precisely because of the complex and heterogeneous *bricolage* character of state dealings with the paradox of customary law, it is desirable to attempt some systematization of the strategies utilized by states and their officials to engage customary law. Such a typology could be devised in many ways and with various subdivisions. Taking inspiration from a number of other overlapping classificatory attempts – e.g. those devoted to government policies on traditional leadership (Bako-Arifari 1999: 5–15; Hlatshwayo 1998; Ubink 2008: 21–22; Hinz 2008: 61–63), to the modes in which private international law deals with non-state law (Michaels 2005), and to the transnational legal tools for managing hybridity (Berman 2007) – we propose a simple typology comprising four principal modes by which states address customary law: *ignorance, awareness, recognition* and *rejection*.

Ignorance refers to the widespread, though unacknowledged fact that the state, as instantiated in the various practices of its officials, simply does not know all (if any) of the alternative normative regimes (including the customary ones) within its jurisdiction. Ignorance is a logical necessity, but states may also behave more deliberately as if (some) alternative normative orders did not exist. Ignorance may comprise a true lack of knowledge or a more or less intentional pretence of not knowing, and the term thereby points to the various possible usages to which such an approach can be put. The boundaries of ignorance are porous and fluid, and thus allow for the strategic exploitation of an official lack of knowledge on the side of the state. In its more extreme manifestations, ignorance arguably constitutes merely the flipside of the official ideology of legal centralism, as discussed above: the conscious refusal of the state to recognize normative orders other than its own as 'law'.

Acknowledgement constitutes the counterpart to ignorance as the generic term for three other principle modes of state engagement with customary law, which all officially take note of the reality of alternative legal orders, but do so in different ways: *Awareness* consist of a variety of possible strategies by the state to officially announce its knowledge and acknowledgement of the existence of customary law, but does not entail the explicit accommodation or recognition of customary law within the realm of state law and legal practice. In some cases, publicly documented awareness can overlap with ignorance because customary law may still be ignored for all intents and purposes. However, quite often, more nuanced and implicit engagements emerge under the mode of awareness. For instance, both state officials and actors within the realm of the customary might observe each other carefully and, depending on the wider political, economic and cultural context, adapt their specific decisions or their practices more generally to what they anticipate as the current and likely next moves of the respective other actor. Thus, state and non-state law might, to varying extents, engage with each other dialectically, without officially recognizing or mandating such a form of interaction. In this process, the state might *de facto* grant customary regimes some limited autonomy as long as certain thresholds of deviation (continuously renegotiated in practice) are not crossed. Finally, the state might also *de facto* incorporate (and thereby co-opt) leading figures from the realm of custom into mixed participation arrangements. Even when such individuals are incorporated, not in their customary capacity, but as 'ordinary citizens', such behaviour in practice may bridge the gap between state and non-state arenas and thereby increase the local legitimacy of the state.

Within the broad field of *recognition* as another mode of acknowledgement, the state officially and expressly attempts to accommodate, to varying degrees and through different registers, at least some aspects of customary law within state law. This can take different forms: in the weak register of *deference*, the state actively tolerates a limited normative autonomy of communities by granting them a private space, for instance through invoking the idea of a personal law (as when recognizing the validity of a customary marriage) (Berman 2007: 1205–1206). However, as Michaels (2005: 1233) succinctly puts it, such 'private orderings enter the substantive law of the state at the time of enforcement as fact. Customs, expectations, and the like must be taken into account in applying the state's laws; but the state does not recognize them as constituting law in and of themselves'. This changes in the register of *delegation*, where the state treats customary orders as legal ones separate from state law, but still denies them full autonomy. In other words, the state integrates parts of customary law and customary courts into the state system, but does so under circumscribed legal conditions – that is, as long as they do not contravene superior state law (such as that found in a constitution, existing legislation or case law), public policy or general repugnancy provisions evoking humanity, civilization or natural justice. Thus, delegation transforms non-state law into subordinated or sub-state law (ibid.: 1234–1235), and can be seen as comprising many versions of the weak legal pluralism and state law pluralism that characterized the colonial period. In the process of recognizing customary law as sub-state law, legalistic devices such as reports of commissions of enquiry, ethnographic works and attempts at restatement play an important role. Finally, recognition can take the strong form of *incorporation*, in which certain parts or aspects of customary law are incorporated into state law itself, thus ceasing to be legally autonomous and becoming part of state law proper. This happens, for instance, when the state regulates and determines certain aspects of customary law through its own legislation, codification and court precedents. Evidently, the extent to which the harmonization of customary and state law is attempted through incorporation differs greatly. As Allot explained in 1984:

> *Unification* is different from *integration*. Unification imposes a uniform law; integration creates a law which brings together, without totally obliterating, laws of different origins [...] Integration might therefore seem a useful halfway house towards full unification. It implies that variant laws remain in being, but there is an attempt to standardise their effects and remove conflicts between them.
>
> (Allott 1984: 65)

Thus, the state may recognize customary law either through treating it as fact (deference); through acknowledging and validating its existence as an independent legal order, yet only subject to and subordinated under superior state law (delegation); or through turning versions of customary law into state law itself (incorporation). In all three instances, however, state recognition operates as a jurispathic act, transforming what is living customary law into some version of official customary law.

Finally, the state may also acknowledge customary law through the mode of *rejection*. Here the state explicitly denies both the legality and the legitimacy of a non-state normative order and attempts to suppress it. Evidently, the extent to which states go in their attempt to reject certain aspects of customary law or customary institutions varies considerably. States may declare only certain customary practices to be illegal, as happened with colonial attempts to suppress witchcraft detection practices (see Chapters 3 and 4 of this volume). States may deny the jurisdiction of customary courts, as was widespread in British colonies for criminal law cases (Mamdani 1996: 116); or they may attempt to abolish the entire institution of traditional authorities, as was attempted after independence in Guinea, Somalia, Tanzania and Mozambique (see Chapters 3, 6, 7 and 8 of this volume). Sometimes, however, states may officially reject customary laws, but in everyday practice exhibit an attitude closer to awareness or even ignorance. Hence, rejection is marked by behaviour that ostensibly insists that an alternative normative order should not or must not exist, even though the actual enactment of this declared 'will to suppress' might vary greatly.

This rough typological sketch comprising the modes of ignorance, awareness, recognition and rejection as ideal-types can be seen, on one level, as institutionalized strategies, sometimes even explicit rules, of how states engage with customary law. Drawing on a common characterization of institutions as 'the rules of the game in a society' (North 1990: 3), these official norms formally define the arena in which state officials, at any moment in time, are meant go about their mundane practices of state-making. Yet these official rules of the game constitute only one set of norms to which public servants might orient their behaviour.

As Tom de Herdt and Jean-Pierre Olivier de Sardan argue, 'players can just play within the rules of the game, but their strategies usually also include, every now and then, playing with the rules *themselves*' (De Herdt and Olivier de Sardan 2015a: 1, original emphasis). In a manner akin to Michael Lipsky's (1980) argument about patterns of practice deriving from the often considerable discretion of bureaucrats interacting with citizens in their daily work, Olivier de Sardan introduces the analytical level of 'practical norms'. Such norms consist of 'the various informal, *de facto*, tacit or latent norms that underlie the practices of actors which diverge from the official norms' (Olivier de Sardan 2015: 26). These practical norms, so maintain De Herdt and Olivier de Sardan (2015a: 3), cover the often large gap between official norms and effective practices of real governance in Africa. To get on with their daily work, state officials flexibly orient themselves towards the 'rules of the game' on the level of official norms, while also playing 'the game of the rules' on the level of practical norms. To the extent to which the practical norms orienting the practices of state officials stay sufficiently within the realm of the underlying official norm, such bureaucrats can be said to make use of *de jure* discretion; this would be the case, for instance, if, under the official norm of awareness, a public servant ventured to incorporate traditional leaders into a state process by addressing them as eligible citizens rather than as traditional leaders. In contrast, state officials might be described as using their *de facto* discretion, when co-opting these actors expressly as traditional authorities; to do so would constitute a shift from the official norm of awareness to the practical norm of recognition. Such a shift from the official to the practical could be construed as 'illegal', or at least 'illegitimate'.[7]

In sum, state officials navigate the rules of the game and the game of the rules on the two interrelated levels of official and practical norms, both of which can be described usefully in terms of the modes of ignorance, awareness, recognition and rejection. It is through skilful and flexible manoeuvring within and between norms and modes of engagement that state officials attempt to process the paradox of customary law in Africa and somehow get their work done.

Chapter overview: when the state has to deal with customary law

When apartheid ended, the South African state initiated a land restitution process redressing historical dispossessions based on race. Using the case of a successful land claim, Olaf Zenker (Chapter 2) focuses on the challenges encountered by officials when dealing with customary law in order to implement restitution law. Drawing on Michael Lipsky's concept of 'street-level bureaucrats' – that is, the public servants who manage intrinsic state problems (especially conflicting policies) in their direct interaction with citizens through discretion – he suggests that South African restitution officials, as 'bush-level bureaucrats', additionally manage challenges extrinsic to the state, namely claims to chiefly rule under customary law.

While South Africa's new constitution officially *recognizes* traditional leaders and customary law, the land laws of the 1990s mostly officially *ignored* them, acknowledging only the individual rights of citizens. Therefore, in the case discussed by Zenker, restitution officials harmonized overlapping claims by organizing the democratic election of a land claims committee. Many of the restitution officials had been anti-apartheid activists

---

[7] According to Tony Evans (2010: 33), *de jure* discretion and *de facto* discretion are typically distinguished on the basis of their origins: in *de jure* discretion, the capacity to decide is given formally by a higher order authority, whereas in *de facto* discretion, the power to act is not officially recognized, but arises circumstantially from the absence of effective control.

and deeply mistrusted chiefs as corrupted colonial collaborators. Hence, their work was not only guided by the practical norm of *ignorance* towards customary rule, but also by its *de facto rejection*: acknowledging the local chief as a citizen-beneficiary, they actively prevented his election onto the committee. However, they failed to get written consent by the chief to be represented by the committee, as legally prescribed. When the chieftaincy argued years later that its land claim had been stolen by the committee, no chiefly consent form could be found and the bureaucrats who had come into place in the meantime lacked personal knowledge of the case history to know any better. Hence, officials started seeing the chief as the legitimate representative of the claim – yet in his capacity as citizen-beneficiary, not as chief. Still following the official norm of *ignorance* within restitution law, this 'recognition' of the chief-as-citizen had *de facto awareness* effects, which previous bureaucrats had prevented, and fuelled further demands by the chief to also rule over the land as chief. This shift towards a *de facto* empowering of the chief took place in the context of increasingly neo-traditionalist legislation, *recognizing* and thereby re-empowering traditional authorities in numerous areas affecting land. Given these changed political conditions, bush-level bureaucrats increasingly found they had to give in to the demands made by chiefs, shifting their practical norms from *rejection* to *awareness* in order to get their work done. Nevertheless, restitution law remains governed officially by *ignorance* towards customary law.

In Chapter 3, Helene Maria Kyed looks at the dilemmas of claiming sovereignty in legal pluralistic contexts in post-civil war Mozambique. When the FRELIMO (Frente de Libertação de Moçambique) government came to power after years of civil war in 1992, the state *rejected* traditional authorities and customary law as obstacle to modern rule. Yet, the state remained weak in many parts of the country. Moreover, RENAMO (Resistência Nacional Moçambicana), the former contender in the civil war and now the main opposition party, used ties to chiefs to widen its power base. Therefore, from 2000 onward, the state's position changed considerably with the introduction of new legislation which led to *recognition* of chiefs as important local actors. Yet the *recognition* of the state extended officially only to small-scale administrative tasks like tax collection, assistance with conflict settlement and judgements in family law and other civil matters. This limited *delegation*, however, contrasted with the *de facto awareness* of state officials – specifically police officers – exhibited towards customary orders. *Awareness* was expressed in a variety of practices, ranging from the transfer of cases to chiefs to police acting themselves like chiefs. Kyed explains too how the game of the rules was played with regard to witchcraft accusations. While witchcraft was officially outlawed by the state, which therefore continuously displayed *rejection* with regard to this aspect of custom, the supernatural was still important for most ordinary people. Local police officers thus engaged with matters related to witchcraft instead of ignoring them; they *de facto* recognized the issues at hand and thereby acted outside the law in order to strengthen the state. Moreover, to keep the face of the state, police officers and even traditional authorities denied the 'illegal' engagement of the police with the supernatural. Occasionally they referenced the overarching power of the state as a deterrent to such an illegal engagement, even though the state's power remained largely nominal.

A similar dynamic involving state officials handling customary law is outlined in Chapter 4 by Cherry Leonardi concerning colonial southern Sudan. There, British officers had to establish what they understood as legal order in a context in which compensatory justice and belief in magic dominated. Officially, *recognition* of customary law in the context of indirect rule confined chiefs' legal authority to their capacity as colonial aides in the administration of minor civil cases. Yet chiefs did not abandon their knowledge or application of customary law which settled even severe criminal cases through compensation payments and took witchcraft seriously. What were the British officers to do about the continued invocation of customary law by their colonial aides? While *ignorance* was the preferred option of some officers higher up the administrative hierarchy, lower-level officers exhibited a mixture of *awareness* and *recognition*. These officers used *de facto* discretion to promote and prioritize 'custom' because they realized the need to satisfy public opinion in a setting where the colonial state was weak. In order to also satisfy their superiors, they proposed that in severe cases (like murder) – where the decisions of statutory and customary law would have diverged greatly – the verdict should be separated from the sentence. Under statutory law, a verdict of murder should have carried a death sentence or at least imprisonment, but if the verdict and sentence were separated, the latter could be reduced on grounds of 'custom' to allow for compensation payments. This form of *de facto recognition* (at least concerning sentences in severe cases) reached its limits in witchcraft cases, because these challenged the judicial monopoly of the state in the most problematic of ways. Following a *de facto awareness* mode, state officials developed pragmatic solutions to punish people for instigating the fear of witchcraft, the practice of which was itself officially *rejected* under the repugnancy clause. In another practical engagement with witchcraft, colonial officers analysed allegedly poisonous 'magical' substances, making the results public. In this way, colonial administrators showed people that they took their concerns about witchcraft seriously, while simultaneously following legal procedures in line with their own sense of rationality.

Katrin Seidel keeps the focus on South Sudan in Chapter 5, but deals with the contemporary approaches of and challenges for state actors in the emerging state. The negotiation of plural legal and political orders is characteristic for the world's youngest state (as of 2017). The drama of South Sudan is that after decades of civil war and shortly after its independence, the new state is again embroiled in internecine fighting. This, however, hopefully halts the elaboration of a final and permanent constitution only temporarily. According to the 2011 Transitional Constitution of the Republic of South

Sudan (TCRSS), *recognition* is offered to traditional authorities and local (i.e. customary) law as part of the state system. The vague constitutional provisions, however, do not reflect the importance of local law on the ground and as part of the nation-building ideology of 'unity in diversity'. After the protracted oppression of southern Sudanese local cultures by the previous government in Khartoum, when *rejection* was the state's way of dealing with customary law, the new South Sudan is compelled to respect local traditions. The challenges emanating in this situation are related to, first, the question of harmonizing customary law. The state seeks to make local law conform to human rights, particularly with regards to women's rights. Second, is the question of how the appeal system within the court hierarchy will work. On paper, a neat hierarchy of courts has been established with local law being applied until the level of the county court, chaired by the paramount chief. The appeal system then involves the county judge and, if necessary, higher courts presided over by state officials. But how shall legal practitioners trained in statutory law decide an appeal case originally based on customary law? While the official approach here is clearly one of *recognition* involving the attempt to *delegate* or *incorporate* customary law, the state is still too weak to implement its legal framework. It remains to be seen which stand state officials will take when it comes to handling customary law once the situation in South Sudan calmed down again and state formation in the legal sphere proceeds.

In Chapter 6, writing about Guinea, Anita Schroven provides a *longue durée* perspective on institutional changes and certain continuities concerning the state's engagement with customary law. Initially, French colonial rulers offered conditional *recognition*. Yet, as in other colonial contexts, the official structure confined chiefs to the role of administrative aides who organized tax payments and forced labour. Toward the end of colonial rule, the Guinean leadership under Sékou Touré demanded more political rights and the abolishment of colonial chieftaincy. Thus, *rejection* was the way elites of the newly independent state (in 1958) dealt with customary law. Yet, also during the postcolonial modernization phase following the ideology of Pan-Africanism and socialism, people belonging to chiefly families gained powerful positions in the hierarchy of the single party state. In the more recent context of decentralization policies which are supposed to foster participatory democracy and strengthen the state in rural areas, the elected local councillors in the Communautés Rurales de Développement (CRD) or Communes Urbaines (CU) (the basic building blocks of the decentralized political framework) often belong to old chiefly families. In this way, the customary order prevails in new forms and state actors must engage it, now following the mode of *awareness*, but not without a certain amount of *ignorance*. As Schroven shows, state officials who are not close to the chiefly families in certain locales face difficulties and cannot work effectively. Thus, while customary law is deemed officially irrelevant and elected councillors are expected to provide governance in rural areas, the reality is that the state is bound to compromise and rule in accordance with the local customary structures that have been engrained in new administrative set-ups.

The dynamics surrounding land dispute settlements in Tanzania outlined by Rasmus Hundsbæk Pedersen in Chapter 7 are remarkable in the sense that they indicate the increasing relevance of statutory arrangements. Since 1999, *recognition* of customary authorities is entailed in statutory laws concerned with the settlement of land disputes. While most other chapters report cases in which state recognition was an attempt to legalize the *de facto* predominance of customary law, Pedersen's research shows that the majority of the dramatically increased number of land conflicts since 2009 have been dealt with by state institutions, mainly courts. Comparing conflict settlement in the years before and after 2009, it becomes clear that customary dispute-settlement mechanisms have fallen out of fashion. Pedersen explains both the growing number of land conflict cases and the predominance of statutory dispute settlement with reference to increased migration into fertile areas. This brings people of different ethnic backgrounds together in villages and small towns – a context in which it is hard to settle land disputes using customary authorities. While intra-ethnic disputes are still frequently settled by elders, and state *recognition* of customary law in this regard provides a practically working framework, inter-ethnic conflicts are taken mainly to state institutions. Pedersen therefore describes the growing *ignorance* of customary law by local actors which, since it is emanating from the behaviour of ordinary people, does not produce the paradoxical practices of state actors described in most other chapters.

Chapter 8, by Markus Virgil Hoehne, focuses on legal and political friction in Somaliland. He shows the policultural state at work. The established literature describes Somaliland as a functioning Hybrid Political Order (HPO), but Hoehne argues that in fact two such orders exist, and that they do not necessarily complement each other. The basis of Somaliland's peace- and state-building process is *recognition* of customary law. Under the previous Somali dictatorship, customary law was *rejected* as 'tribal' and backward, but it was promoted after the secession of Somaliland as part of the 'local traditions' considered to be effective in conflict settlement. In 1993, traditional authorities were even installed as part of the government with seats in the Upper House (*Guurti*). However, over the years, traditional authorities in government have been co-opted increasingly by professional politicians, which diminished their legitimacy in the eyes of many ordinary people. The second HPO is identified by Hoehne in the extensive margins of Somaliland. There, the delivery of justice as well as questions of war and peace rest mainly in the hands of the traditional authorities who administer customary law. They do not hold official positions, but state officials cooperate with them and seek their assistance (e.g. to arrest suspects). Many cases, including homicide, are also *de facto* delegated by courts to elders and customary proceedings, since the judgements of elders carry greater weight and are therefore more easily implemented than court decisions (which betray the prevailing sense of compensatory justice). State officials therefore use *de facto* discretion to get the job of justice done at all. In matters of everyday governance, a mixture of *awareness* and *recognition* characterizes the engagement of the state with customary law. This in contrast to the situation of police officers in Mozambique described by Kyed, because elders in Somaliland are addressed openly and involved as accepted non-state actors in legal cases. Hoehne's case study of a major armed conflict in eastern Somaliland, causing death and displacements between 2010 and 2014, demonstrates how the two HPOs collide: state officials from the centre, who were used to co-opt traditional authorities in government, tried to settle the dispute ignoring customary approaches. But they met elders whose power and legitimacy was unbroken in this marginal area of Somaliland. Dispute resolution failed, which led to further violence. The chapter thus shows the limitations of official attempts to merge statutory and customary orders.

In her afterword (Chapter 9), Janine Ubink reviews important aspects of the previous chapters and connects them with wider discussions in legal and political anthropology, focusing on recognition, legibility through recording and operating the plural legal setting. She emphasizes that both state actors and authorities administering customary law are entangled in their struggle for power. Recognition, as part of liberal statecraft, will therefore always entail a reordering of power and authority. Ubink also emphasizes the jurispathic nature of the state and underlines how indeed all attempts of the state to make customary law legible will 'kill off' what is 'alive' within living customary law. Finally, the reality in plural legal settings is that besides different layers of state and non-state law (including 'official customary law' and 'living customary law') also multiple and partly competing versions of living customary law exist on the ground, between and even within communities. This makes the task of state officials dealing with it extraordinarily challenging.

Conclusion

Customary laws and traditional authorities continue to play highly diverse, important, contested roles in contemporary African states. The modern state and its law, transplanted under colonialism, have had a profound impact on these customary regimes. Previous scholarship has been crucial in demonstrating how colonial (re)imaginations of 'custom', co-produced continuously in the negotiations between colonizing and colonized actors of all sorts, have often facilitated and entrenched colonial rule and the advancement of economic interests of various rulers, contributing, ultimately, to the global expansion of capitalism. Yet, as we argued in this introductory chapter, in focusing primarily on the impact that the state has had on *non-state laws*, such instrumentalist renderings of the complex interrelation of the modern state and customary law have left important questions unanswered.

These questions come into sight when the prevailing analytical gaze is reversed. We have argued for a focus on how the interactions between state and non-state normative orders have shaped the everyday practices of *the state itself*. As we showed, the (mis)appropriation by the state of other normative forms and logics – as embodied, for instance, in the kingdom of custom – has not been merely a question of the strategic and intentional transformation of the state's normative Other to the advantages of metropolitan, colonial and African political and economic elites. Such forms of (mis)recognition have also emerged simply from the practical difficulties unfolding in the attempt to conjoin the different forms and logics of the state and of customary law in Africa. To put it bluntly, even if such political and economic interests for misconstruing African customary law had not existed, any appropriation, by a modern state, of customary law would have still led to the latter's necessary transformation.

This is so because the political and legal pluralism within the state's jurisdiction appears *to the state* in the form of 'the paradox of customary law'. State officials working in ostensible orientation towards the fundamental values, laws and policies of the state – which currently presents itself across the continent in some liberal and policultural variant – must deal, somehow, with the reality of customary law and traditional authorities in their everyday work. They must address 'custom', even though the form and logic of customary rule is not easily compatible and often incommensurable with the form and logic of the state. More specifically, we suggested that this paradox of customary law takes the form of a predicament resulting from three interrelated paradoxical conundrums: first, that of liberal statecraft; second, that of jurispathic state recognition; and third, that of the policultural state at work.

In their conjuncture, these three conundrums offer various practical possibilities for state officials which are, however, as ambiguous as they are self-defeating. The paradox of customary law cannot be resolved, but merely processed in piecemeal ways that deparadoxify certain problems (at least temporarily) but also simultaneously create new problems. In order to understand in more concrete terms how state officials actually process this paradox, we suggested an analytical framework that distinguishes between the four modes of *ignorance, awareness, recognition* and *rejection* as types of state engagement. We suggested that state officials orient themselves towards these modes of engagement both on the level of 'official norms' (the rules of the game) and on the level of 'practical norms' (the game of the rules).

Looking at the contributions to this volume in this framework, a few comparative observations can be made. One point is that African states, both during and after colonialism, have evidently made use of all modes of engagement on the level of official norms as enshrined in state laws and policies. The *rejection* of customary law has focused on the entire institution of traditional authorities, as in their formal abolition in Tanzania (Pedersen), Guinea (Schroven), Somalia (Hoehne) and Mozambique (Kyed) after independence. However, often such rejection has merely targeted certain aspects of customary law, as with widespread attempts to legally prohibit customary witchfinding activities in colonial southern Sudan (Leonardi) or in contemporary Mozambique (Kyed). In many contexts, customary law has also been formally *recognized* by the state in one way or the other: this was evidently the case during colonial indirect rule, when the scope and content of officially recognized customary law varied enormously locally and historically, as within the conditional *recognition* in colonial southern Sudan (Leonardi) and Guinea (Schroven). In the course of the more recent wave of democratizsation and decentralization in Africa since the 1990s, many states have switched to, or expanded, the official *recognition* of customary regimes, typically under a policultural rhetoric of accommodating diversity. This happened, as the chapters show, in the respective state-building projects in Somaliland (Hoehne), South Africa (Zenker), Mozambique (Kyed) and the new South Sudan (Seidel), but also through the recent recognition of customary authorities in Tanzania with regard to land dispute settlement (Pedersen).

While the mode of *awareness* has played an important role as a practical norm (see below), the case studies in this volume do not exhibit extensive forms of official *awareness*. The somewhat ambiguous toleration, by state institutions, of members of chiefly families taking up offices in Guinea, as described by Schroven, is perhaps the most 'official' strategy of awareness manifest in the presented case studies. Here, the state officially *is aware of* specific functions for elders, and it seems to allow the chiefly heritage of some actors to play a legitimizing role in formal politics. Still – officially – customary law has been discounted. Finally, the chapters also demonstrate the formal role that *ignorance* can play. This appears again in Guinea (Schroven), and in South Africa in the prevailing constraints on the application of customary law in land restitution (Zenker). This latter case also highlights the heterogeneous nature of modern statehood because the *ignorance* of custom within restitution law has coexisted uneasily with the overall constitutional *recognition* of customary law as one of the official laws of the land and a trend towards more expansive neo-traditional *recognition* in other domains.

Such heterogeneity prompts attention to the practical norms orienting the actual practices of state officials, especially as they attempt to handle the state's legal inconsistencies. As the case studies demonstrate, officials have used their *de jure* discretion to implement the official norms, but have often also made use of their *de facto* freedom to transgress these same norms. Contrary to widespread stereotypes of weak, failing and corrupt states in Africa, our studies find that much of the transgressive work of state officials has operated in the service of, rather than against, the state. Precisely because of the paradox of customary law, officials have often bent (some) rules of the state in order to acquire a (basic) legitimacy on the ground through which they are able to implement (other) state rules. In many cases, this game of the rules has been played in ways that have allowed state officials (and sometimes chiefs) to 'keep face' and to create a discourse of legality, as Leonardi mentions in her chapter. In turn, such a discourse of legality has helped reconciling actually inconsistent legal practices. As mentioned above, this kind of discretion is frequently related to the practical mode of *awareness*, in which officials draw on their knowledge of customary law, without officially accommodating or *recognizing* custom within the realm of state law or legal practice. This was so in the colonial past (Leonardi), and it is still the case in the postcolonial present (Kyed).

Where the state has officially recognized customary law, a *de jure* practice of *recognition* appears relatively straightforward as well. However, the realities have often been more complex: while the state might have offered only a circumscribed *recognition*, in practice, state officials have often been forced to concede a more extensive *de facto recognition* to appease local expectations. Such was the case with witchcraft in colonial southern Sudan (Leonardi) and also in postcolonial Mozambique (Kyed). The hybrid political order in the margins of Somaliland (Hoehne) provides another example for such *de facto recognition*, where elders are accepted as non-state actors in legal cases officially falling under the jurisdiction of the state.

South Africa constitutes, in some way, an exception to the historical developments characterizing other states in this volume. Many African states that became independent in the 1950s and 1960s initially followed a discourse of liberal or socialist modernization, attempting to leave behind the tradition of customary rule through more or less extensive attempts at official *rejection* (or at least *ignorance*); by the 1990s, this negative attitude was increasingly giving way to official *recognition*, as outlined above. By contrast, becoming independent only in the 1990s during the era of democratization, decentralization and African constitutionalism, South Africa officially *recognized*, in principle, customary law in its new constitution *right away*. This *recognition*, however, came against a backdrop of deep suspicion of chiefs who had served as colonial puppets and the generally ambivalent attitude towards traditional authorities of the governing African National Congress Party (ANC). Against this backdrop, Zenker's chapter presents a land claim, in which officials *de facto rejected* customary rule and effectively sidelined a chief (at least initially), even though customary law was at the same time officially *recognized* in principle and merely *ignored* within the official laws dealing with restitution.

Last but not least, *de facto ignorance* of customary law has also been utilized. The case of South African land restitution illustrates this: officials have stayed within their *de jure* discretion by *de facto* ignoring custom, just as restitution law has officially required them to do. Such *de facto ignoring* of customary regimes that should be *rejected* by law, has been a common strategy, as within the widespread colonial approach to handling witchcraft accusations (Leonardi). Finally, Pedersen provides an interesting case of *de facto ignorance* of customary law in Tanzania: while the state has officially *recognized* customary law in land matters since 1999, many disputes are actually brought before state courts. Here, ordinary people increasingly *ignore* the rule of custom in a move towards state 'legalism from below' (Eckert 2006), which reduces rather than increases the practical problems of state officials who can more easily 'do the state' as the reign of custom diminishes.

As Schroven's chapter demonstrates through its *longue durée* perspective on Guinea, change may occur over time in official state laws and policies regarding customary law and in practical norms, without necessarily involving a changeover in people. That is, in differed frameworks, the same individuals and types of people may be addressed as 'chiefs', 'male elders', 'community leaders', 'citizens eligible to stand for election', and so on. A person from the same group might end up being selected for a (transformed) office, even though the norm motivating the selection has changed explicitly or implicitly. This brings to the fore the trivial but consequential fact that social life is multivalent, allowing it to be framed – legally and otherwise – in multiple, overlapping and often contradictory ways. Precisely for this reason, officials succeed in appearing to follow the official rules of the game, while covering up the practical norms that truly animate their game of the rules. And precisely for this reason, too, state officials, in turn, are unlikely to solve the paradox of customary law, but can merely engage continuously in its reprocessing: when the state decides to treat all people as equal, some may complain that their customary law is thereby *ignored*, creating a potential reason for reprocessing the paradox of customary law; when the state decides to *acknowledge* such customary law in any of the ways discussed above, it may be accused of thereby jurispathically transforming custom beyond 'recognition', creating another potential reason for processing this paradox anew; and when the state at work attempts to exclusively implement state laws and policies on the ground, it might thereby paradoxically have to deal with local custom first, simply because doing the state might otherwise not be possible.

The intrinsic deficit in the capacity of state officials to process the paradox of customary law, in all its various forms, does not mean that all state engagements with custom are all equally (in)valid. Rather, our point is to show that how state officials actually go about processing this paradox in their different historical contexts results in different forms of path-dependent connectivity for subsequent state and non-state practices. Moreover, our point is to underscore that these linked state and non-state practices do not come about only to serve some political and economic interests. They also come about because of the intrinsic problems that issue from officials' attempt to conjoin, in practice, the different forms and logics of the state and of custom in order to get their own work done as representatives of the state.

References

Allott, A.N. 1984. What is to be done with African customary law? The experience of problems and reforms in Anglophone Africa from 1950. *Journal of African Law* 28(1/2), 56–71.
Anders, G. 2010. *In the shadow of good governance: an ethnography of civil service reform in Africa*. Leiden: Brill.
Anders, G. and Zenker, O. (eds). 2015. *Transition and justice: negotiating the terms of new beginnings in Africa*. Malden: Wiley-Blackwell.
Anderson, B. 1991 [1983]. Imagined communities: reflections on the origin and spread of nationalism. Rev. and extended. London: Verso.
Bako-Arifari, N. 1999. *Traditional local institutions, social capital and the process of decentralization: a typology of government policies in developing countries*. Working Papers on African Societies. Berlin: Arabische Buch.
Baldwin, K. 2016. *The paradox of traditional chiefs in democratic Africa*. Cambridge: Cambridge University Press.
Bayart, J.-F. 1993. *The state in Africa: the politics of the belly*. London: Longman.
Bayart, J.-F., Ellis, S. and Hibou, B. 1999. *The criminalization of the state in Africa*. Oxford: James Currey.
Beek, J., Göpfert, M., Owen, O. and Steinberg, J. (eds). 2017. *Police in Africa: the street level view*. London: Hurst.
Bellagamba, A. and Klute, G. (eds). 2008. *Beside the state: emergent powers in contemporary Africa*. Köln: Rüdiger Köppe.
Benda-Beckmann, F. von 2002. Who's afraid of legal pluralism? *Journal of Legal Pluralism and Unofficial Law* 34(47), 37–82.
Bennett, T.W. 2008. 'Official' vs 'living' customary law: dilemmas of description and recognition, in *Land, power and custom: controversies generated by South Africa's Communal Land Rights Act*, edited by A. Claassens and B. Cousins. Cape Town: Legal Resources Centre, 138–153.
Benton, L.A. 2002. *Law and colonial cultures: legal regimes in world history, 1400–1900*. Cambridge: Cambridge University Press.
Berman, P.S. 2007. Global legal pluralism. *Southern California Law Review* 80, 1155–1238.
Berry, S. 1992. Hegemony on a shoestring: indirect rule and access to agricultural land. *Africa* 62(3), 327–355.
Bierschenk, T. and Olivier de Sardan, J.-P. 2003. Powers in the village: rural Benin between democratization and decentralization. *Africa* 73(2), 145–173.
Bierschenk, T. and Olivier de Sardan, J.-P. (eds). 2014. *States at work: dynamics of African bureaucracies*. Leiden: Brill.
Blundo, G. and Le Meur, P.-Y. (eds). 2009. *The governance of daily life in Africa: ethnographic explorations of public and collective services*. Leiden: Brill.
Boden, D. 2005. Plurisme juridique en droit international privé. *Archives de Philosophie du Droit* 49, 275–316.
Buur, L. and Kyed, H.M. (eds). 2007. *State recognition and the democratization of Sub-Saharan Africa: a new dawn for traditional authorities?* Basingstoke: Palgrave Macmillan.
Chabal, P. and Daloz, J.-P. 1999. *Africa works: disorder as political instrument*. Oxford: James Currey.

Chanock, M. 1985. *Law, custom, and social order: the colonial experience in Malawi and Zambia*. Cambridge: Cambridge University Press.
Chanock, M. 2001. *The making of South African legal culture, 1902–1936: fear, favour, and prejudice*. Cambridge: Cambridge University Press.
Claassens, A. and Cousins, B. (eds). 2008. *Land, power and custom: controversies generated by South Africa's Communal Land Rights Act*. Cape Town: Legal Resources Centre.
Comaroff, J.L. and Comaroff, J. 2004. Criminal justice, cultural justice: the limits of liberalism and the pragmatics of difference in the new South Africa. *American Ethnologist* 31(2), 188–204.
Comaroff, J.L. and Comaroff, J. Forthcoming. Chiefs, capital, and the state in contemporary Africa: an introduction, in *The politics of custom: chiefship, capital, and the state in contemporary Africa*, edited by J.L. Comaroff and J. Comaroff. Chicago, IL: University of Chicago Press.
Cover, R.M. 1983. The Supreme Court, 1982 term – foreword: nomos and narrative. *Harvard Law Review* 97(4), 4–68.
De Herdt, T. and Olivier de Sardan, J.-P. 2015a. Introduction: the game of the rules, in *Real governance and practical norms in sub-Saharan Africa: the game of the rules*, edited by T. De Herdt and J.-P. Olivier de Sardan. London: Routledge, 1–16.
De Herdt, T. and Olivier de Sardan, J.-P. 2015b. *Real governance and practical norms in sub-Saharan Africa: the game of the rules*. London: Routledge.
Diala, A.C. 2017. The concept of living customary law: a critique. *Journal of Legal Pluralism and Unofficial Law* 49(2), 1–23.
Dijk, R. van and van Rouveroy van Nieuwaal, E.A.B. 1999. Introduction: the domestication of chieftaincy in Africa: from the imposed to the imagined, in *African chieftaincy in a new socio-political landscape*, edited by E.A.B. van Rouveroy van Nieuwaal and R. van Dijk. Hamburg: LIT-Verlag, 1–20.
Doornbos, M.R. 2006. *Global forces and state restructuring: dynamics of state formation and collapse*. Basingstoke: Palgrave Macmillan.
Eckert, J.M. 2006. From subjects to citizens: legalism from below and the homogenization of the legal sphere. *Journal of Legal Pluralism* 53–54, 45–75.
Eriksen, T.H. 2002. *Ethnicity and nationalism: anthropological perspectives* (2nd edition). London: Pluto Press.
Evans, T. 2010. *Professional discretion in welfare services: beyond street-level bureaucracy*. Farnham: Ashgate.
Galanter, M. 1981. Justice in many rooms: courts, private ordering, and indigenous law. *Journal of Legal Pluralism and Unofficial Law* 19, 1–47.
Gebauer, M. 2007. Orde public (Public policy), in *Max Planck Encyclopedia of Public International Law – Oxford Public International Law*, edited by Rüdiger Wolfrum. Oxford: Oxford University Press.
Griffiths, J. 1986. What is legal pluralism? *Journal of Legal Pluralism* 24, 1–55.
Hagmann, T. and Hoehne, M.V. 2009. Failures of the state failure debate: evidence from the Somali territories. *Journal of International Development* 21(1), 42–57.
Hagmann, T. and Péclard, D. 2010. Negotiating statehood: dynamics of power and domination in Africa. *Development and Change* 41(4), 539–562.
Hamilton, C. 1998. *Terrific majesty: the power of Shaka Zulu and the limits of historical invention*. Cambridge, MA: Harvard University Press.
Herbst, J.I. 2000. *States and power in Africa: comparative lessons in authority and control*. Princeton, NJ: Princeton University Press.

Himonga, C.N. 2011. The future of living customary law in African legal systems in the twenty-first century and beyond, with special reference to South Africa, in *The future of African customary law*, edited by J. Fenrich, P. Galizzi and T.E. Higgins. Cambridge: Cambridge University Press, 31–57.

Himonga, C.N. and Nhlapo, R.T. (eds). 2014. *African customary law in South Africa: post-apartheid and living law perspectives*. Capte Town: Oxford University Press Southern Africa.

Hinz, M.O. 2008. Traditional Governance and African customary law: Comparative observations from a Namibian perspective, in *Human Rights and the Rule of Law in Namibia*, edited by N. Horn and A. Bösl. Windhoek: Macmillan Namibia, 59–87.

Hlatshwayo, B. 1998. Harmonizing traditional and elected structures at the local level: experiences from four Southern African Development Community countries, in *Traditional authority and democracy in Southern Africa*, edited by M. d'Engelbronner-Kolff, M.O. Hinz and J.L. Sindano. Windhoek: New Namibia Books, 131–154.

Hobsbawm, E. and Ranger, T.O. 1983. *The invention of tradition*. Cambridge: Cambridge University Press.

Hooker, M.B. 1975. *Legal pluralism: introduction to colonial and neo-colonial laws*. Oxford: Clarendon Press.

Krämer, M. 2016. Neither despotic nor civil: the legitimacy of chieftaincy in its relationship with the ANC and the state in KwaZulu-Natal (South Africa). *Journal of Modern African Studies* 54(1), 117–143.

Kurtz, D.V. 2001. *Political anthropology: power and paradigms*. Boulder, CO: Westview.

Kyed, H.M and Buur, L. 2007. Introduction: traditional authority and democratization in Africa, in *State recognition and the democratization of Sub-Saharan Africa: a new dawn for traditional authorities?*, edited by L. Buur and H.M. Kyed. Basingstoke: Palgrave Macmillan, 1–28.

Kymlicka, W. 1995. *Multicultural citizenship: a liberal theory of minority rights*. Oxford: Clarendon Press.

Leonardi, C. 2013. *Dealing with government in South Sudan: histories of chiefship, community and state*. Woodbridge: James Currey.

Lipsky, M. 1980. *Street-level bureaucracy: dilemmas of the individual in public services*. New York: Russell Sage Foundation.

Logan, C. 2009. Selected chiefs, elected councillors and hybrid democrats: popular perspectives on the co-existence of democracy and traditional authority. *Journal of Modern African Studies* 47(1), 101–128.

Luhmann, N. 1991. Sthenographie und Euryalistik, in *Paradoxien, Dissonanzen, Zusammenbrüche: Situationen offener Epistemologien*, edited by H.U. Gumbrecht and K.L. Pfeiffer. Frankfurt am Main: Suhrkamp, 58–82.

Luhmann, N. 1995. The paradoxy of observing systems. *Cultural Critique* 31(2), 37–55.

Lutz, G. and Lindner, L. 2004. *Traditional structures in local governance for local development*. Bern: Institute of Political Science, University of Bern.

Mamdani, M. 1996. *Citizen and subject: contemporary Africa and the legacy of late colonialism*. Princeton, NJ: Princeton University Press.

Mauss, M. 1990 [1924]. *The gift: the form and reason for exchange in archaic societies*. London: Routledge.

Meagher, K. 2012. The strength of weak states? Non-state security forces and hybrid governance in Africa. *Development and Change* 43(5), 1073–1101.
Merry, S.E. 1988. Legal Pluralism. *Law and Society Review* 22(5), 869–896.
Merry, S.E. 1991. Review essay: law and colonialism. *Law and Society Review* 25(4), 889–922.
Michaels, R. 2005. The re-*state*-ment of non-state law: the state, choice of law, and the challenge from global legal pluralism. *The Wayne Law Review* 51, 1209–1259.
Michaels, R. 2009. Global legal pluralism. *Annual Review of Law and Social Science* 5, 243–262.
Migdal, J.S. and Schlichte, K. 2005. Rethinking the state, in *The dynamics of states: the formation and crises of state domination*, edited by K. Schlichte. Aldershot: Ashgate, 1–40.
Modood, T. 2007. *Multiculturalism: a civic idea*. Cambridge: Polity.
Moore, S.F. 1978. *Law as process: an anthropological approach*. London: Routledge and Kegan Paul.
Moore, S.F. 1986. *Social facts and fabrications: customary law on Kilimanjaro, 1880–1980*. Cambridge: Cambridge University Press.
North, D.C. 1990. *Institutions, institutional change and economic performance*. Cambridge: Cambridge University Press.
Ntsebeza, L. 2005. *Democracy compromised: chiefs and the politics of the land in South Africa*. Leiden: Brill.
Obarrio, J. Forthcoming. Third contact: invisibility and recognition of the customary in northern Mozambique, in *The politics of custom: chiefship, capital, and the state in contemporary Africa*, edited by J.L. Comaroff and J. Comaroff. Chicago, IL: University of Chicago Press.
Olivier de Sardan, J.P. 2015. Practical norms: informal regulations within public bureaucracies (in Africa and beyond), in *Real governance and practical norms in sub-Saharan Africa: the game of the rules*, edited by T. De Herdt and J.-P. Olivier de Sardan. London (Routledge), 19–62.
Pels, P. 1996. The pidginization of Luguru politics: administrative ethnography and the paradoxes of indirect rule. *American Ethnologist* 23(4), 738–761.
Popitz, H. 2017. *Phenomena of power: authority, domination, and violence*. New York: Columbia University Press.
Pospisil, L.J. 1971. *Anthropology of law: a comparative theory*. New York: Harper & Row.
Ralser, E. 2003. Plurisme juridique et droit international privé. *Revue de la recherche juridique – Droit prospectif* 28, 2547–2576.
Ranger, T.O. 1983. The invention of tradition in colonial Africa, in *The invention of tradition*, edited by E. Hobsbawm and T.O. Ranger. Cambridge: Cambridge University Press, 211–262.
Ranger, T.O. 1993. The invention of tradition revisited: the case of Africa, in *Legitimacy and the state in twentieth-century Africa: essays in honour of A.H.M. Kirk-Greene*, edited by T.O. Ranger and O. Vaughan. Basingstoke: Macmillan, 62–111.
Ray, D.I. and van Rouveroy van Nieuwaal, E.A.B. 1996. Introduction: the new relevance of traditional authorities in Africa. *Journal of Legal Pluralism* 37–38, 1–38.
Ribot, J.C. 2002. *African Decentralization: Local Actors, Powers and Accountability*. Democracy, Governance and Human Rights Paper no. 8. Geneva: United Nations Research Institute for Social Development.

Roberts, R.L. and Mann, K. 1991. Law in colonial Africa, in *Law in colonial Africa*, edited by K. Mann and Roberts, R.L. Portsmouth, NH: Heinemann, 3–58.

Rösel, J. and von Trotha, T. (eds). 1999. *Dezentralsiierung, Demokratisierung und die lokale Repräsentation des Staates*. Köln: Rüdiger Köppe.

Rouveroy van Nieuwaal, van E.A.B. and van Dijk, R. (eds). 1999. *African chieftaincy in a new socio-political landscape*. Hamburg: LIT-Verlag.

Schlee, G. 2004. Taking sides and constructing identities: reflections on conflict theory. *Journal of the Royal Anthropological Institute* 10(1), 135–156.

Scott, J.C. 1998. *Seeing like a state: how certain schemes to improve the human condition have failed*. New Haven, CT: Yale University Press.

Skalník, P. 1996. Authority versus power: democracy in Africa must include original African institutions. *Journal of Legal Pluralism* 37–38, 109–121.

Snyder, F.G. 1981a. Colonialism and legal form: the creation of 'customary law' in Senegal. *Journal of Legal Pluralism* 19, 49–90

Snyder, F.G. 1981b. *Capitalism and legal change: an African transformation*. New York: Academic Press.

Snyder, F.G. 1984. Customary law and the economy. *Journal of African Law* 28(1/2), 34–43.

Spear, T. 2003. Neo-traditionalism and the limits of invention in British colonial Africa. *The Journal of African History* 44(1), 3–27.

Starr, J. and Collier, J. 1989. Introduction: dialogues in legal anthropology, in *History and power in the study of law: new directions in legal anthropology*, edited by J. Starr and J. F. Collier. Ithaca, NY: Cornell University Press, 1–28.

Tamanaha, B.Z. 1993. The folly of the 'social scientific' concept of legal pluralism. *Journal of Law and Society* 20(2), 192–217.

Tamanaha, B.Z. 2000. A non-essentialist version of legal pluralism. *Journal of Law and Society* 27(2), 296–321.

Teubner, G. 1996. Global Bukowina: legal pluralism in the world society, in *Global law without a state*, edited by Gunther Teubner. Aldershot: Ashgate, 3–17.

Trotha, T. von 1996. From administrative to civil chieftaincy: some problems and prospects of African chieftaicy. *Journal of Legal Pluralism* 37–38, 79–107.

Ubink, J. 2008. *Traditional authorities in Africa: resurgence in an era of democratization*. Leiden: Leiden University Press.

Ubink, J. 2011a. Stating the customary: an innovative approach to the locally legitimate recording of customary law in Namibia, in *Customary justice: perspectives on legal empowerment*, edited by J. Ubink. Rome: International Development Law Organization, 131–150.

Ubink, J. 2011b. The quest for customary law in African state courts, in *The future of African customary law*, edited by J Fenrich, P. Galizzi and T.E. Higgins. Cambridge: Cambridge University Press, 83–102.

Vanderlinden, J. 1989. Return to legal pluralism: twenty years later. *Journal of Legal Pluralism* 28, 149–157.

Weber, M. 1978 [1921]. *Economy and society*, 2 vols, edited by Guenther Roth and Claus Wittich. Berkeley, CA: University of California Press.

West, H.G. and Kloeck-Jenson, S. 1999. Betwixt and between: 'traditional authority' and the democratic decentralization in post-war Mozambique. *African Affairs* 98(393), 455–484.

Woodman, G.R. 1969. Some realism about customary law – the West African experience. *Wisconsin Law Review* 1969, 128–152.

Woodman, G.R. 1996. Legal pluralism and the search for justice. *Journal of African Law* 40(2), 152–167.
Woodman, G.R. 2011. A survey of customary laws in Africa in search of lessons for the future, in *The future of African customary law*, edited by J Fenrich, P. Galizzi, and T.E. Higgins. Cambridge: Cambridge University Press, 9–30.
Woodman, G.R. 2012. Legal pluralism in Africa: the implication of state recognition of customary laws illustrated from the field of land law, in *Pluralism and development: studies in access to property in Africa*, edited by H. Mostert and T. Bennett. Claremont, South Africa: Juta, 35–58.
Young, C. 2012. *The post-colonial state in Africa: fifty years of independence, 1960–2010*. Madison, WI: University of Wisconsin Press.
Zenker, O. Forthcoming. Mind the gaps: renegotiating South African legal pluralism within the post-apartheid state, in *Negotiating normative spaces in Africa*, edited by K. Seidel and H. Elliesie. London: Routledge.

2 Bush-level bureaucrats in South African land restitution

Implementing state law under chiefly rule

Olaf Zenker

Introduction

The first free democratic elections in South Africa in 1994 marked a new beginning, promising to redress past injustices and to reconcile a deeply racialized and divided society in order to build a better future for all. This new era was founded on a profoundly altered constitutional order, first based on the (interim) Constitution of the Republic of South Africa (Act 200 of 1993), then on the current Constitution of the Republic of South Africa (Act 108 of 1996). This order also comprises a new property clause, simultaneously protecting existing property rights and providing for a substantial land reform programme. Subsections 25(4)–(9) of the current property clause explicitly demand the restitution of former land rights, a more equitable access to land through land redistribution and legally secure land tenure through tenure reform, mostly to be achieved through Acts of Parliament.

With regard to land restitution, the corresponding Act of Parliament – the Restitution of Land Rights Act (Act 22 of 1994) – provides a set of criteria, according to which claimants are entitled to restitution (i.e. restoration of the land or equitable redress). The claimant can be an individual (or a direct descendant) or a community (or part of a community), whose rights in land were derived from shared rules determining access to land held in common by such a group. The claimant had to be dispossessed after 19 June 1913[1] because of racially discriminatory laws and practices. Finally, claimants should not have received just and equitable compensation and had to lodge their claim before 31 December 1998.[2] Significantly,

---

1 This was the day of the promulgation of the Natives Land Act (Act 27 of 1913), first legalizing massive dispossessions country-wide by introducing racial zones of possible land-ownership and by restricting black reserves to only 7 per cent of South African land (later to be extended to 13 per cent).
2 On 29 June 2014, President Jacob Zuma signed the Restitution of Land Rights Amendment Act of 2014 (Act 15 of 2014), which reopened the lodgement period and extended it until 30 June 2019. However, on 28 July 2016, the Constitutional Court declared this Act as entirely invalid from the date of the judgment due to the unconstitutional public

restitution was explicitly not limited to former freehold ownership of land, but also included unregistered rights of labour tenants and sharecroppers, customary law interests and rights of beneficial occupation of not less than 10 years prior to dispossession. The Restitution Act further established the Commission on Restitution of Land Rights, including the Chief Land Claims Commissioner and the Regional Land Claims Commissioners, as well as the specialist Land Claims Court (LCC) as its key players.

Since 1995, commission officials have thus validated and verified lodged claims and, if legitimate, mediated between claimants and usually white landowners in order to settle on a largely market-oriented agreement, in which the state buys the land and, based on certain conditions, hands it over to the claimants. Originally, the LCC was established to grant restitution orders in every case. However, owing to the slow progress in handling claims, amendments to the Restitution Act shifted the judicial to an administrative approach in 1999. Now, the minister, and by delegation the land claims commissioners and their officials, have the power to facilitate and conclude settlements by agreement, and only claims that cannot be resolved this way take the judicial route through the Court.

While land restitution in South Africa has received considerable academic attention, most research has focused on the perspectives of claimants and scrutinized the restitution process, so to speak, from the receiving end (e.g. James 2007; Manenzhe and Lahiff 2007; Fay 2009; Walker et al. 2010). Relatively few studies have been primarily concerned with the inner workings of restitution as a state-bureaucratic process (e.g. Walker 2008; Dodson 2010; Mostert 2010). This involves both the concrete work of the judiciary, interpreting and developing restitution law in courts, and the executive such as the Commission on Restitution of Land Rights, tasked with processing and implementing this law (e.g. Zenker 2015a, 2015b, 2015c). This is not to say, of course, that judicial and administrative processes have been ignored. However, such processes tend to be depicted as framework conditions within generalized summaries, subsequently allowing for claimant

---

consultation process. While prohibiting the acceptance of any new claims after that date, the Constitutional Court also maintained the validity of those new claims already lodged since 2014. But these were put on hold and the Commission interdicted from processing them, until all old claims lodged before 1998 have been processed or new legislation has been enacted by Parliament. The Government subsequently made clear that the re-opening of lodgement of claims remains its policy. The Government Gazette of 7 April 2017 published a notice, inviting public comment on a new draft Restitution of Land Rights Amendment Bill, which Mr P.J. Mnguni, MP (ANC), intended to introduce in Parliament during the second quarter of 2017 as a private member bill. However, at the time of writing (July 2017), the bill has not yet been before Parliament.

dramas to unfold in descriptive detail, without being scrutinized as fields of daily work and agency in themselves.

This chapter aims for such a focused investigation of daily processes within the state bureaucracy working on South African land restitution. It deals specifically with the implementation of restitution law through officials working for the Commission on Restitution of Land Rights, who interact directly with claimants, current landowners and other citizens. Drawing on Michael Lipsky's work on the dilemmas of the individual in public services (Lipsky 2010), these officials can be described as 'street-level bureaucrats', characterized by both direct interaction with citizens as clients of public services, hence constituting an interface between the state and the citizenry, and by their 'substantial discretion in the execution of their work' (ibid.: 3). Lipsky argues that notoriously limited resources, ambiguous and conflicting abstract goals of their agencies, the concomitant absence of clear performance measures and highly complex situations on the ground lead to a situation, in which street-level officials have relative autonomy from organizational authority and exercise wide discretion. This, as Lipsky puts forward as a central thesis, *de facto* turns the day-to-day actions of street-level bureaucrats, rather than their agency's official statements, into the ultimate determinant of state policies (ibid.: 13–25).

Lipsky's work points to crucial problems and dilemmas characterizing the concrete workings of state bureaucracies and the implementation of state law. As I will argue below, however, it seems more appropriate to conceive the decisions and routines of street-level bureaucrats as merely one crucial arena of *de facto* policy-making, interlinked through chains and networks of translation (Rottenburg 2009: xxxi–xxxiii) to several other such arenas made up of processes within the bureaucracies, in parliament, cabinet, congresses of ruling parties and the like. Nevertheless, Lipsky reveals important ambiguities that are intrinsic to state bureaucracy (see also Best 2012; Zenker 2015a). What is more: in South African land restitution, such street-level workers often have to leave the metropolitan 'streets' behind, travelling into rural areas, where land – 'the bush' as the metaphorical other of 'the street' – is under claim. This is, of course, not merely a spatial move for officials but also connotes a shift within the still bifurcated state (Mamdani 1996) from dealing with prototypically urban 'citizens' under state law towards addressing rural 'subjects' still also living under powerful structures of 'customary law' and chiefly rule. In other words, in addition to the *intrinsic* problems of public services (as described by Lipsky), these 'bush-level bureaucrats' are confronted as well with *extrinsic* challenges, arising from the fact that they have to implement state law within areas of overlapping and contentious political authority and legal jurisdiction. It is this paradoxical situation, in which state officials somehow have to deal with 'customary law' in order to implement state law regarding land restitution, that constitutes the subject matter of this chapter.

I will use a case study on the twists and turns related to officials' attempts to settle and finalize the communal land claim on the farm 'Kafferskraal'[3] and 16 surrounding farms in Limpopo Province in order to provide an answer to the question of how state representatives, in practice, process this paradox and thereby, more or less, get their work done. In order to allow for a better understanding of the dynamics unfolding in this case, it is important to highlight right from the start the very contested nature of 'traditional authorities' and 'customary law' in post-apartheid South Africa due to the profound co-optation and transformation of these institutions under colonialism. As discussed in the introductory chapter to this volume (Zenker and Hoehne 2018), 'customary law' in South Africa and beyond emerged through continuous processes of unequal renegotiations between various subgroups of the colonizers and the colonized about the form and content of 'custom'. As described in more detail below, massive legal interventions by the colonial state in South Africa ensured that colonial officers could, at will, recognize, change and relocate 'tribes', appoint and dismiss 'chiefs' and empower them to apply 'customary law' in civil matters. In this process, what had constituted the living customary law under pre-colonial chiefs, who had depended on the more or less voluntary support of their followers, transformed into a state-backed regime of official customary rule. In this process, the control over land also increasingly resided in the hands of local chiefs as the alleged 'owners' of the land. Against this backdrop, it is hardly surprising that many anti-apartheid activists became deeply suspicious of these so-called 'traditional authorities' and, upon entering the state bureaucracy under President Nelson Mandela during the 1990s, preferred to bypass them through focussing exclusively on the rights of South African citizens. However, as we will see below, this tide began to turn in the late 1990s: under President Thabo Mbeki and his successor, President Jacob Zuma, more and more neo-traditionalist pieces of legislation were introduced in Parliament that re-empower chiefs (Ntsebeza 2005; Claassens and Cousins 2008; Claassens 2014; Zenker undated, forthcoming). As the case study of this chapter demonstrates, this development has led to increasingly ambiguous and conflicting policy goals also for the implementation of the officially unaffected restitution law.

In the following, I will first give a brief historical overview of the colonial dispossession of the Ndzundza Ndebele in that area, which provides the backdrop for the lodgement of various land claims during the 1990s. I will then study in detail the strategies utilized by commission officials to handle

3   The name of this farm has appeared on successive title deeds since 1872. The word 'kaffer' is, of course, an offensive term for African people and 'kraal' refers to an enclosure for cattle within an African homestead. However, as I discuss elsewhere in more detail (Zenker 2014), the fact of this pejorative name was used to positive effect by the claimants during their court case against the white landowners opposing their claim, arguing that the name proved the continued residence of African people on the land. Locally, the wider area is known among Africans as 'Mahlungulu'.

'customary law' through exclusion and inclusion. It will finally become evident that far from posing merely an extrinsic problem to the daily work of bush-level bureaucrats, 'customary law' has also increasingly constituted a challenge from within, more and more jeopardising the success of implementing restitution law in South Africa.

Preparing the ground for land restitution: the colonial dispossession of the Ndzundza Ndebele of Mahlungulu

The restitution case analysed in this chapter is concerned with a number of overlapping land claims related to a total of 17 neighbouring farms, including the so-called 'Kafferskraal' farm, which are situated on the edge of the highveld escarpment approximately 200 kilometres to the northeast of Pretoria. Located along the Stoffberg-Groblersdal corridor, the area formerly belonged to the Transvaal Province under apartheid, then to the new Mpumalanga Province in post-1994 South Africa, before reaching its current location within neighbouring Limpopo Province after rezoning in 2005. In isiNdebele, the language spoken by the Ndebele[4] on whose land claims I will concentrate here, the place is known as 'Mahlungulu'.

Mahlungulu and surrounding areas have a complex and shifting settlement history. During the first half of the nineteenth century, intense contestation and competition characterized the region, as three powerful South African kingdoms – the Pedi, the Swazi, and the Zulu – jockeyed for predominance. The interplay of colonial penetration, especially in the form of arriving Boer Voortrekkers in the 1840s, the emergence of new African kingdoms, wars and migration in the aftermath of the Difaqane[5] sent further shock waves throughout the region (Delius 2007: 137). In 1852, Boer settlers established the 'Zuid-Afrikaansche Republiek (ZAR)' in what later became known as the South African province of 'Transvaal', comprising the area at issue as its eastern part. The Boers wanted to own and control the land and further distribute it to white settlers. They attempted to buy land from various kings and chiefs, occupied pockets of land that did not fall under the control of any particular chief and subordinated smaller African chiefdoms and communities. In this process, the ZAR issued title deeds for what it regarded as its land (in Mahlungulu and far beyond) to the growing number of immigrating white *burghers* (citizens) (Delius and Hay 2009: 51–52).

---

4   The overall Transvaal Ndebele have been classified into Northern and Southern sections, of which the Northern Ndebele subsequently came to be substantially influenced by Northern Sotho language and cultural forms. Thus, the name 'Ndebele' is often used as shorthand only for the Southern section, as is the case in this text (see Delius 1989: 228–229).
5   The Difaqane, also called Mfecane, refers to a self-generated process of violence, migration, and political change within African society during the early 19th century (see Delius 2007: 107–111).

Much earlier in their history, the Ndebele had divided into the two kingdoms of Manala and Ndzundza (Delius 1989: 229). By the 1840s, Ndzundza Ndebele had established a significant kingdom under King Mabhoko, with various fortified mountain strongholds in the area. Against a number of failed Boer attempts to subdue the kingdom, Ndzundza power reached its heights in the late 1860s and 1870s. However, in 1883 the fate turned, when the Ndzundza lost the protracted Mapoch War against the Boers. King Nyabela and other members of the royal family were imprisoned and all Ndebele land was confiscated, subdivided, and handed over to Boers, who had fought during the war (van Vuuren 2010: 10–11). The population of the kingdom was dispersed among the ZAR burghers and indentured for a period of five years (1883–1888) (Delius 1989: 232). However, the imprisoned Ndzundza leadership organized for the escape of Nyabela's brother Matsitsi, who was sent to 'Kafferskraal' to re-establish chiefly guidance and the male initiation ritual (*ingoma*), an important Ndebele institution until today (Delius 1989: 241; van Vuuren 2010: 11–12).

The farm 'Kafferskraal' had been in white titled ownership since 1872, with its subdivision into three separate portions being in existence with changing owners from at least 1902. While white owners never actually lived on the farm, generations of Ndzundza Ndebele resided and worked on 'Kafferskraal', including Matsitsi and his chiefly successors, who regularly organized male initiation schools on the farm and exercised judicial functions there. At various points in the 1920s and 1930s, Ndzundza leaders also attempted to buy a portion of 'Kafferskraal' from willing white sellers, but were prevented from doing so by the Natives Land Act (Act 27 of 1913). Against this backdrop, and after some changes in white ownership of 'Kafferskraal', most members of the local Ndebele community were finally evicted by the late 1930s on the basis of the Native Trust and Land Act (Act 18 of 1936), being removed to the north to the state-owned farm Goedgedacht and surrounding areas in the Nebo district (today Limpopo Province) that, as reserve land, later became part of the Lebowa homeland. Based on the Bantu Authorities Act (Act 68 of 1951), a proclamation in the Government Gazette on 2 August 1957 defined these Nebo farms as Ndzundza Ndebele 'tribal areas' and established the 'Ndebele Tribal Authority' under the then Chief Maphepha I Poni Jafta Mahlangu. This Ndebele Tribal Authority continues to exist as a state-recognized form of traditional leadership until today.

Excluding chiefly rule from state law: the early implementation of land restitution from the mid-1990s until the mid-2000s

When apartheid came to an end and land restitution was put into practice in the mid-1990s, numerous individuals and groups from Ndebele, but also Pedi and Tswana backgrounds lodged separate and often overlapping claims for land in and beyond the Mahlungulu area. Given that many of these overlaps involved competing claims that promised a conflictual and protracted settlement process, the then Regional Land Claims Commissioner for Mpumalanga and Northern Province, Durkje Gilfillan, decided in late 1997 to single out and start with claims on the farm 'Kafferskraal'. This was done on the assumption that since all claimants seemingly belonged to the same Ndzundza Ndebele community, this case would be easier to settle than competing claims on surrounding farms. In addition, a dispute between one landowner and some of his farm labourers belonging to the claimant community further justified priority treatment according to §6(2)(d) of the Restitution Act.[6]

A community claim regarding 'Kafferskraal' had been submitted on 6 November 1997 by a man called Simon Shabangu. Based on a first research report produced by the project officer, Peter Ntshoe, according to Rule 3 of the 'Rules of the Commission', the Regional Land Claims Commissioner, Durkje Gilfillan, established *prima facie* validity of this community claim. Accordingly, she published in the Government Gazette on 2 January 1998 the proscribed notice concerning the restitution claim by Simon Shabangu on behalf of the so-called 'Sibuyela Ekhaya' ('We Are Going Home') Committee for all three portions of 'Kafferskraal'. A first meeting of all interested parties, including the current landowners, was held on 16 July 1998, during which the rule-3-report of the Commission was presented. In the course of this and subsequent stakeholder meetings, it became clear that while the owner of portion 1 agreed after initial opposition to sell his portion (as he subsequently did in 2002), the white owners of portion 2 and 3 continued to contest the validity of the claim. The Regional Land Claims Commissioner thus referred the case to the LCC on 19 January 2000, since no agreement could be reached.

The white landowners subsequently lost both the case in the LCC and their appeal case in the Supreme Court of Appeal (SCA). However, the SCA did remit to the LCC for further consideration the question, whether the claimants had been compensated justly and equitably in the past in terms of the relocation farms in Nebo. The landowners subsequently reached a settlement with the claimants (made an LCC order on 21 August 2006), in which all parties consented to the transfer of the two remaining 'Kafferskraal' portions on the condition that the issue of past compensation would again be taken into account, when the outstanding claims by the same community

---

6   Interviews with Durkje Gilfillan on 26 August and 2 September 2010 and interview with Peter Ntshoe, the project officer mainly in charge of this land claim at the time, on 6 November 2010. In addition to basing my knowledge of this case on interview data referred to below, it derives also from studying the extensive court files (that I compiled from multiple, incomplete sources) as well as from participant observation in the context of a 'multi-sited ethnography' (Marcus 1995) following this case intermittently between January 2010 and March 2012.

regarding the above-mentioned 16 neighbouring farms would be adjudicated by the LCC (several of which were also owned by the same white farmers).[7]

While Simon Shabangu's community claim had actually mentioned only 'Kafferskraal', it was Chief Mphezulu Jack Mahlangu of the Ndebele Tribal Authority, who had earlier lodged a separate community claim on 18 September 1995 regarding 'Kafferskraal' and the surrounding 16 farms (van Vuuren 2010: 10). While his claim form ambiguously referred to the claimants as the 'Ndebele Tribe' and the 'Ndebele Tribal Authority', an annexed memorandum explicitly requested 'the government to release this land (i.e. the 17 farms) to its rightful owner Ikosi M.J. Mahlangu'. As mentioned before and discussed below in more detail, this idea that, in African culture, the chief – rather than the community – is the rightful owner of the land has, of course, a long tradition within colonial (mis)understandings of 'customary law' (Gluckman 1965: 76) and remains a highly contested legacy in contemporary South Africa (Zenker forthcoming). As such, this chiefly expectation was to cause considerable problems for the implementation of postcolonial restitution law by bush-level bureaucrats.

This is so because the statutory provisions affecting land restitution strongly emphasize individual rights of citizens even in communal land claims. Thus, the Communal Property Associations Act (Act 28 of 1996), according to its preamble, enables 'communities to form juristic persons, to be known as communal property associations in order to acquire, hold and manage property on a basis agreed to by members of a community in terms of a written constitution'. Apart from similar entities like trusts, such communal property associations (CPAs) constitute the main form, in which land restored through restitution is communally held. According to §9(1) of the Act, CPA constitutions must accommodate fair and inclusive decision-making processes, equality of membership, democratic processes and fair access to the property of the association. While traditional authorities are not legally prevented from holding key positions within CPAs and trusts, and often in fact do so (Derman et al. 2010: 310), by law they must be democratically elected onto the committee like any other member. Common templates for such CPA constitutions even explicitly restrict the permitted proportional representation of traditional leaders on the committee (Klug 2006: 131–142). Thus, all in all, 'chiefs were not formally included in the restitution process' (Hellum and Derman 2009: 129) – at least not in the legislation of the 1990s.

Against this backdrop, the Regional Land Claims Commissioner, Durkje Gilfillan, brought together Simon Shabangu and Chief M.J. Mahlangu in

---

7 See the unreported judgment of the LCC, in re Ndebele-Ndzundza Community regarding the farm Kafferskraal 181 JS, Case No. LCC 03/2000, 21 August 2006. For a detailed discussion of the judicial proceedings and the relationship between claimants and white landowners in this case see Zenker (2014).

late 1997 and made them agree to combine their land claims and work together in the 'Kafferskraal' case.[8] As Gilfillan explained to me, as a former anti-apartheid activist she was sceptical of chiefs as representatives of claimant communities anyway and hence usually established and interacted directly with elected communal spokespeople:

> During my time at the Commission, my approach was to look only at the people who had lived on the land – irrespective of who they paid allegiance to as chiefs! That's their own thing. They can pay allegiance until the cows come home. I couldn't care less. But in terms of rights in land, not allegiance to a chief, but it's the rights in land that indicate whether you were part of what claimant group. And I mean, they were then settled under various chiefs. So, you had three or four chiefs, claiming the same piece of land. Because they all said, 'Oh, no, but the people, they are my people, therefore it's my land!' And it doesn't work that way. In other words, I said, 'It's irrespective of what chief you have. If you want him, pay allegiance to the chief. That's fine; of course, you can do that. That's not tied to the fact that you live on a particular piece of land!' Because that was one of the problems with the apartheid system. In customary law, the chief is the chief through the people. It was in apartheid law that chieftainship then became tied to the land. [...] The chief then came basically into the position of an [land]owner.[9]

Given that, by state law, the claim was to be represented by an elected land claims committee, Gilfillan gazetted the 'Kafferskraal' case in the name of Simon Shabangu on behalf of the elected Sibuyela Ekhaya Committee rather than in the name of the chief. The democratic election of the Sibuyela Ekhaya Land Claims Committee with its chairperson Simon Shabangu was later repeated under the auspices of bush-level bureaucrats and formally documented in a community resolution dated 29 October 1998. However, the continual cooperation between the elected committee and the Ndebele Tribal Authority under the overall representation of Simon Shabangu apparently did not come about so easily. Peter Ntshoe, also a former anti-apartheid activist, had been the main project officer in this early phase of the 'Kafferskraal' claim, compiling both the initial rule-3-report and the subsequent 'investigation report' in terms of Rule 5 of the Rules of the Commission. He recalled in 2010:

> Now the challenge I faced: Chief Mahlangu felt he was the claimant on behalf of the tribe. And I said: 'No, you are a descendant of one of the people who were removed. Therefore, I have to facilitate the formation of a democratically elected land claims committee'. And I must say that

8   Interview with Peter Ntshoe on 6 November 2010.
9   Interview with Durkje Gilfillan on 26 August 2010.

did not take place in one meeting. It took me several meetings with Chief Mahlangu and his royal council to convince them that that had to happen. I joined the Commission in 1997 and went directly into the 'Kafferskraal' case; so from 1997 until, I think it happened in 1998, and then finally they agreed. [...] So first I got an agreement with the Chief and the royal council. Then I called a meeting with all claimants including the Chief and the council in the farm school opposite 'Kafferskraal' in 1998. During that meeting, I and three other commission colleagues explained the restitution process, told them about the Act and how claimants are defined. I also explained the available options: land, financial compensation etc. And we explained that we need to elect a land claims committee because the committee that was there was actually an interim committee. Shabangu was part of that committee called 'Sibuyela Ekhaya'. Then I had another community meeting in KwaDlaulale in 1998, where we called the whole community including parts living elsewhere. [...] The Chief had not been there at the first meeting at the school, but Chief Mahlangu was at the second meeting at the tribal office in KwaDlaulale. We then had the third meeting again at the school [on 29 October 1998], where we elected the land claims committee also called 'Sibuyela Ekhaya'. And Shabangu was again elected as the chairperson.[10]

Bush-level bureaucrats such as Gilfillan and especially Ntshoe thus seemingly managed during these early years to stick to their exclusive commitment to individual rights of citizens enshrined in state law through effectively containing and excluding chiefly rule from the implementation of land restitution. They thereby not only handled this *extrinsic* challenge to their work as bush-level bureaucrats through ignoring the logic of 'customary law' and tribal leadership, but also effectively succeeded in sidelining members of the Ndebele Tribal Authority, who were legitimate claimants in their own right, as potential representatives of the claimant community.

Nevertheless, tensions were not as easily resolved as it superficially appeared. In the course of the LCC litigation against the 2 white landowners, the court ordered Peter Ntshoe and the attorney of Sibuyela Ekhaya, Nicolaas Muller, to consolidate all other existing land claims to 'Kafferskraal' into only one community claim, as is the common procedure with overlapping claims. For this, any other claim either had to be joined in terms of the 'Rules of the Land Claims Court' or be formally withdrawn by its claimant(s). It is significant that Ntshoe and Muller managed to consolidate a total of 15 individual claims into the community claim by 6 March 2002, but did not obtain any written confirmation from the Ndebele Tribal Authority to formally join Sibuyela Ekhaya. This proved to have considerable consequences for more recent developments.

10 Interview with Peter Ntshoe on 6 November 2010.

Including the chief as chief claimant within state law: recent implementation since the mid-2000s

On several occasions in 2010, I talked separately to the bush-level bureaucrats Durkje Gilfillan and Peter Ntshoe, as well as to the Sibuyela Ekhaya attorney, Nicolaas Muller. All agreed retrospectively that it would have been better to get written confirmation from Chief Mahlangu and the Ndebele Tribal Authority about officially joining the Sibuyela Ekhaya community claim. While Muller had apparently believed this to have actually happened in the form of the letter discussed below,[11] Ntshoe claimed that such written confirmation seemed unnecessary because 'at the time, it did not seem to be a problem, as Chief Poni, his council and Simon Shabangu were together during the meetings anyway'[12] and hence evidently made common cause up until the mid-2000s. Maybe, however, there was also some half-conscious recognition among bush-level bureaucrats that getting the chief and his council to grudgingly consent to an elected committee had been difficult enough; demanding an official withdrawal in favour of Sibuyela Ekhaya was possibly asking for too much.

Interestingly enough, the white landowners opposing the validity of any 'Kafferkraal' claim turned out to be less lenient. They worried from early on whether the community claims by Sibuyela Ekhaya and the Ndebele Tribal Authority were one and the same. Thus, in their 'Request for further particulars', dated 30 November 2001, their lawyers asked in §§1.2 and 1.3:

> 1.2 Does the Claimant Community resort under the Ndebele Tribal Authority and Ikosi M.J. Mahlangu, who lodged a claim in respect of the farm Kafferskraal 181 JS and 16 other farms on September 1995?
>
> 1.3 If so, has the current claim before Court been authorised by the Ndebele Tribal Authority, and if so, when and in what manner was it so authorised? Full particulars and the relevant documentation are required.

The response by Sibuyela Ekhaya in the 'Further Particulars', dated 11 February 2002, was revealingly ambiguous, stating in §§1.2 and 1.3:

> 1.2 Yes but the claimant does not purport to the act on behalf of the Ndebele Tribal Authority.
>
> 1.3 It is contended on behalf of the claimant that it does not require formal authority from the Ndebele Tribal Authority. However, the Ndebele Tribal Authority is indeed acutely aware of the claim and has given permission insofar as it may be necessary. Insofar as

---

11 Interview with Nicolaas Muller on 13 October 2010.
12 Interview with Peter Ntshoe on 6 November 2010.

documentation is required it is contended on behalf of the claimant that such permission was given orally but a written confirmation of same will be obtained in due course and will be filed as part of the papers before Court.

A letter was indeed filed with the LCC by attorney Muller a good week later, on 20 February 2002. While the cover letter proclaimed that 'written confirmation of the recommendation by the Ndebele Tribal Authority as mentioned in paragraph 1.3 of Claimants Further particulars' was being delivered, the letter itself, however, actually consisted in a formal recommendation by the Ndzundza Ndebele King Mayitjha III N.C. Mahlangu. In terms of the 'customary' logic of tribal hierarchy, Chief Mahlangu of the Ndebele Tribal Authority in Nebo did indeed fall under then King Mayitjha III ka Mabhoko, residing in Weltevreden near Siyabuswa. Yet what was at issue here was not 'customary law', but state law: what the landowners demanded in terms of restitution law was a formal declaration by the Ndebele Tribal Authority to withdraw, as a competing claimant, its own valid land claim in favour of the comprehensive Sibuyela Ekhaya community claim. This did not take place, and bush-level bureaucrats did not seem to notice the difference or at least did not intervene. This might have been related to the fact that Peter Ntshoe left the 'Kafferskraal' case precisely at that moment in time (i.e. in early March 2002), starting to work on other land claims in Mpumalanga,[13] while new project officers ignorant of such subtle differences joined this project.

Since 1966, Chief M.J. Mahlangu had actually acted as chief in Nebo only on behalf of the rightful heir, his nephew Poni Jafta Mahlangu (i.e. his elder brother's son).[14] In 1997, Poni succeeded M.J. Mahlangu, becoming the new Chief Maphepha II Poni Jafta Mahlangu. During the LCC trial on 1 November 2002, taking place in Groblersdal rather than in Randburg, Chief Poni was present in the gallery, as reported by several independent observers. Furthermore, given that the owner of portion 1 had meanwhile sold his land to the state, a huge handover ceremony was organized for portion 1 for 16 November 2002 (i.e. in the middle of the ongoing trial regarding portions 2 and 3). Being one of the earliest handovers, the Commission reported specifically about this event in its annual report 2002/2003 (Commission on Restitution of Land Rights 2003: 18) and even SABC 3 covered it in its TV News. As visible in this TV footage, available in the SABC archives, and supported by various of my interlocutors (including Poni himself), Chief Poni and at least four other members of the tribal council did participate in the event as well.[15]

---

13 Interview with Peter Ntshoe on 6 November 2010.
14 See van Vuuren (1992: 188).
15 Interview with Chief Poni and other members of the Ndebele Tribal Authority on 15 February 2012.

However, recent changes in the composition of the tribal council in Nebo and the fact that Chief Poni, a friend of liquor, has been rarely present in meetings of the Ndebele Tribal Authority has given the land claims regarding the 17 farms in Mahlungulu a new direction. In about 2005, the Ndebele Tribal Authority suddenly started complaining to the Land Claims Commission, asserting that it had been completely sidestepped and left ignorant since the 1990s about any restitution developments regarding the 17 farms (including 'Kafferskraal') and that its claim had been 'stolen' by Sibuyela Ekhaya.[16] Broader political developments in South Africa had meanwhile created an environment conducive to such an endeavour of including the chiefly claim more firmly into state law as the chief land claim.

In 2005, the area under claim was rezoned from Mpumalanga into Limpopo Province, and all claims were thus transferred to new officials in the provincial office of the Limpopo commission. After some back and forth between different officials, Jacob Tshabangu became the new project manager in 2010 of all land claims (about 500) that had been transferred from Mpumalanga. Amidst repeated complaints by the Ndebele Tribal Authority, Tshabangu scrutinized the files and research reports, soon realizing that the case number for the 17 farms claimed on behalf of the Ndzundza Ndebele community (KRP 12156) did indeed belong to the claim lodged by the Ndebele Tribal Authority rather than to the one of Simon Shabanga. Furthermore, Tshabangu discovered that a certain Sipho Mahlangu – himself Ndzundza Ndebele Chief in a different area in the former KwaNdebele homeland and CPA chairperson for one of the 17 farms – had given a misleading affidavit in 2006 in support of Sibuyela Ekhaya, creating the false impression of legitimately representing the claim of the Ndebele Tribal Authority.[17]

Sibuyela Ekhaya, in turn, had meanwhile changed its name and structure, establishing CPAs or trusts for the each of the 17 farms and maintaining the unity of Mahlungulu by what they now called a 'motherboard'. This motherboard was represented by Simon Shabangu, while also being chairperson of the 'Kafferskraal' trust.[18] With all the tacit knowledge of consecutive project officers and worrying amounts of file pages lost in the process of interprovincial transfer, the sole information available to Jacob Tshabangu consisted in the written Commission files regarding the Mahlungulu claims. Based on this data, Jacob Tshabangu expressed his irritation to me about the fact that Simon Shabangu declared representing the overall Mahlungulu claim for all Ndzundza Ndebele (while his own claim form only mentioned 'Kafferskraal'), without having any written mandate from the tribal authority

---

16 Interview with members of the Ndebele Tribal Authority on 6 September 2010.
17 Interview with Jacob Tshabangu on 30 August 2011.
18 Interview with committee members of the KwaMahlungulu Motherboard on 7 September 2010.

for such an action amidst the vehement insistence of that tribal council that they had never given Shabangu any such powers.[19]

In June 2011, Tshabangu was replaced in the Limpopo office by Makhanana Senwana as the responsible project manager for the claim by the Ndebele Tribal Authority. 'Kafferskraal' became a renewed matter of concern, as members of the tribal council and of the 'Kafferskraal' trust finally seemed to agree to cooperate.[20] Makhanana Senwana and her team organized a number of meetings with all known claimant groupings related to 'Kafferskraal', in which the parties expressed their willingness to consolidate their land claims into a single community claim. However, new friction emerged, when Simon Shabangu refused to make public the details of the current trust arrangement on 'Kafferskraal'.[21]

When I left the field in March 2012, bush-level bureaucrats of the Limpopo Commission declared their intention to verify all over again, who was a legitimate beneficiary in 'Kafferskraal' in the first place and how it came that the Ndebele Tribal Authority had apparently been left out as a rightful claimant in terms of state law – a puzzling fact for the Limpopo officials, which their files could not account for. Hence, while still meeting the *extrinsic* challenge of having to deal with chiefs by means of ignoring the 'customary' logic of chiefly rule, bush-level bureaucrats in Limpopo reversed the earlier strategy of their Mpumalanga colleagues in now including the chief – not as *chief*, but in his function as the chief *land claimant* under state law.

When extensively discussing the matter with members of the Ndebele Tribal Authority, they insisted again and again that the state had to hand over the lands from Simon Shabangu, and the various committees under his motherboard, to the Chief as only the latter was 'the rightful owner of the land'. When I pointed out that under current state law the Chief could not easily become the owner of restituted land anyway, but that a committee had to be elected in any case, some council members aggressively insisted that in the olden days such challenges to chiefly power would have been solved through 'taking up arms, fighting and killing'. For now, I was told, the Ndebele would continue playing the state game of talking to the Commission and working through the courts, but if this did not produce the desired outcomes of returning the land from ordinary Ndebele such as Simon Shabangu to the Chief, then no-one could guarantee that 'the children', i.e. Ndebele people subject to the Chief, would not resort to violence.[22]

---

19 Interview with Jacob Tshabangu on 30 August 2011.
20 Interview with members of the Ndebele Tribal Authority on 24 August 2011.
21 Interviews with Makhanana Senwana on 7 February 2012 and with members of the Ndebele Tribal Authority on 15 February 2012.
22 Interviews with various members of the Ndebele Tribal Authority on 6 September and 25 October 2010, 24 August 2011 as well as 31 January and 15 February 2012.

Recognizing 'customary law' within state law pluralism: towards an increasingly ambiguous context of implementing land restitution

Different sets of bush-level bureaucrats, while officially ignoring 'customary law', have thus first excluded the chief as *chief*, and then included the Ndebele Tribal Authority again in its capacity as chief *claimant* in their paradoxical attempt to practically deal with 'customary law' in order to implement state law on land restitution. However, as the last section showed, this did not really succeed in taming the underlying alternative – and ultimately incommensurable – logic of 'customary law' that some supporters of Ndebele chiefly rule seem to aspire for Mahlungulu and beyond. Thus, merely held more or less at bay, chiefly rule as the embodiment of a different understanding of political authority and legal jurisdiction has continued constituting an *extrinsic* challenge to the work of bush-level bureaucrats in land restitution.

The situation has been even more complex, however, since 'state law' in general has, of course, for a long time, itself been infused with state law pluralism (Griffiths 1986; Woodman 1996; Oomen 1999) and hence contained 'customary law' as a seed for additional *intrinsic* problems. In other words, 'customary law' has not only constituted an extrinsic challenge for the state as 'living customary law' within deep legal pluralism, but also produced intrinsic difficulties in the form of 'official customary law' within state law pluralism (see Zenker and Hoehne 2018 in this volume). As Bennett (2006: 17) observes, 'customary law' was recognized during South African colonialism first in Natal (1849), then in the Eastern Cape (1879), Transvaal (1885) and Southern Bechuanaland (1895). Sources of this official 'customary law' have consisted in formal codes (in Natal since 1878), reports by commissions of inquiry (e.g. 1873 and 1883), ethnographic presentations such as Maclean's Compendium (MacLean 2009 [1858]) or Schapera's Handbook of Tswana Law and Custom (Schapera 1955) and precedent judgments handed down in the Native High Court (in Natal), the Native Appeal Court (in Transkei) and, since 1927 until its abolishment in 1986, the Native Appeal Court (Bennett 2004: 5; 2008: 140–141).

After the establishment of the Union of South Africa in 1910, the Natives Land Act (Act 27 of 1913) introduced racial zones of exclusive landownership and restricted black reserves to only 7 per cent of South African land – extended by the Native Trust and Land Act (Act 18 of 1936) to (still only) 13 per cent of South African lands. Meanwhile, a system of state administration for the African population was established. The Native Administration Act (Act 38 of 1927) modified and consolidated the system of chiefly rule and 'customary law'. It placed all chiefs under the Governor-General as the white 'supreme chief', who had the right to establish and modify tribes, delineate their areas, appoint and dismiss chiefs and headmen, remove tribes from one area to another, establish native commissioners' courts for criminal and civil matters, as well as to authorize chiefs to settle civil disputes according to 'customary law' (Platzky and Walker 1985: 88). While the powers of chiefs were thereby, to some extent, restricted, their authority in local African administration was also officially recognized, for instance regarding the right to control land allocation in the reserves. With the advent of apartheid, the powers of chieftaincy were further expanded through statutes such as the Bantu Authorities Act (Act 68 of 1951) (Levin and Mkhabela 1997: 156–157).

Given this implication of chiefs into the mechanisms of colonial oppression and the growing popular opposition against them during the 1980s (Ntsebeza 2005: 15), it is perhaps surprising that traditional leaders and 'customary law' continued to be recognized in post-apartheid democratic South Africa. Yet §211 of the current Constitution of 1996 explicitly recognizes the 'institution, status and role of traditional leadership, according to customary law', allows systems of 'customary law' to function and requires courts to apply 'customary law' where that law is applicable – all, however, subject to the Constitution and any applicable legislation. Thus, principally recognizing the institution of traditional leadership, the Constitution leaves it to further legislation to define the concrete roles, functions and powers of chiefs. However, for almost the first decade of post-independence, the ANC-led government proved ambivalent and hesitant towards these issues (Ntsebeza 2005: 256–257). While tribal authorities have continued to exercise the right, obtained under colonialism, to allocate land (usually in the form of quitrents called 'Permissions-to-Occupy') in the former 'homelands' (Oomen 2005: 70), the impact of 'customary law' *within* state law pertaining to land restitution proved still rather limited throughout the 1990s. As described before, statutory provisions affecting land restitution strongly emphasized individual rights under state law only and structurally bypassed chiefs in the control and allocation of land. During the first 5 years under Mandela's presidency, the Department of Land Affairs (DLA) under Minister Derek Hanekom also comprised many former land activists and human rights lawyers (such as Durkje Gilfillan and Peter Ntshoe), many of whom were 'anti-chief' and had 'very little patience with chiefs, unless they had high popular legitimacy' (Oomen 2005: 72; Zenker undated).

However, under the presidency of Mbeki since 1999, the political tide began to turn towards 'African Renaissance'. Minister Hanekom was replaced by the 'Africanist' minister with a tribal background, Thoko Didiza, who was much more sympathetic to the interests of tribal authorities (Oomen 2005: 75). Numerous former officials, including bush-level bureaucrats like Durkje Gilfillan, left or had their contracts not renewed (Lodge 2002: 79, Zenker undated). In line with this general trend to neo-traditionalism, in 2003 the Parliament passed the Traditional Leadership and Governance Framework Act (Act 41 of 2003), which defined 'traditional leadership' in §1 as 'the customary institutions or structures, or customary systems or procedures of governance, recognised, utilised or practised by traditional communities'.

Furthermore, it recognized both traditional communities and traditional councils, giving these councils broad but largely unspecific functions in the field of development and the administration of their communities in accordance with 'custom' and tradition (Oomen 2005: 69). The Act thereby effectively endorsed the tribal authorities set up under the Bantu Authorities Act (1951) as a legitimate foundation for a post-1994 traditional order (Ntsebeza 2005: 14). The subsequent Communal Land Rights Act (Act 11 of 2004) then envisioned traditional councils as having the authority to administer and allocate land in so-called 'communal lands', including land in former homelands, but also land restituted or redistributed to communities.

The Communal Land Rights Act (2004) was assented, but not enacted, by President Mbeki on 20 July 2004, given that several rural communities, supported by legal activists, from early on had expressed their opposition and intention to challenge the constitutionality of this Act (Claassens and Cousins 2008; Zenker 2012, undated). In 2010, the Constitutional Court did indeed declare the Act invalid due to its improper procedural enactment.[23] Despite this fiasco, however, several other neo-traditional bills have been introduced in Parliament. These include the Traditional Courts Bill (B1 of 2017), which was reintroduced into the legislative process in January 2017 after having been submitted and withdrawn already two times since 2008 due to massive protest from civil society. Many legal activists have feared that this legislation might give chiefs even more judicial powers than they had under apartheid (Law Race and Gender Research Unit 2011; Mnisi Weeks 2011; Claassens 2014).

This recent wave of retribalizing legislation, resuscitating chiefly powers in South Africa's 'communal' countryside, has directly impacted on the work of bush-level bureaucrats implementing land restitution, and has challenged it from within, even though – officially – this legislation does not deal with land restitution. As Peter Ntshoe put it:

> One must also say, and that's my own personal view, from the experience that I have: the government of South Africa did not want to come clear in terms of what should happen about the chiefs. When they give instructions to us as the bureaucrats, to ourselves as officials, they will say: 'the law is law; law is law'. But when they meet with the chiefs, then they will say: 'no, we need to look at that, because, you know, this is our tradition'. And that creates problems for us as officials. Because as officials we look at the Act, and say: 'this is the Act'. [...] The politicians don't want to come up rightly to say to the chiefs: 'we have a legislation that says one, two, three – as the officials are saying!' You know. They want to please traditional authorities. So that, come the elections, traditional authorities will support them. But we have a legislation in

---

23 See *Tongoane and Others v National Minister for Agriculture and Land Affairs and Others* 2010 (8) BCLR 741 (CC), §§98–127 and 133.

place! And anything as officials, anything that we do, we do that within the parameters of the Restitution Act; we do that within the parameters of the Constitution of South Africa; anything that we do! So, you know, when it comes to the tribal authority, it is a bit of a grey area. [...]. I think the politicians want to amend the CPA Act and make it more favourable to chiefs because in all these areas, where there are tribal authorities, there are disputes. The dispute is about who should administer the land! [...] The CPA Act says, the *people* should administer the land. [...] And the Traditional Leadership Act gives the *chiefs* power; it does not talk about 'administering the land', but it talks about 'development'. [...] Now how do you develop, if you do not administer? [...] That's why we have these types of conflicts between elected CPA committees and chiefs everywhere! It's an endemic problem![24]

Thus, attempts by bush-level bureaucrats such as Peter Ntshoe, Jacob Tshabangu and Makhanana Senwana to implement restitution law against the *extrinsic* challenge of chiefly rule have been further complicated through the *intrinsic* problem of an increasingly incompatible recognition of 'customary law' within state law pluralism related to land issues, especially in recent years. While the state law on restitution as such has not (yet) been changed, hardly reconcilable other statutes have been added, increasing ambiguity and introducing conflicting directives into the work of bush-level bureaucrats. The controversy, whether elected communities (as demanded by the CPA Act) or chiefs (as provided for by the Traditional Leadership Act), should administer the land, is a case in point. But even when legislation such as the Communal Land Rights Act (2004) was not yet enacted and subject to a constitutional challenge, the declared intention of Parliament to transfer to chiefs land only recently restituted to CPAs already gave traditional authorities more bargaining power in local conflicts over land.

Under such conditions of increasingly ambiguous and conflicting policy goals and highly complex situations on the ground, bush-level bureaucrats indeed continue to exercise considerable discretion in their day-to-day decisions, and thereby contribute to defining *de facto* state policies, as Lipsky observed. But these ground-level officials do so under profoundly transformed policy conditions, which are themselves the outcome of *de facto* policy productions occurring in higher-level arenas that are situated well beyond the reach of 'the bush'.

Conclusion: when bush-level bureaucrats have to deal with 'customary law'

In this chapter I have used the case study of a communal land claim regarding the restitution of 17 farms in the Mahlungulu area of (now) Limpopo

---

24 Interview with Peter Ntshoe on 6 November 2010.

Province in order to provide some answer to the question of how state representatives, in practice, handle the paradox of dealing with 'customary law' in order to implement state law. I built on Lipsky's notion of street-level bureaucrats, dealing directly with citizens as clients of public services and using their discretion to *de facto* define state polices. Yet I proposed that, apart from the *intrinsic* challenges related to acts of policy translation *within* state bureaucracies, officials in South African land restitution also face the *extrinsic* problem of dealing with chiefs who insist on ruling in rural areas.

Following some exemplary 'bush-level bureaucrats' into their work related to the land claims in and around the 'Kafferskraal' farm, I noticed two main strategies used over time: during an early phase lasting from the mid-1990s until about the mid-2000s, officials attempted to implement the exclusive focus on individual rights of citizens inscribed into restitution law not only through ignoring, but also through *de facto* rejecting and excluding any chiefly rule under 'customary law' that, by law, they were meant to merely ignore. For that, they could build on both relatively consistent legal provisions emphasizing individual rights even within communal land claims and on a political climate sceptical of traditional authorities and in support of a transformative agenda. During a more recent phase since the mid-2000s, a different set of bush-level bureaucrats – largely ignorant of earlier tensions and negotiated agreements between the elected committee and the traditional council due to procedural mistakes and lost knowledge through the inter-provincial transferral of this case – took a different route: based on the papers, they included the chief as the chief *land claimant*, while continuing to exclude him as the proclaimed *chief* of the land; in other words, they included him as *citizen-beneficiary* rather than as chief. Nevertheless, this new state backing of the chief as chief *land claimant* could be (mis)construed as also constituting some form of state recognition of the chiefly claim to locally rule over the land *as chief* – an effect that previous generations of restitution officials had successfully managed to prevent.

While the state, in its attempt to deal internally with the externality of 'customary law', could evidently not solve the paradox of customary law, but merely process and reposition it (Luhmann 1991), the increased recognition of 'customary law' within state law that also deals, one way or the other, with questions of access and control of land has further increased the tensions and also transformed them into an additionally intrinsic challenge. Bush-level bureaucrats have been increasingly confronted with irreconcilable policy goals, in which their discretion theoretically increases, but – progressively lacking the force of law – practically implodes. This reveals that the arena of bush-level bureaucrats, while surely constituting an important juncture of *de facto* policy-making, as Lipsky pointed out, is but one node in a much longer chain or larger network of translations (Rottenburg 2009), in which the matters of policy become reworked and revised in arena-specific ways that – from the point of view of bush-level bureaucrats – often systematically cannot make sense.

To these explicit strategies utilized by bush-level bureaucrats in order to deal with the incommensurable logic of 'customary law' can be added another more implicit 'strategy', deriving from the paradoxical fact that in South African land restitution – as in other contexts where state capacity does not live up to its promises (e.g. Haller and Merten 2008) – 'the state' is simultaneously present and absent: in rural restitution conflicts, the state is *present* in its self-conception as the sole and ultimate lawmaking authority on land governance (subject to the Constitution), whereas it is *absent* most of the time when it comes to its ability to actually enforce its law. Yet this relative failure of what could be described as a 'palimpsest state', inscribing its rules in a gesture of exclusivity, while *de facto* allowing incommensurable authorities to scratch off, overwrite and overrule the state monopoly in its absence, has, of course, instrumental potential as well. It allows bush-level bureaucrats under the conditions (and pretence) of limited resources to deal with 'customary law' in concrete settings also through sitting it out and *not* dealing with it at all.[25] In other words, the state can to some extent also *de facto* simply ignore the problem of 'customary law' *and* state law, thereby outsourcing this 'conflict of laws' to non-statal actors in local arenas who, in turn, find themselves in the unenviable position of now having to process this paradox. But that is the subject for another analysis.

References

Bennett, T.W. 2004. *Customary law in South Africa*. Lansdowne: Juta.
Bennett, T.W. 2006. The conflict of laws, in *Introduction to legal pluralism in South Africa* (2nd edition), edited by J.C. Bekker, C. Rautenbach and N.M.I. Goolam. Durban: LexisNexis Butterworths, 15–27.
Bennett, T.W. 2008. 'Official' vs 'living' customary law: dilemmas of description and recognition, in *Land, power and custom: controversies generated by South Africa's Communal Land Rights Act*, edited by A. Claassens and B. Cousins. Cape Town/Athens, OH: Legal Resources Centre/Ohio University Press, 138–153.
Best, J. 2012. Bureaucratic ambiguity. *Economy and Society* 41(1), 84–106.
Claassens, A. 2014. Denying ownership and equal citizenship: continuities in the state's use of law and 'custom', 1913–2013. *Journal of Southern African Studies* 40(4), 761–779.
Claassens, A. and Cousins, B. (eds). 2008. *Land, power and custom: controversies generated by South Africa's Communal Land Rights Act*. Cape Town/Athens, OH: Legal Resources Centre/Ohio University Press.
Commission on Restitution of Land Rights. 2003. *Annual report 2002/03*. Pretoria: Department of Land Affairs.

---

25 This strategy to internally deal with conflicting demands is similar to the one exhibited by the 'cunning state' as described by Shalini Randeria (2007), which plays off conflicting demands emanating from the domestic and the transnational spheres by strategically feigning lack of (sufficient) state capacity to both audiences.

Delius, P. 1989. The Ndzundza Ndebele: indenture and the making of ethnic identity, in *Holding their ground: class, locality and culture in 19th and 20th century South Africa*, edited by P. Bonne, I. Hofmeyr, D. James and T. Lodge. Johannesburg: Witwatersrand University Press, 227–258.

Delius, P. 2007. *Mpumalanga: history and heritage.* Scottsville: University of Kwazulu-Natal Press.

Delius, P. and Hay M.A. 2009. *Mpumalanga: an illustrated history.* Johannesburg: Highveld.

Derman, B., Lahiff, E. and Sjaastad, E. 2010. Strategic questions about strategic partners: challenges and pitfalls in South Africa's new model of land restitution, in *Land, memory, reconstruction, and justice: perspectives on land claims in South Africa*, edited by C. Walker, A. Bohlin, R. Hall and T. Kepe. Athens: Ohio University Press, 306–324.

Dodson, A. 2010. Unfinished business: the role of governmental institutions after restitution of land rights, in *Land, memory, reconstruction, and justice: perspectives on land claims in South Africa*, edited by C. Walker, A. Bohlin, R. Hall and T. Kepe. Athens, OH: Ohio University Press, 273–287.

Fay, D. 2009. Land tenure, land use, and land reform at Dwesa–Cwebe, South Africa: local transformations and the limits of the state. *World Development* 37(8), 1424–1433.

Gluckman, M. 1965. *The ideas in Barotse jurisprudence.* New Haven, CT: Yale University Press.

Griffiths, J. 1986. What is legal pluralism? *Journal of Legal Pluralism* 24, 1–55.

Haller, T. and Merten, S. 2008. 'We are Zambians – don't tell us how to fish!' Institutional change, power relations and conflicts in the Kafue Flats fisheries in Zambia. *Human Ecology* 36(5), 699–715.

Hellum, A. and Derman, B. 2009. Government, business and chiefs: ambiguities of social justice through land restitution in South Africa, in *Rules of law and laws of ruling: on the governance of law*, edited by F. von Benda-Beckmann, K. von Benda-Beckmann and J.M. Eckert. Aldershot: Ashgate, 125–150.

James, D. 2007. *Gaining ground? 'Rights' and 'property' in South African land reform.* Abingdon: Routledge-Cavendish.

Klug, H. 2006. Community, property and security in rural South Africa: emancipatory opportunities or marginalized survival strategies? In *Another production is possible: beyond the capitalist canon*, edited by B. de Sousa Santos. London: Verso, 123–145.

Law Race and Gender Research Unit. 2011. *The Traditional Courts Bill (B15-2008): a summary of concerns.* Cape Town: University of Cape Town.

Levin, R. and Mkhabela, S. 1997. The chieftancy, land allocation, and democracy, in *'No more tears …': struggles for land in Mpumalanga, South Africa*, edited by R. Levin and D. Weiner. Trenton: Africa World Press, 153–173.

Lipsky, M. 2010. *Street-level bureaucracy: dilemmas of the individual in public services.* New York: Russell Sage Foundation.

Lodge, T. 2002. *Politics in South Africa: from Mandela to Mbeki.* Cape Town: David Philip.

Luhmann, N. 1991. Sthenographie und Euryalistik, in *Paradoxien, Dissonanzen, Zusammenbrüche: Situationen offener Epistemologien*, edited by H.U. Gumbrecht and K.L. Pfeiffer. Frankfurt am Main: Suhrkamp, 58–82.

MacLean, J. 2009 [1858]. *A compendium of Kafir laws and customs.* Newcastle upon Tyne: Cambridge Scholars Publishing.

Mamdani, M. 1996. *Citizen and subject: contemporary Africa and the legacy of late colonialism*. Princeton, NJ: Princeton University Press.

Manenzhe, T. and Lahiff, E. 2007. *Restitution and post-settlement support: three case studies from Limpopo*. Cape Town: PLAAS.

Marcus, G.E. 1995. Ethnography in/of the world system: the emergence of multi-sited ethnography. *Annual Review of Anthropology* 24, 95–117.

Mnisi Weeks, S. 2011. The Traditional Courts Bill: controversy around process, substance and implications. *South African Crime Quarterly* 35, 3–10.

Mostert, H. 2010. Change through jurisprudence: the role of the courts in broadening the scope of restitution, in *Land, memory, reconstruction, and justice: perspectives on land claims in South Africa*, edited by C. Walker, A. Bohlin, R. Hall and T. Kepe. Athens, OH: Ohio University Press, 61–79.

Ntsebeza, L. 2005. *Democracy compromised: chiefs and the politics of the land in South Africa*. Leiden: Brill.

Oomen, B. 1999. Group rights in Post-Apartheid South Africa: the case of the traditional leaders. *Journal of Legal Pluralism and Unofficial Law* 44, 73–103.

Oomen, B. 2005. *Chiefs in South Africa: law, power and culture in the post-apartheid era*. Oxford: James Currey.

Platzky, L. and Walker, C. 1985. *The surplus people: forced removals in South Africa*. Johannesburg: Ravan Press.

Randeria, S. 2007. The state of globalization: legal plurality, overlapping sovereignties and ambiguous alliances between civil society and the cunning state in India. *Theory, Culture and Society* 24(1), 1–33.

Rottenburg, R. 2009. *Far-fetched facts: a parable of development aid*. Cambridge, MA: MIT Press.

Schapera, I. 1955. *A handbook of Tswana law and custom*. London: International African Institute.

Van Vuuren, C.J. 1992. Die aard en betekenis van 'n eie etnisiteit onder die Suid-Ndebele. PhD thesis, Universiteit van Pretoria, South Africa.

Van Vuuren, C.J. 2010. Memory, landscape and event: how Ndebele labour tenants interpret and reclaim the past. *Anthropology Southern Africa* 33(1–2), 9–18.

Walker, C. 2008. *Landmarked: land claims and land restitution in South Africa*. Athens, OH: Ohio University Press.

Walker, C., Bohlin, A., Hall, R. and Kepe, T. (eds). 2010. *Land, memory, reconstruction, and justice: perspectives on land claims in South Africa*. Athens, OH: Ohio University Press.

Woodman, G.R. 1996. Legal pluralism and the search for justice. *Journal of African Law* 40(2), 152–167.

Zenker, O. 2012. The juridification of political protest and the politicisation of legalism in South African land restitution, in *Law against the state: ethnographic forays into law's transformations*. Cambridge, edited by J. Eckert, B. Donahoe, C. Strümpell and Z.Ö. Biner. Cambridge: Cambridge University Press, 118–146.

Zenker, O. 2014. New law against an old state: land restitution as a transition to justice in post-apartheid South Africa? *Development and Change* 45(3), 502–523.

Zenker, O. 2015a. De-judicialization, outsourced review and all-too-flexible bureaucracies in South African land restitution. *The Cambridge Journal of Anthropology* 33(1), 81–96.

Zenker, O. 2015b. Failure by the numbers? Settlement statistics as indicators of state performance in South African land restitution, in *A world of indicators: the making of governmental knowledge through quantification*, edited by R. Rottenburg, S.E. Merry, S.-J. Park and J Mugler. Cambridge: Cambridge University Press, 102–126.

Zenker, O. 2015c. South African land restitution, white claimants and the fateful frontier of former KwaNdebele. *Journal of Southern African Studies* 41(5), 1019–1034.

Zenker, O. Undated. Politics by other means revisited: legal activism and land reform in post-apartheid South Africa. Unpublished manuscript.

Zenker, O. Forthcoming. Mind the gaps: renegotiating South African legal pluralism within the post-apartheid state, in *Negotiating normative spaces in Africa*, edited by K. Seidel and H. Elliesie. London: Routledge.

Zenker, O. and Hoehne, M.V. 2018. Processing the paradox: when the state has to deal with customary law, in *The state and the paradox of customary law in Africa*, edited by O. Zenker and M.V. Hoehne. London: Routledge, 1-40.

Statutes

Natives Land Act (Act 27 of 1913)
Native Administration Act (Act 38 of 1927)
Native Trust and Land Act (Act 18 of 1936)
Bantu Authorities Act (Act 68 of 1951)
(Interim) Constitution of the Republic of South Africa (Act 200 of 1993)
Restitution of Land Rights Act (Act 22 of 1994)
Communal Property Associations Act (Act 28 of 1996)
Constitution of the Republic of South Africa (Act 108 of 1996)
Traditional Leadership and Governance Framework Act (Act 41 of 2003)
Communal Land Rights Act (Act 11 of 2004)
Restitution of Land Rights Amendment Act of 2014 (Act 15 of 2014)
Traditional Courts Bill (B1 of 2017)

Case law

In re Ndebele-Ndzundza Community regarding the farm Kafferskraal 181 JS, Case No. LCC 03/2000, 21 August 2006 (unreported)
Tongoane and Others v National Minister for Agriculture and Land Affairs and Others 2010 (8) BCLR 741 (CC

3 State police and tradition in post-war Mozambique

The dilemmas of claiming sovereignty in legal pluralistic contexts

Helene Maria Kyed

Introduction

In 2000 the Mozambican state recognized traditional leaders as counterparts in local administration and in law and order enforcement. The 2004 Constitution also recognizes legal pluralism and thereby the existence of different norms and institutions for the resolution of conflicts. The state nonetheless maintains the sovereign authority not only to use force and make final decisions over severe crimes, but also in determining the validity of such norms and institutions. As such the state entitles itself to prohibit those practices that either compete with or contradict state law. As explored extensively in the Africanist literature on chieftaincy, this means that state recognition of the customary and traditional leadership simultaneously misrecognizes and transforms empirical reality. In Mozambique this regards particularly the exclusion from law of spirits and invisible forces. Commonly left out in the scholarly debate, however, is the question of what such processes of (mis-)recognition imply for the state (i.e. for the everyday operations of state officials and for state authority in general). This is the theme of this chapter.

Two positions have dominated the discussion of the state recognition of traditional authority in Africa. The first argues that chieftaincy has become completely encapsulated over time by the state apparatus, turning present-day chiefs into little more than state bureaucratic inventions (Costa 1999; Serra 1997; Mamdani 1996; Herbst 2000; Ntsebeza 1999). The second holds that chiefs have become hybrid authorities, as they both draw legitimacy from the state as well as represent a traditional culture that follows an entirely different logic than the modern state (Ray and van Rouveroy van Nieuwaal 1996; von Trotha 1996; van Dijk and van Rouveroy van Nieuwaal 1999; Quinlan 1996; Sklar 1999). Yet neither of these positions address whether state practices may also be (re)shaped through interactions with chiefs. The state seemingly remains unchanged, either as a distinct domain separated from traditional authority or as a powerful entity that has eroded traditional authority through different forms of indirect rule.

This chapter challenges both these positions. It shows that attempts to co-opt chieftaincy to consolidate state authority considerably reshape everyday state practices. Focus is on the daily operations of the state police and on public events where state authority and tradition is ritually staged. This focus goes to the heart of the dilemmas of claiming sovereignty in legal pluralistic contexts, as it addresses how transgressions of social order(s) are handled and perceived. The context is Sussundenga District, which is a rural former war-zone, where there were intense battles between the then rebel movement Renamo (Resistência Nacional Moçambicana) and the Frelimo (Frente de Libertação de Moçambique) government military, during the 16 year civil war (1978–1992). Here state sovereignty was highly contested after the war, and the presence of the Frelimo government and the state apparatus was very meagre. In the 2000s when I did fieldwork there, it was still one of the Renamo strongholds of Manica province in the central part of Mozambique.

A key finding from ethnographic fieldwork since 2002 is that the local state police, after the recognition of chiefs, began to handle an increasing number of social and traditional cases as well as resolve crimes using resolution mechanisms that mimic those of chiefs. This is paradoxical, because the police themselves have been very determined to establish a strict boundary between 'state' and 'traditional' jurisdictions: the state police are only supposed to resolve crimes; chiefs and other community authorities are to handle only traditional and social cases. There are a number of reasons why the police go beyond their official mandate.

At the heart of the issue is a contradiction between local-customary and state-legal conceptions of transgressions. In particularly the importance of invisible forces and the need for compensational justice contradict what the state-legal system officially can provide. The police's popular legitimacy and their authority vis-à-vis chiefs depend on them adjusting to such local conceptions. Failure to acknowledge spiritual arguments in criminal cases, for instance, can mean that the police loose power and control, simply because people turn their backs on the state and seek other dispute resolution forums (Jacobs 2012: 203). This reflects the precariousness of police authority in a legally pluralistic context where sovereignty is not the monopoly of the state alone. Police officers face a dilemma. They are caught between having to act as State and getting the job done by drawing on the 'local ways'. The legitimacy of state officials, and thereby also the constitution of their authority, depends on constantly separating, mixing and moving between 'state' and 'tradition', between the formal and the informal. The result is 'microstates' within the State. Microstates are characterized by having their own combination of different local and extra-local, historical layers of operational logics and styles of behaviour because local state officials 'exert their own personal differences on them [the operational logics]' (Santos 2006: 50). Before going into the details of how this is played out in practice, I provide a brief historical background to the recognition of traditional authority in the context of post-war state formation.

State formation processes and the dilemma of tradition

The different state formation processes in Mozambique since Portuguese colonial rule have, as in many other African countries, been in a constant ambiguous relationship with 'tradition' and chieftaincy. In important respects, state formation has centred on domesticating this non-state domain of authority. Official strategies have moved between excluding, substituting or even criminalizing traditional authorities, to including them and appropriating their legitimacy to consolidate and expand state sovereignty. Yet in all periods there has *de facto* been a mixture of recognition and suppression of traditional authorities, because mechanisms to tame their powers were never really successful and full recognition would be a denial of state sovereignty. There is therefore a long history of state officials, colonial as well as post-colonial, both relying on 'tradition' and denying their dependency on this domain of authority.

Mozambique is one of the few countries in Sub-Saharan Africa where at Independence in 1975 a complete ban was issued on traditional chiefs and customary law, including all religious and spiritual practices (Kyed and Buur 2007). In Frelimo's socialist-revolutionary regime (1975–1990), chiefs were not only presented as detrimental to the modernization of society, but also seen as allies of colonial power due to the history of indirect rule (Araújo 2012; O'Laughlin 1997). The anti-traditionalist and state-centric position however came to coexist quite quickly with a more moderate approach towards indigenous justice. Frelimo replaced the chiefs with village and neighbourhood level People's Courts (*Tribunais Populares*) consisting of judges elected from among the populations. These courts were allowed to judge according to local norms and customs, however excluding 'superstitious' elements such as witchcraft and spirit possessions. They were also expected to ensure loyalty to the Frelimo party-state. As noted by Santos, the creation of the People's Courts could in fact be seen as a way to selectively co-opt 'traditional cultures', in order to make them serve the socialist-revolutionary goals of Frelimo (Santos 2006: 49). This project largely failed.

At least as far as the central parts of Mozambique are concerned chiefs and other traditional practitioners such as healers continued to operate. The popular courts only existed in some areas and during the 16 year civil war (1978–1992) between Frelimo and Renamo many of them disappeared due to open combat or to the establishment of Renamo control. The latter capitalized in part on criticizing Frelimo's anti-traditionalist politics and on claiming that it would restore chieftaincy (Kyed 2007a; Alexander 1997). Renamo soldiers relied extensively on traditional healers, rituals and collaboration with some of the chiefs to aid them in the war. Like many civilians, soldiers resorted to 'powerful medicines and amulets obtained from powerful traditional healers, which created a shield of invisibility around the person' (Meneses 2012: 81). At the same time, Frelimo state officials increasingly relied unofficially on chiefs for information and advice to do their daily work.

Some saw the denial of witchcraft as absurd (Alexander 1994: 48–49). Local state officials also supported spiritual ceremonies in situations of famine, drought and intensified insecurity (Meneses 2012: 78). This should be seen in light of significant parts of rural populations seeing the war as ultimately caused by the failure to observe traditional spiritual practices (ibid: 81). Renamo capitalized on this by casting its insurgence as a 'war of the spirits' (Kyed 2007a: 77; Bertelsen 2016). In short, criminalization was gradually accompanied by subtle, yet silenced forms of recognition and incorporation of the traditional spiritual domain of authority and social ordering.

Irrespectively, an even more state-centric approach to security and justice sector reform came to dominate after the war ended in 1992 and Mozambique embarked on a liberal-democratic transition. Apart from a few studies on the extent to which traditional authorities were (still) important in society, reform focused exclusively on reforming and strengthening formal state institutions in accordance with the rule of law and human rights.[1] A strong emphasis was on depoliticizing and professionalizing the police and judges.[2] This meant removing from the justice system, all the lay judges and any references to local norms and customs. The stated goal was to make the formal system more effective and re-extend it to the vast territories of the country where it had been weakened or disappeared due to the war. Traditional chiefs and other traditional practitioners were not criminalized as during the socialist-revolutionary period, but simply ignored in policies. Implicitly it was assumed that they would become irrelevant once the state system was in place. This did not happen. In fact, they came out strengthened at the end of the 1990s when the Frelimo government had gradually changed its sceptical attitude towards traditional leaders.

In 2000 Decree 15/2000 was passed. It allowed for the state recognition of traditional chiefs and other locally legitimate leaders, as 'community authorities'. These authorities should help state officials perform a range of administrative tasks, such as taxation, as well as assist in conflict resolution. In return they received uniforms and since 2005 also a monthly subsidy from the state.[3] Traditional healers are now also allowed to practice traditional medicine and organize themselves, although official law still does not recognize witchcraft (West 2005; Meneses 2004; Bertelsen 2016). The former village-level Popular Courts are still not part of the formal justice system, but under the new label of 'community courts', promises have been made to strengthen their status. The new 2004 Constitution consolidated this shift

---

1 These studies were funded by US donors and hosted by the Ministry of State Administration. For more details on these and media debates on traditional authority during the 1990s see Kyed (2007a) and West and Kloeck-Jensen (1999).
2 On post-war police reform see Baker (2002), Seleti (2000) and Kyed (2017). On justice sector reform see Kyed (2007a).
3 For detailed accounts of the implementation of Decree 15/2000 in central Mozambique see Kyed (2007a), Kyed and Buur (2007) and Buur and Kyed (2006).

away from the state-centric approach of the 1990s, with its article 4 on the state recognition of Legal Pluralism.[4] There were at least three reasons for this shift in official policy.

First, the low success rate of state-centric post-war reform efforts made it clear that state institutions needed, for pragmatic reasons, to collaborate with actors among the population to do their job. If they did not do so other authorities, like the chiefs, would simply continue to operate in a shadowy fashion rather than support the state. Ongoing unofficial collaboration with chiefs by the police and administrations underscored this need. Many local level officials also made calls for formal recognition in the media and at workshops (Kyed 2007a). This was secondly supported by wider changes in international donor policies towards the acknowledgement (at least rhetorically) of non-state policing actors and informal justice.[5]

Thirdly, and importantly, domestic political divisions and the competition for government power in the new liberal-democratic setup, sparked contestations over the issue of traditional authority. Studies coming out in the late 1990s argued for the continued significance of traditional leaders in administration, conflict resolution and national identity formation (Lundin 1995). These results instigated intensive media and parliamentary debates, between the ruling party, Frelimo and the opposition, Renamo. While Frelimo was internally split on the issue, Renamo continued to argue for full recognition of traditional authority. However, after the 1999 elections, when Renamo almost won the majority, a number of influential members of the Frelimo government changed their attitude towards chiefs. This was likely influenced by them being convinced that Renamo's success in rural areas was because of their alliances with chiefs. On the ground, this national party political feud was matched, in Frelimo strongholds, by conflicts between chiefs and the former Frelimo village secretaries. In Renamo strongholds there were pockets of resistance by chiefs to the reestablishment of state police and administrations. In the southern part of Sussundenga district, for instance, state officials and Frelimo cadres were chased out by disgruntled chiefs when they tried to set up new offices (Kyed 2007a; Alexander 1994). These issues pushed the last sceptics within Frelimo to agree on passing Decree 15/2000.

Recognition of chiefs was therefore driven by both political and administrative concerns. Central have been efforts to consolidate state sovereignty in areas where this was highly contested, such as Sussundenga district.

---

4 Article 4 of the Constitution states that the state recognizes the 'various normative systems and the resolution of conflicts' that go beyond the formal legal system. Article 212 further calls for the development of institutional and procedural mechanisms that link formal courts with other mechanisms of justice (Republica de Moçambique 2004: Article 4 and Article 212).

5 On this shift in international donor policies see Albrecht et al. (2011), Harper (2011) and Kyed (2011).

Undermined have, however, been concerns with the dilemmas of sociocultural diversity and popular versus state conceptions of justice and order. In fact, as I have discussed extensively elsewhere, legislation supporting legal pluralism postulates an unproblematic relationship between state-legal and traditional norms, and ignore overlapping jurisdictions and claims to authority (Kyed 2009a, 2009b). At the same time there is no codified customary law in Mozambique, which makes it a matter of practical judgment to decide what falls outside of state-legal jurisdictions. In everyday practice local state officials have therefore had to deal with the paradoxes and dilemmas on their own. This has in itself conditioned the way that state authority is being constituted.

The local state – embracing tradition, claiming stateness after the war

When in 2001 Decree 15/2000 was first implemented in the rural areas of Sussundenga district the state police were only cautiously re-establishing a presence. As recalled by one Chief of Police 'we were not allowed to be aggressive towards people. We just remained seated and if someone did a crime we would call them in politely to the station and tell them that it was illegal, but we would not arrest them.' Few people came to the police with cases at the time. The police were at worst feared or simply viewed as irrelevant. They were associated with war and militarized governance, having operated side by side the Frelimo government army with the mandate to prosecute the enemies of the state, rather than service the population (Baker 2002).

Chiefs were by far the preferred option in resolving even severe criminal offences. They did so in collaboration with their *madodas* (councils of elders), their *ma-auxilliares* (young police assistants) and the *wadzi-nyanga* (healers, singular *nyanga*). There were also remnants among these of Renamo soldiers and the *mujhibas*, who constituted Renamo's civilian police force during the war. These actors performed the role as 'informal sovereigns', making 'decisions on life, death, punishments, rewards, taxation and territorial control' (Hansen and Stepputat 2005: 31). Yet they did not represent an integrated system of governance, but 'a palimpsest of contested sovereignties, codes, and jurisdictions', co-existing horizontally and partly overlapping (Comaroff and Comaroff 2006: 9). The local state (i.e. police and administrations) could be seen as part of this horizontal palimpsest, being itself *de facto* a partial and incomplete sovereign despite its formal sovereignty status.

What the 'informal sovereigns' had in common was a history of opposition to the Frelimo state. They also shared sovereignty claims that drew on a spiritual idiom of power and evil doing, which had been banned by the state. In this idiom, power derives from the ancestral spirits, who are believed to be indispensable to the wellbeing of the land and the people, but which, when dissatisfied can cause much harm and misfortunes.⁶ Such dissatisfaction can emerge when it is not the right person(s) who take up leadership positions, as was for instance evident in the conflicts over chieftaincy after the war, or when the right ceremonies are not performed (Kyed 2007a). But the spiritual idiom also has a dark side, of invisible evil forces that the living can tap into, consciously or unconsciously, to boost their power, protect themselves or transgress the order of things. As I address in more detail below, this idiom informed local perceptions of transgressions or evil-doing (*kushaisha*) as both having visible and invisible dimensions. The state police were ill-equipped to engage with the invisible forces.

In fact, until 2001 some places were still completely no-go areas for the police, because of the fear of armed opposition by Renamo and, as some officials admitted, because of the 'strong spirits' in those places. These places only became assessable as chiefs were recognized and alliances with them allowed for the setting up of police posts and administrations.

Recognition of traditional leaders

The recognition ceremonies of chiefs during 2002 in many instances provided the first visit of state officials after the war to areas outside of the main administrative villages and towns (Buur and Kyed 2005). Recognition of tradition paved the way for (re)constituting the state in the hinterlands. In this process state administrative concerns merged with beliefs in the spiritual power of the ruling lineages. This is reflected in a state official's comment on the recognition of an apparently ill-suited chief for the execution of state-administrative tasks:

> Their norms and beliefs ... their tradition is like that when there are problems. They interpret the following: when it is not the real one [leader] there are many contradictions with the spirits in the area and we [state officials] also acknowledge that as important in pursuing development and administration. We have to respect the ancestral spirits so that conflicts do not arise.⁷

After this comment the official asked us to turn off the tape recorder. He spoke around ten minutes about a lion who – possessed by a spirit – had caused so much trouble at night that it had prevented the reopening of a road, because the state had failed to ask the chief to perform the right ceremonies for the ancestral spirits. The reason why he did not want to be

---

6 This is not to say that chiefs only draw on spiritual idioms in their claims to authority as discussed in Buur and Kyed (2006). Skills to engage in everyday administration and conflict resolution as well as references to state recognition and law were also important sources of legitimacy.
7 Interview, Dombe administrative post, 2 September 2002.

recorded for this story, he told us, was that state officials do not really believe in these things with the spirits, after which he added: 'but they [the spirits] do exist here, they do'. This reflected how state officials, in general, both embraced and distanced themselves from tradition.

The recognition ceremonies for the chiefs of the area openly performed the ambiguous unification of 'tradition' and 'state'. This was theatrically staged with rituals of offerings to the ancestral spirits that served to communicate to the spirits that the chief was now officially installed. State officials participated by drinking *doro* (locally brewed beer) with the elders from the same calabash, an act that symbolizes hospitality and reconciliation after a conflict. Yet this unification was combined with acts and speeches by state officials that signified a hierarchical distinction between state and tradition, between government leaders and chiefs. The Police commander spoke about how the police are in charge of resolving all criminal cases and that chiefs should bring such cases to them; the district administrator talked about obeying government orders and respecting the leaders and laws of the Government. The physical dressing up of the chiefs in state paraphernalia and the inscription of their names into the state register, which followed the offerings to the spirits, also gave the sense that tradition became 'fixed' within a state-defined order.

Through the different acts and speeches the State embraced 'tradition', but only to reconstitute itself, as a distinctive sovereign authority. Nowhere was this more evident than in the District Administrator's speech about respect for authority. Here he drew an analogy between chiefly authority and Frelimo leadership ('the heroes who brought our nation to Independence'), tapping into the familiar idiom of power associated with family and ancestral spirits, yet insinuating the superiority of the Frelimo government:

> You have to learn to respect the authorities like you respect your father. The chief is like your father ... he is the father of the community, that has existed always and will always exist from generation to generation ... the chief is the representative of the state, of our nation before the community. The chief has to respect the law of the state and the heroes that brought our nation to independence. They are the fathers of all the people, whom you have to respect like you respect your own father.[8]

The ceremonies ended off with a miniature national celebration, where everyone was gathered around the chief's new flagpole to sing the national anthem, an anthem that very few knew how to sing. This was followed by the consumption of local traditional brewages and food prepared for the official state visitors, marking the new partnership between chiefs and state officials. Now one thing is how tradition and stateness is managed within

---

8 Fieldnotes, District Administrator's Speech, July 2002.

public events, which constitute relatively controlled state spaces. Another matter concerns everyday state governance. Next, I address the everyday work of state police officers.

State police officers: making and breaching jurisdictions

As I have explored extensively elsewhere (Kyed 2007a, 2009b), efforts to expand state law and order after the recognition of chiefs were done on two interrelated fronts: informal outsourcing of policing to chiefs and juridical-institutional (re)ordering of the jurisdictions of justice and policing providers. Chiefs were obliged to localize 'troublemakers', to arrest and question suspected law-breakers, and bring them to the police station. Yet along with this 'outsourcing', chiefs were strictly prohibited from actually resolving criminal cases and from using physical force, unless this was directly supervised by police officers. They were also prosecuted by the police if they were caught failing to turn in criminals to the police or provide information about suspects. Three concrete cases from 2004–2005 illustrated that failure to abide by police rules could lead to severe physical punishments, days in detention and/or physical work for the police. Such punishments were not based on official court decisions, but executed, informally, by the local police.

The informal outsourcing of policing was thus ambiguously structured by attempts to claim state police monopoly over the use of force, and over defining and prosecuting crimes. This was the formal juridical-institutional element. Criminal cases included those defined as 'crimes against the state' and thus as punishable by the state alone: homicide, fights in which blood is spilt, rape, stabbings, larger thefts involving the use of weapons and violence, the use and production of drugs, and arson.[9] The police conversely established that conflicts and transgressions not defined as 'criminal' were to be resolved only by those authorities recognized by the state (i.e. the 'community authorities', which were the chiefs in the rural areas and the community courts in the villages). Such cases were by the police referred to as 'social' and 'traditional' cases. The former included: adultery, smaller fights, minor threats and slander, divorce, debt, and land disputes between neighbours. The latter covered specific customs (such as sleeping in the bush, violating sacred places, marriage payment or *lobolo*) and it intriguingly also included *uroi* (witchcraft) and *vuli* (evil spirit possession) although accusations of such are illegal. This meant that the police on the one hand redefined 'traditional cases' by prohibiting chiefs from resolving those transgressions that were defined as crime,

---

9   These crimes corresponded more or less to the *crimes públicos* (public crimes) in the Penal Code which in judicial language means that prosecution is independent of the victim and where it is the state that lays the charges. These crimes also cover the highest penalties. They are different from *crimes particulares* (particular crimes) – such as minor slander and minor thefts – which, for prosecution by the formal court, depend on the victim taking the case to court.

such as 'the taking of life' and 'the burning of homes'. On the other hand they recognized illegal parts of 'tradition' like witchcraft accusations. The police also allowed *wadzi-nyanga* (healers) to handle such matters. This combination of embracing 'tradition' and claiming state sovereignty over significant areas of social life was a recurring paradox in the everyday practices of state police officers. The ideal goal of distinct jurisdictions between the 'traditional' and the 'state' constantly met obstacles.

Chiefs continued to make final decisions in criminal matters, amounting to no less than 21 per cent of the criminal cases that I encountered during 2004–2005.[10] This can be compared to the police handling only 7.5 per cent of the crimes without the involvement of chiefs or other local authorities, although they did take part in settling 59 per cent of the cases.[11] Noticeably, only 13.5 per cent of these crimes ended up in the official courts. Of even more interest to the present discussion is that the police took part in handling a growing number of the so-called traditional (26 per cent) and social cases (24 per cent). Of the traditional cases, all were related to witchcraft and spiritual problems. Besides this, the police resolved a high number of criminal cases on their own, without sending them to the official courts. This they did partly by mimicking the practices of chiefs. First I illustrate how this took place in practice, before discussing why the police breached their own rules by drawing on what they themselves defined as a separate domain of traditional authority.

Everyday state police resolutions outside official law

Spending days at the local police posts during fieldwork in 2004 and 2005 revealed an ever increasing crowd of people sitting outside, from early in the morning, waiting to be seen by an officer with any type of case. Police officers did not just listen to people's social problems and spiritual issues and then sent them to a chief or a community court, as was otherwise supposed to be the rule. They developed set routines for handling the non-criminal cases. The description below of a fairly ordinary day at a police post in the southern part of Sussundenga district is illustrative:

- *Case 1.* The first case concerned an old divorce case, in which the families of the divorcees disagreed who should have the custody of the couple's

---

10   Aside from this, chiefs were involved in settling 74 per cent of the total number of criminal cases that I encountered, which means that they were also involved in handling cases that ended with the police or where other actors like community courts or healers were involved.

11   These percentages are based on my own data sets, as reliable statistics and records of cases are non-existent in the district. Only criminal cases that ended in court were kept in police files. A total of 326 cases were collected over a seven month period in 2004 and 2005 respectively, on the basis of my presence, at a given time, at the *banjas* of chiefs, police stations, and other rooms of justice, as well as on the basis of the cases that people chose to tell me about.

ten-month-old baby boy. Since the divorce the baby had been living with his father's parents, because, according to them, the mother's family had caused the child to fall ill due to *vuli* within that family. During the police hearing the mother's parents rejected this accusation, and wanted the boy back. In support of their request they referred to a prior community court hearing in the village at which they had won their case. However, the other party had not obeyed the resolution, so the mother's parents had brought the case to the police. After the parties had each spoken, the officer stated that, 'According to the Law a baby of this age has to be with the mother'. The father's parents then claimed that the baby would fall sick if it was returned to its mother. The officer first responded by telling them off for handling the case in an uncivilized way, but then himself hinted that future *uroi* (witchcraft) might emerge if they did not return the baby: 'You have to give it back, because if something bad happens to the baby you [the parents of the baby's father] could be accused of these things of tradition.' In the end they agreed to hand over the baby.

- *Case 2.* This case concerned the failure to pay *soro u mundo* (the price of life) of a child who had died due to *uroi*.[12] The case had initially been resolved at a Chief's *banja* (court), but the compensation decreed to the victims had still not materialized. They now wanted the police to enforce the compensation that had been agreed. After hearing the two parties, the officer convinced the accused family that they had to pay. Indicating that he was well aware that such cases can end in criminal self-redress, he added: 'It is very important that you pay ... because these cases can become very dangerous and then one of you might end up in prison.' However, he refused to enforce payment at the police station, saying that 'We the police cannot do this with pay'. Instead he sent a letter notifying a Chief to oversee the payment.
- *Case 3.* Elias described a case that had begun two months earlier, when his nephew fell sick. The parents of the sick child, Tobias and Maria, had been told by two *wadzi-nyanga* that it was Elias' wife, Inês, who had bewitched the child. Elias agreed to take his wife to a *nyanga*. She was accused, but the *nyanga* added that, without consciously knowing, she had been given a medicine by an old woman to kill the nephew. Tobias had then decided to take the case to a smaller police post near his village. The police notified the parties and, after a hearing, the officer ordered Inês and the old woman to remove the medicine. The old woman denied the accusations and said she wanted to go to another *nyanga*. The officer decided to send the parties to the sub-chief because only a chief can send

---

12 *Soro u mundo* is the penalty traditionally imposed by chiefs for taking life (physically or invisibly), which involved a non-negotiable sum to be paid to the family of the victim. This symbolized a pardon to the spirit of the diseased. If not paid it could cause future misfortune for the family of the offender as the spirit would revenge on them for instance by possession one of them.

people to a *nyanga*. At the *nyanga* the old woman was acquitted and Inês accused instead. Back at the *banja*, the sub-chief imposed a fine of MZM 900 (approximately 30 USD) on Elias for falsely accusing the old woman. Elias did not want to pay the fine, arguing that the *nyanga* had been 'a liar'. Two weeks later the nephew died. Tobias informed the sub-chief about this, who reacted by sending two of his police to arrest Elias. The father of Inês also arrived at the *banja* of the sub-chief. During the hearing, he insisted that they consult another *nyanga* before any compensation was paid. He wanted to make sure that Inês really was an *umroi* (witch). But the sub-chief refused. Elias and his father-in-law left the *banja* angry and without paying anything. Subsequently Elias was threatened by Tobias and the old woman, who wanted the money. After this last information the police officer intervened, asking 'What are you trying to bring forward here? Who are you accusing?' Elias responded: 'We are accusing the sub-chief of solving the case badly ... that he refuses to send us to the *nyanga*'. The officer responded by writing a notification to the sub-chief, stating aloud that 'You have to appear here together with sub-chief Sanguene, Snr. Tomas and Senhora Maria this coming Friday the 26th of August and resolve this case here at the police station.'

- *Case 4.* João explained that his fifteen-year-old daughter was asked a year ago by a man to marry her. But he refused because his daughter was too young. However, one day she ran away to the man and got pregnant. Two weeks earlier, she was expelled by her parents-in-law. After hearing this, the police officer asked: 'Why have you come here with this case?' João wanted the man to take responsibility for the pregnancy and pay *lobolo*. The officer asked for the man's name, wrote another notification and ended by stating: 'You can tell him [the accused] that if he does not appear here on the 26th of August, then he will have two cases. One for making a young woman pregnant, and another for abusing the police [failing to turn up at the police station] ... if he does not come we will arrest him and educate him [moving his hands to show that he meant beating him with the *sjamboko* or baton]. That's all. You can now go.'

These four cases reflect the three main situations for taking non-criminal cases before the local state police. First, the police was used as an appeal institution when a resolution issued by a *banja* or community court had not materialized. On other occasions, as in Case 3, the accused went to the police because of dissatisfaction with a verdict provided by a *banja*. Finally, as in Case 4, victims turned to the police as a first option because they did not believe that a *banja* could make the accused turn up for a hearing, but believed the police could. The police assisted people first by ensuring that the accused was brought to trial, and secondly, by helping to materialize a verdict. In doing so police officers combined the resolution mechanisms of chiefs with the use of state bureaucratic artefacts and references to the state police's monopoly on force.

The first thing the police did after a hearing was to issue a notification obligating the accused to appear at the police station for a hearing. This practice also resembled a common practice of the chief's *banjas*. It nonetheless differed in the sense that the notification came from the State and was authorized with the official stamp of the Polícia de República de Moçambique (the Police of the Republic of Mozambique – PRM). As João (Case 4) stated to us in an interview after the hearing, this marked a clear difference from the chiefs. He was convinced that when the accused received the notification he would comply, because 'He will see that it [the notification] comes from the state … and then he will be too afraid not to turn up … you know, as he [the officer] said there the police will *sjambokear* him [beat him with a baton] if he does not come.' Although resolution of non-criminal cases did not involve conventional police arrests, the notifications were presented as an *order* attached to the threat of state-police enforced sanctions. Notably, as in Case 4, this threat was attached to the use of force, which was indeed applied when the police found it necessary.[13] That police notifications were effective was underscored by the fact that in only one of the incidents I came across did the accused completely fail to turn up.

In terms of verdicts, the police did not hand down sentences, as judges in the official courts do, but played the role of mediators in supporting resolutions. They listening to the parties and concluded by supporting one of their proposals. The police officers thereby adjusted to the parties' own notions of what was appropriate justice, rather than basing judgments on written law. When trying to convince the parties to abide by a resolution they did however refer to state law. They did so often interchangeably with warnings of the potential risks of future *uroi* inflictions if the accused did not abide by a verdict. These practices strikingly resembled those that I observed in the *banjas* (Kyed 2007a). The police officers however differed from chiefs by refusing to enforce the final verdicts. Their support ended with writing police notifications with the verdict and the names, which were issued as 'tickets' to be 'cashed in' at the *banja* of a chief or a community court. They 'returned' *uroi* cases, which required (another) *nyanga* consultation, to chiefs, because, as was explained, 'only a chief can send people to a *nyanga*'. Even though the notifications provided no guarantee, they did put extra pressure on the chief and the accused party to materialize a verdict.

These practices of the police suggest that, although they drew on the traditional domain of justice enforcement, their capacity to facilitate resolutions of non-criminal cases was dependent on also enacting the distinctive authority of the police as State. By referring traditional and social cases (back) to the community authorities, the police also re-enacted the

---

13 In 2004 I encountered three incidents in which the accused (two of *uroi*, one of *lobolo* payment) were punished with the *sjamboko* because they only turned up at the police station after a second notification.

boundaries between distinct domains of authority, the 'traditional' and the 'state'. In my sixty interviews with members of the population it also became apparent that the police were summoned in non-criminal cases because of how they differed from the chiefs by being state representatives. 85 percent stated that 'it is because the police are quicker than the chief'. This was related to the police's ability to make people appear for hearings and pay compensation. Both were tied to the state police's instruments of force and capacity for physical violence. This was captured in statements such as: 'People here believe that the police are very quick ... because they can beat people and put them in the cells.'[14] Hence it was the specific stateness of the police that made them relevant in resolving non-criminal cases.[15] Yet to bring such cases before the police only really made sense in the first place, because the police adjusted themselves to local perceptions of transgressions and demands for justice.

Similar dynamics regarded the conclusion of criminal cases by the local police (i.e. without any official court hearing). A core difference was that when it came to crimes the police did enforce the verdicts, which included compensational payments in money for stolen goods and fines in cases such as rape, physical aggression and arson. This was done in direct response to the wishes of the victims and their families, just as I observed it in the *banjas*. The police commonly gave the option to open a criminal process, but then allowed the parties to have it resolved differently at the police post. It was also common for the police officers to allow – albeit they would never officially admit to it or put it in their records – the spiritual idiom of power and evil-doing to influence the handling of criminal offences.[16] In one case for instance the police took into consideration that the accused of arson claimed that his crime was due to having been possessed by an evil spirit sent by a neighbour who had fought with his father over a piece of land. The officer on duty judged that the man should help rebuild the house he had burnt. Simultaneously, the officer recognized the aspect about the spirit, and sent that part of the case to be resolved by the chief. Thereby, the officer also recognized the neighbour as a perpetrator. The police also on some

---

14   Interview, male resident of Gudza chieftaincy, approximately 60 years old, August 2005.

15   In hearing these kinds of cases the police officers did not receive any payment for case resolution as in the chiefs' courts. This was also highlighted as an advantage by persons seeking the police rather than the chiefs. The state police in Mozambique are otherwise notorious for corrupt practices, especially in relation to the extortion of money during patrols as well as in handling larger organized crimes. During my fieldwork in Maputo a discourse of corruption was much more prevalent in explaining the failure of police to properly resolve crimes, as they would, it was widely believed, receive payment to release suspects without charges. In Sussundenga during 2004–2005 this was also heard of, but did not dominate popular perceptions of the state police. What was shared was a perception that police decisions are negotiable, and not stringently attached to the letter of law.

16   On similar police practices in Gorongosa District, also a former war zone and Renamo stronghold, in the neighbouring province, see Jacobs (2012).

occasions allowed a criminal case to be reclassified as a traditional case in response to the requests of the victims or their families. The below case is illustrative:

- *Case 5.* One couple accused a young man for having 'taken the virginity' of their sixteen-year-old daughter. At a *banja* it was established that the young man should pay a fine of MZM 4000 (130 USD) for having slept with the girl without marriage arrangements and he was also ordered to pay an equivalent amount in *lobolo*. But he failed to pay, and then the parents took the case to the police. Here the case was immediately defined as 'rape against minors', and thus as a public crime that must be prosecuted. In conformity with official law, the police sent the girl for hospital examination and arrested the man. From the hospital the police got proof that the girl had been raped, and explained to the man that 'what you have done is a crime ... now you have to go to prison ... we must open a criminal process'. However, the parents of the girl protested against this decision, whereafter the officer asked 'what is it you want then?' Before anyone could answer he looked at the youngsters, asking 'Do you want each other? Do you want to marry?' The parties all agreed that the young man should pay the fines and begin the marriage arrangements, but before they left the officer reminded them that 'he could go to prison for this crime'.

As in the above case, it is clear that cases could have various meanings depending on their interpretation according to different sets of rules and to the interests of the people involved. The police allowed for flexibility in the interpretation of a case, in accordance with the wishes of the victims. This commonly resulted in punishments that are typically associated with the *banjas*, namely compensatory forms of justice. However, the police often combined these forms of justice with types of punishments that rural residents associated with the state police: physical force, public work for the police and/or detention in the cells for a few days. These additional, extra-legal punishments constituted an important distinction between how the police resolved crimes and how the chiefs resolved crimes. The chiefs lacked the power to effectively implement rulings against the will of the contenders.

The question is why the police went through all the trouble of resolving an ever-increasing number of cases, including those that according to their own definitions were under the jurisdiction of chiefs and other community authorities.

Why did the state police resolve witchcraft and crimes locally?

Police dealings with non-criminal cases completely contradicted the shared opinion expressed to me by chiefs, police officers and the population alike:

the police do not know of *uroi* and do not have the mandate to deal with it, and; the police do not interfere in 'social' problems.[17] Such opinions may reflect that the police's dealings with traditional cases are relatively new or have increased in the post-war era. What is certain, however, is that the opinions reflect the paradoxes faced by police officers in trying to consolidate state sovereignty in a context where such authority is challenged and where state law does not correspond well with local conceptions of transgressions and justice demands.

The District Commander of Police stated again and again to me that the police cannot deal with *uroi* but also stressed: 'Really, if the practices of *uroi* diminish, then I also think that crime will diminish. But this *uroi* is for the chief to resolve, because it is outside the law.'[18] At the same time he took no measures to discipline officers who did handle *uroi*. I also overheard him several times speaking to parties within his police station about the dangers of spirits and *uroi* in criminal cases, when he passed by to oversee hearings. The police had to adjust themselves to local conceptions of transgressions to be relevant and legitimate. Many officers themselves, albeit very reluctantly, shared such conceptions, while also trying to act as State.

As touched upon earlier, popular understandings of transgressions in Sussundenga were intimately related to the realm of spirits and invisible evil forces. Any wrongful act visible to the eye of a normal person can potentially have an invisible dimension in the form of a spirit possession or it can result from or lead to an invisible act of evil-doing. For instance, in the case referred to earlier the man, it was believed, had committed arson, because he was possessed by an evil spirit (*vuli*), which was the result of a conflict that his father had been involved in and that had never been properly resolved. In other cases *uroi*, manifested by illness, madness or even death was interpreted as revenge over visible crimes (such as arson, rape, theft and murder) that had not been resolved in the right way. People who failed to pay *lobolo* or to resolve their dispute with neighbours could suffer a similar fate. Yet in other cases, the failure to identify and deal with the perpetrator of *uroi* could lead to counter-*uroi* with the help of the *wadzi-nyanga* or imply criminal self-redress (including witch hangings and killings in extreme cases). Failure to resolve cases could cause a vicious circle of evil-doing (*kushaisha*) and misfortune, manifested by both invisible and visible acts. To end this vicious circle justice must be dispensed. In Sussundenga justice meant compensation to the victim so as to 'return' what has been taken or destroyed (material items, virginity, wife, land, child). This also symbolizes a reconciliation of the parties. When *vuli* and *uroi* is involved justice also requires exorcism performed by a *nyanga* to 'remove' what has been given or sent. This is also

---

17 85 percent of my sixty interviewees said the police should only be summoned in criminal cases. The remaining 15 percent asserted that the police had the mandate to resolve *uroi* only if the 'case got out of hand' or 'the accused got nervous' at a *banja*.

18 Interview, Chief Commander of Police, Sussundenga, 31 August 2004.

seen as a kind of cure or restoration of the person inflicted, including when that person is a criminal perpetrator. Only in extreme cases, such as the repeated commitment of severe crimes or *uroi* inflictions did people regard the removal of a perpetrator from the chieftaincy as a desirable form of justice – i.e. in the form of imprisonment or eviction. In fact, imprisonment of the perpetrator was seen not only to conflict with the principles of compensatory justice and reconciliation: it also potentially reinforced a vicious circle of evil-doing. The source of evil-doing remained with the perpetrator, but worse still, it could also inflict a family member. For instance in one case the mother of a convict of homicide became possessed by an evil spirit because the victims of the deceased were not compensated for the death. Imprisonment both signalled the lack of compensatory justice and aggravated the state of the perpetrator and his kin.[19] To end the circle of evil-doing, the parties must return to the traditional domain of justice enforcement, because only here can both the visible and invisible dimensions of the case be dealt with.

The above explains the difficulty of separating cases into criminal, traditional and social ones, as these are overlapping and interlinked. People do not use separate categories, but one word for problem or case (*ndava*) and for transgression or evil doing (*kushaisha*). When helping to resolve *uroi* or a social dispute the police are therefore also engaging in crime prevention. The resentment for imprisonment, associated with official court rulings, also helps to explain why the police resolved crimes *outside* state law, allowing for compensations and reconciliations to occur. This relates not only to spiritual beliefs, but also to questions of survival and wellbeing.

The police officers understood perfectly well that when a person ends in prison there is little guarantee that the victims will be compensated for their loss of material items or in worse cases for the loss of family members. People are not privately insured and therefore have no other choice but to cover loses by consulting the perpetrator or his/her kin. Police officers are themselves residents of the area and are not well-off people with private insurance, as salaries for police are low in Mozambique. Understanding local economic needs is crucial, and the police gain legitimacy from it.

Achieving legitimacy in the everyday work of police officers was intimately linked to the fragile authority of the state as such in the former war zones. This was clear when a chief of police explained to me why he heard social and traditional cases:

> We cannot just send people away. We need to show that the police are there for the people. This is very important in these areas, you know …

---

19 Geschiere (1996) mentions a similar perception of imprisonment in eastern Cameroon, but more precisely in regard to the imprisonment of witches and sorcerers, which followed the involvement of the official courts in prosecuting people accused of being witches. The point he draws is that, when these offenders return from prison, they are even more feared than they were before. This is due to the perception that the state can only punish witches, not cure them: the state cannot neutralize their powers, as the healers can (ibid: 321ff.).

were some of the people have had this thing of not collaborating with the police because of the war. It is to regain the trust of the people.[20]

Settling non-criminal cases provided a concrete space for addressing the precarious authority of the police in particular and of state sovereignty more generally. When people took a case to the police, this in itself was an act recognizing the specific authority and enforcing power of the police as State. Like the population, the police officers also constantly articulated to me how distinct they were from chiefs:

> It is clear that people do this [take uroi and social cases to the Police] because the police have instruments that can ensure obedience to law and order. When a person is notified by the police, they become very scared because he knows that if he does not obey he will end in prison ... or be educated [beaten] ... and the chiefs do not have any instrument really to make the undisciplined fear them. We are the ones who have the power to deal with those undisciplined.[21]

This statement further underlines the paradox of how police officers were compelled into operating *outside* the law in order to enact state sovereignty. This was nurtured by a context where the police were *de facto* competing with chiefs over the authority to make final decisions in even severe forms of transgressions. Whereas the police had the State instruments of force, the chiefs had the upper hand when it came to dealing with the invisible forces. The authority of the police always remained precarious in this area. Since severe crimes were also associated with invisible forces, police authority was even contested in their 'own' area of jurisdiction. In exceptional situations all the police had were the instruments of force. This was evident in the extra-legal punishments of chiefs when these were openly caught challenging state sovereignty.

In sum the practices of the local state police *outside* of official state law can be explained by the inadequacy of official state law as well as by the uncertainty of state sovereignty in the former war zones. First, the police acted in 'the local' way to gain popular legitimacy in a context where popular conceptions of transgressions did not correspond well with state-legal norms. This was also influenced by police officers' own beliefs in spirits and invisible forces, and in their first-hand experience with the livelihood conditions of the population. Second, resolving traditional cases as State was an opportunity for the local police to demonstrate the sovereign power of the state in a pluralistic context where such power is highly fragile. This was done through the threat and use of physical force and detention. The use of official notifi-

---

20 Interview, Chief of Police, 25 July 2004.
21 Interview, Chief of Police, 26 September 2005.

cations and stamps served as symbolic markers of this power. This power could also be converted into personal gains and ambitions for the individual officers, such as access to land and favours in the local area, but taking bribes in resolving petty crimes and non-criminal cases were not an issue spoken about.[22] Now what kind of state authority is constituted through such everyday practices? I conclude this chapter by addressing this question.

Towards a conclusion: microstates within the state

In this chapter, I have shown how the recognition of traditional authority in post-war Mozambique has contributed considerably to state (re)formation in the former war zones. Yet in this process state practices have also considerably changed and even approximated those of chiefs. Most surprisingly, the state police began to increasingly resolve cases related to the very domain of spirits and evil-doing that the state *de jure* has tried to silence and suppress. State sovereignty, while constantly enacted, has however remained precarious.

The result of the local state practices described in this chapter, I suggest, is 'microstates' within the State, to borrow a phrase from Santos (2006). Microstates are characterized by having their own combination of different local and extra-local, historical layers of operational logics and styles of behaviour because local state officials 'exert their own personal differences on them [the operational logics]' (ibid.: 50). Microstates have developed because of the inability of local state institutions to guarantee their own efficiency by relying alone on formal procedures and the codified law existing in the present (ibid.: 54). In Sussundenga the most pervasive local idiom (or logic in Santos's sense) was the spiritual idiom of power and evil doing.

Instead of straightforwardly consolidating a distinct and hierarchically defined domain of state authority vis-à-vis the chiefs, as otherwise intended, the police became localized, adjusting to the specificities of the particular context. This involved them acting *outside* the law. The paradox is that the extra-legal practices of the police were exactly made effective because of officers' ability also to act as State. These observations suggest that 'microstates' should be understood as characterized by a continuous movement between the informal – acting *outside* the law – and the formal – acting with reference to the law. They are also characterized by consolidating their own specific power positions, while at the same time contributing to the larger national project of constituting state sovereignty. This, according to Das and Poole (2004), is a general feature of the state in the 'margins'.

In the margins the extra-legal practices of state officials are made effective because state officials are also able to refer to the 'supposedly impersonal or neutral authority of the state' (Das and Poole 2004: 14). The extra-legal

---

22 In larger crimes and cross-border smuggling into Zimbabwe there was talk about bribes and systematic corruption among the police.

practices 'represent at once the fading of the state's jurisdiction and its continual refounding through its (not so mythic) appropriation of private justice' (ibid.). The flipside, as evident in Sussundenga, is the prevalence of state violence within everyday state operations. This is because state sovereignty remains incomplete or partial and therefore needs to be constantly re-enacted and displayed (Das and Poole 2004; Comaroff and Comaroff 2006). To constitute authority the police and other state representatives have to constantly engage in 'an active and contested process of assertion, legitimization and exercise' (Lund 2006: 679).

In a sense what this points to is that not only traditional, but also state authority becomes 'hybrid' as a result of state efforts to recognize and incorporate the chiefs. This insight differs from the dominant literature on chieftaincy, which has tended to focus alone on the hybridity of traditional authority, yet without considering how state authority may too be transformed through the same processes of interaction (Ray and van Rouveroy van Nieuwaal 1996; von Trotha 1996; van Dijk and van Rouveroy van Nieuwaal 1999; Quinlan 1996; Sklar 1999). In a more recent body of literature on fragile states and peace building, the concept of hybridity also includes the local state, and is used to describe not only singular forms of authority, but the whole political order (Boege et al. 2009; Brown et al. 2010; Clements et al. 2007; Lambach and Kraushaar 2008). The concept of 'hybrid political order' here describes pluralistic contexts 'in which diverse and competing claims to power and logics of order coexist, overlap and intertwine' (Boege et al. 2009: 10). In this order the state does not enjoy a 'privileged position as the political framework that provides security, welfare and representation; [rather] it [the state] has to share authority, legitimacy and capacity with other structures' (ibid.). This opens up for new ways of viewing the state, as itself more plural, or multi-layered, and therefore as more capable of sharing responsibilities with other institutions, than is the case with the dominant monolithic conception of state sovereignty. The concept of 'hybrid political order' is indeed very appealing, as it allows for unpretentious forms of pluralism and shared sovereignty. But is it a realistic *de jure* model for society and does it really capture the whole picture of what goes on in former war zones such as Sussundenga?

In Sussundenga, local state authority and chieftaincy did not merge into similar hybrid formations. As argued by Das and Poole (2004: 14), local state officials in the margins 'do not so much embody 'traditional' authority as a mutation of traditional authority made possible by the intermittent power of the state'. Claiming distinctiveness is exactly an important feature of constituting authority, for both state officials and chiefs – even in the very situation that hybridity is apparent. Hybridity coexists with acts of boundary-marking between what is 'state' and what is 'tradition'. Acts of boundary-marking do not convey equality or shared sovereignty. They are structured around efforts to assert superiority and, to borrow from Comaroff and Comaroff's (2006: 35) definition of sovereignty, 'autonomous, exclusive control over the lives, deaths, and conditions of existence of those who fall within a given purview, and to extend over them the jurisdiction of some kind of law'. We should also recall that boundary-marking was always underpinned by the very violence upon which sovereign power is ultimately founded (Hansen and Stepputat 2005).

As Hannah Arendt (1998: 234) reminds us, 'sovereignty, the ideal of uncompromising self-sufficiency and mastership, is contradictory to the very condition of plurality'. This, I suggest, helps us to understand the paradoxes faced by local state officials in legally plural contexts such as Sussundenga: they are caught between local requirements and the national quest for sovereign power. Because of the violence this paradox yields a *de jure* 'hybrid political order' would indeed be desirable. However, that would require a fundamental rethinking of the concept of state sovereignty as applied in the international order today.

References

Albrecht, P., Kyed, H.M., Harper, E. and Isser, D. (eds). 2011. *Perspectives on involving non-state and customary actors in justice and security reform*. Rome: International Development Law Organisation (IDLO).

Alexander, J. 1994. Terra e autoridade política no pos-guerra em Moçambique: o caso da Província de Manica', in J.P.B.C. Coelho (ed.), *Manica: boletim do arquio histórico de Moçambique*, 16, 5–94.

Alexander, J. 1997. The local state in post-war Mozambique: political practices and ideas about authority. *Africa*, 67(1), 1–26.

Araújo, S. 2012. Toward an ecology of justices: an urban and rural study of Mozambican plurality, in *The dynamics of legal pluralism in Mozambique*, edited by H.M. Kyed, H.M., J.P.B. Coelho, A.N. de Souto and S. Araújo. Maputo: Kapicua, 109–129.

Arendt, H. 1998. *The human condition*, 2nd edition. Chicago, IL: University of Chicago Press.

Baker, B. 2002. *Taking the law into their own hands: lawless law enforcers in Africa*. Burlington, VT: Ashgate Publishing.

Bertelsen, B. 2016. *Violent becomings: state formation, sociality and power in Mozambique*. New York: Berghahn Books.

Boege, V., Brown, A.M. and Clements, K.P. 2009. Hybrid political orders, not fragile states. *Peace Review*, 21(1), 13–21.

Brown, M. A., Boege, V., Clements, K.P and Nolan, A. 2010. Challenging state-building as peacebuilding – working with hybrid political orders to build peace, in *Palgrave advances in peacebuilding: critical developments and approaches*, edited by O.P. Richmond. Basingtoke: Palgrave Macmillan, 99–116.

Buur, L and Kyed, H.M. 2005. *State recognition of traditional authority in Mozambique: the nexus of community representation and state assistance*. Discussion Paper 28. Uppsala: Nordic Africa Institute.

Buur, L. and Kyed, H.M. 2006. Contested sources of authority: re-claiming state sovereignty and formalizing traditional authority in post-conflict Mozambique. *Development and Change*, 37(4), 847–869.

Clements, K.P., Boege, V., Brown, M.A., Nolan, A. and Foley, W. 2007. State building reconsidered: the role of hybridity in the formation of political order. *Political Science*, 59(1), 45–56.

Comaroff, J.L. and Comaroff, J. (eds). 2006. *Law and disorder in the postcolony.* Chicago, IL: University of Chicago Press.

Costa, A. 1999. Segregation, customary law and governance of Africans in South Africa. PhD dissertation, University of Cambridge.

Das, V. and Poole, D. (eds). 2004. *Anthropology in the margins of the state.* New Delhi: Oxford University Press.

Geschiere, P. 1996. Chiefs and the problem of witchcraft: varying patterns in south and west Cameroon. *Journal of Legal Pluralism and Unofficial Law*, 37–38, 307–327.

Hansen T.B. and Stepputat F. (eds). 2005. *Sovereign bodies: citizens, migrants and states in the postcolonial world.* Princeton, NJ: Princeton University Press.

Harper, E. 2011. *Customary justice: from program design to impact evaluation.* Rome: International Development Law Organisation (IDLO).

Herbst, J. 2000. *States and power in Africa: comparative lessons in authority and control.* Princeton, N.J: Princeton University Press.

Jacobs, C. 2012. Spirits at the police station and the district court, in *The dynamics of legal pluralism in Mozambique*, edited by H.M. Kyed, J.P.B. Coelho, A.N. de Souto and S. Araújo. Maputo: Kapicua, 196–213.

Kyed, H.M. 2007a. State recognition of traditional authority. Unpublished dissertation, Roskilde University.

Kyed, H.M. 2007b. The politics of policing: re-capturing 'zones of confusion' in rural Post-war Mozambique, in *The security development nexus. expressions of sovereignty and securitization in southern Africa*, edited by L. Buur et al. Uppsala/Pretoria: Nordic Africa Institute and HSRC, 132–151.

Kyed, H.M. 2009a. The politics of legal pluralism: state policies on legal pluralism and their local dynamics in Mozambique. *Journal of Legal Pluralism and Unofficial Law* 59, 87–120.

Kyed, H.M. 2009b. Traditional authority and localization of state law: the intricacies of boundary making in policing rural Mozambique, in *State violence and human rights*, edited by S. Jensen and A. Jefferson. Abingdon: Routledge.

Kyed, H.M. 2011. Introduction to special issue: legal pluralism and international development interventions. *Journal of Legal Pluralism and Unofficial Law* 63, 1–24.

Kyed, H.M. 2017. Post-war police reform in Mozambique: the case of community policing, in C. O'Reilly (ed.), *Colonial policing and the transnational legacy: the global dynamics of policing across the Lusophone community.* New York: Routledge, 163–182.

Kyed, H.M. and Buur, L. 2007. Introduction: traditional authority and democratization in Africa, in *A new dawn for traditional authorities: state recognition and democratisation in Sub-Saharan Africa*, edited by L. Buur and H.M. Kyed. New York: Palgrave, 1–26.

Lambach, D. and Kraushaar, M. 2008. *Hybrid political orders: the added value of a new concept.* Occasional Paper. Brisbane: Australian Center for Peace and Conflict Studies.

Lund, C. 2006. Twilight institutions: an introduction. *Development and Change*, 37(4), 673–684.

Lundin, I.B. 1995. A pesquisa piloto sobre a autoridade/poder tradicional em Moçambique: um somatória comentado e analisado, in *Autoridade e poder tradicional, volume I.*, edited by I.B. Lundin and F.J. Machava. Maputo: Ministerio da Administração Estatal, 7–32.

Mamdani, M. 1996. *Citizen and subject: contemporary Africa and the legacy of late colonialism.* Princeton, NJ: Princeton University Press.

Meneses, M.P. 2004. Toward interlegality? Traditional healers and the law in postcolonial Mozambique. *Beyond Law* 30, 1–39.

Meneses, M.P. 2012. Legal pluralism and plural memories: the perseverance of spirits in Mozambique, in *The dynamics of legal pluralism in Mozambique*, edited by H.M. Kyed, J.P.B. Coelho, A.N. de Souto and S. Araújo. Maputo: Kapicua, 66–88.

Ntsebeza, L. 1999. *Land tenure reform, traditional authorities and rural local government in post-apartheid South Africa: case studies from the Eastern Cape.* Cape Town: School of Government, University of Western Cape, Programme for Land and Agrarian Studies.

O'Laughlin, B. 2000. Class and the customary: the ambiguous legacy of the Indigenato in Mozambique. *African Affairs* 99, 5–42.

Quinlan, T. 1996. The state and national identity in Lesotho. *Journal of Legal Pluralism and Unofficial Law* 37–38, 377–406.

Ray, D.I. and van Rouveroy van Nieuwaal, E.A.B. 1996. Introduction: the new relevance of traditional authorities in Africa. *Journal of Legal Pluralism and Unofficial Law* 37–38, 1–38.

República de Moçambique. 2004. *Constitução da República*. Maputo: Imprensa Nacional de Moçambique.

Santos, B.S. 2006. The heterogeneous state and legal pluralism in Mozambique. *Law and Society Review* 40(1), 39–75.

Seleti, Y. 2000. The public in the exorcism of the police in Mozambique: challenges of institutional democratisation. *Journal of Southern African Studies* 26(2), 349–364.

Serra, C. 1997. *Novos combates pela mentalidade sociológica.* Maputo: Universidade Eduardo Mondlane.

Sklar, R.L. 1999. The significance of mixed government in southern African studies: a preliminary assessment, in *African democracy in the era of globalization*, edited by J. Hyslop. Witwatersrand, South Africa: Witwatersrand University Press, 115–121.

Van Dijk, R. and van Rouveroy van Nieuwaal, E.A.B. 1999. Introduction: the domestication of chieftaincy: the imposed and the imagined, in *African chieftaincy in a new socio-political landscape*, edited by E.A.B van Rouveroy van Nieuwaal et al. Leiden: African Studies Centre, 1–20.

Von Trotha, T. 1996. From administrative to civil chieftaincy: some problems and prospects of African chieftaincy. *Journal of Legal Pluralism and Unofficial Law* 37–38, 79–102.

West, H.G. 2005. *Kupilikula: governance and the invisible realm in Mozambique.* Chicago, IL: University of Chicago Press.

West, H.G. and Kloeck-Jenson, S. 1999. Betwixt and between: 'traditional authority' and democratic decentralization in post-war Mozambique. *African Affairs* 98, 455–484.

4 Mixing oil and water?
Colonial state justice and the challenge of witchcraft accusations in central Equatoria, southern Sudan

Cherry Leonardi

[O]ne is inclined sometimes to wonder whether witchcraft and the provisions of the Criminal Procedure Code are not like oil and water and will never mix.[1]

(Chief Justice Bennett, Sudan, 1945)

Introduction

Witchcraft accusations have often been seen to epitomize the paradox addressed by this volume: the integration of legal and judicial systems derived from apparently incommensurable cultural logics. Mohamed Diwan (2004) 'treats African disputes about witchcraft as a case study of the conflict between state legal norms and norms underlying popular beliefs', examining 'how these disputes challenge judges to produce fair outcomes when legal cultures clash', for example over 'the judicial practice of punishing individuals who kill alleged witches'. Such a clash of legal and judicial cultures has commonly been traced to the establishment of colonial states in Africa, whose judiciaries demanded a monopoly on juridical violence and empirical proof of crimes, and were thus more likely to prosecute witch-killers than suspected witches. This was not simply a dichotomy between state and popular ideas of justice, but a chasm between entire 'cosmologies' (Lambert 2012; Luongo 2011: 45).

Nevertheless, the recognition of customary law by colonial regimes is also seen to have established enduring systems of legal pluralism and 'composite' justice in postcolonial Africa, systems which are commonly described as 'hybrid'. Witchcraft cases have, however, continued to expose the fault-lines and contradictions within such systems, and hence the limits and problems of the idea of hybridity. While some states have recognized witchcraft as an occult crime and admitted what Diwan terms the 'spectral evidence' of diviners and witchdoctors to identify witches (Diwan 2004; Fisiy and

---

1 Bennett CJ, 28 April 1945, commenting on *Sudan Government v. Deng Diang* (AC-CP-105-45 / UNP-Maj.Ct-41.C.2-45), Sudan Archive Durham (hereafter SAD), Hayes Box 2 File 4.

Geschiere 1990; Fisiy 1998), others have retained colonial legislation against witchcraft accusations and state judicial scepticism towards witchcraft beliefs. In the latter context, it remains impossible to prove in accordance with statutory law and procedure that a person has caused harm to another by supernatural means – the very nature of the offence renders its means and mechanisms invisible to the forensic science of the state (Luongo 2011: 93).

Yet this very problem also ensures that witchcraft cases can reveal a great deal about how justice systems work in practice to overcome or circumvent legal contradictions. The colonial and postcolonial judicial systems in South Sudan do not represent a harmonious fusion of indigenous or customary law with criminal law. The laws and procedures employed by chiefs and magistrates in their courts up to now are not a compound but a mixture. To understand how legal incommensurability is overcome, we must look then not just at the laws and procedures on paper, but at the ways in which judicial authorities and litigants have in practice found solutions. In Sudan's British-derived common law system, these solutions might have in turn become part of a body of case law, and thus a more syncretized legal system. But the solutions represent compromise and pragmatism – the imposition of one law over another; or the mitigation of an offence or sentence; or the transmogrification of an offence in the customary system into a crime in the statutory code – not the fusion or commensurability of laws. Away from any systematic recording of judicial precedent, everyday justice in local courts has relied on similar compromise, and the creativity of judges in translating pragmatic solutions into legal discourse. Their success rests not then on the commensurability of customary and state law, but on their use of legal discourse to explain and justify divergent judicial practice.

This chapter examines how British colonial officials and judges handled witchcraft cases in southern Sudan, particularly in the south-central part of Equatoria Province, and how they sought to translate 'administrative expediency' into legal discourse.[2] In the process however, they also opened up arenas of discourse on the ground, in which multiple local actors were using the language of the law to explain, demand or appeal judicial remedies for witchcraft. The chapter suggests that it was the priorities and strategies of these multiple actors that could intersect and prove commensurable, not the letter of the law. All agreed that the phenomenon of witchcraft represented a danger to social order and public security; that the state had a duty to protect people from this danger; that public opinion should play a key role in informing judicial decisions; that evidence was necessary in order to identify and convict witchcraft practitioners; and that one of the strongest forms of such evidence was the possession and use of poisonous substances.

---

2   This phrase was used by a British colonial official reporting his judgement of a witchcraft or 'poison' case, which is discussed further below. DC Tracey, 'A case of poison', Yei, 31 December 1939, Rhodes House Library, Oxford, MSS Perham 549/5 ff. 1–2.

Of course, each of these areas of shared concern was cut through by fundamental differences in belief and thought systems which maintained considerable incommensurability of colonial and indigenous law and procedure – oil and water did not actually combine. But the common concerns around witchcraft nevertheless generated an *appearance* of commensurability, which was achieved through the creative use of legal discourse by state actors on the ground.

Colonial justice and customary law in Sudan

Sudan was governed not as a British colony, but as the Anglo-Egyptian Condominium, established in 1899 after the Anglo-Egyptian 'reconquest'. In common with other British colonial governments, however, the British administrators of the Sudan Government saw the establishment of law and order as both their immediate priority and as the ideological justification for their rule. The penal and criminal procedure codes immediately adopted in 1899 were based on Anglo-Indian models, as well as on principles of English common law. In personal and family law, both Islamic sharia and customary law were recognized, so far as the latter was 'not repugnant to good conscience'. After 1915 a High Court was established under a British Chief Justice, who sat with other judges as a court of appeals (Dupont 2001: 846). But the vast majority of cases were heard by British administrators acting as magistrates in the provinces and districts, or by the courts of the 'tribal sheikhs' or chiefs. From the 1920s the latter were formally recognized through a series of ordinances, from the 'Power of Nomad Sheikhs Ordinance, 1922' to the 'Chief's Courts Ordinance' for the southern provinces in 1931.

By this time, the wider British ideology of 'Indirect Rule' was vociferously promoting indigenous custom as the basis of successful colonial governance. But the application of customary law by chiefs in southern Sudan was still subject to the scrutiny and oversight of British District Commissioners, and serious criminal cases were still heard by these DCs. As in other parts of British colonial Africa, the so-called customary law was very much the product of dialogue between British officials and the chiefs whom they had appointed (Chanock 1998; Mann and Roberts 1991). The early ad hoc, localized codes of customary law recorded in the 1920s were clearly designed above all to enhance the power and coercive control of the chiefs, who were also equipped with their own armed retainers or 'chiefs' police'. DCs particularly colluded with these courts in the punishment of adulterous wives and the use of corporal punishment, often to the disapproval of more senior government officials.[3]

By the 1930s, however, colonial administrators were also beginning to admit that chiefship was a novel form of government among the previously

---

3   National Records Office, Khartoum (NRO) Mongalla Province 1/1/2.

stateless societies of southern Sudan, and to express some concern that chiefs were abusing their powers. Chiefs began to be tried or censured for illegal activities like poaching and gunrunning, or for 'misappropriating' tax money and other government funds. At the same time colonial officials were increasingly absorbed in amateur ethnography, informed by wider indirect rule ideology, and concerned to document the customs of their districts. Chiefs had learned that reference to custom and historical precedent was the most effective means of justifying their actions and privileges to the colonial government. But others too were beginning to assert alternative versions of history and law – clan heads, elders, rival lineages, church leaders and teachers. British officials became embroiled in disputes and competing discourses, and began to experiment with new administrative units and positions based on clan and kinship (e.g. Nalder 1936, 1937). But the more they sought to know and categorize indigenous society, the more confused they became as to the appropriate means of administration. In the end, the existing chiefship remained – more or less by default – the most pragmatic institution of administration and justice at the local level, with a subordinate hierarchy of sub-chiefs and headmen underneath. Some chiefs by this time had been educated in the Christian mission schools, but the rest were illiterate and relied on clerks, interpreters and messengers to record their court cases and to assist them with the increasingly bureaucratic demands of government (Leonardi 2013).

The court records kept by chiefs and their clerks represented one (often rather frayed) end of a bureaucratic channel of communication that in theory was supposed to ensure that customary justice and law could satisfy local demands for justice and ease the burden of cases on magistrates, without compromising or offending the law and sovereignty of the Condominium government. The chiefs' courts did hear criminal cases, but the sentences they could award were capped at a maximum of two years' imprisonment. DCs, as first-class magistrates, were to regularly inspect chiefs' court records and hear appeals from them, as well as hearing the more serious criminal cases in their districts by convening a Major Court. Appellate and supervisory authority over DCs' magisterial decisions and sentences was similarly exercised by province governors, and in turn ultimately by the Chief Justice and court of appeals, the Legal Secretary and even the Governor-General of Sudan. In practice, the lower their position in this chain, the more that British officials tended to promote and prioritize 'custom' and the need to satisfy public opinion over the official laws and procedures. Each link in the judicial chain of appeal and supervision represented an opportunity for negotiation and interpretation, and only the most serious of cases tended to reach the higher judicial authorities in Khartoum. The latter acknowledged the local, ethnographic expertise of district and province administrators, and respected their administrative priorities – but they also censured ignorance or misapplication of the law codes.

One general tactic to overcome contradictions between custom and state law was to separate the verdict from the final sentence; or, as Comaroff and Comaroff (2004) put it, to separate judgment from justice. In cases of murder, for example, Major Courts were ordered to follow the law in sentencing to death, but when forwarding the case to the Chief Justice as confirming authority, the province governor could recommend that the sentence be reduced on the grounds of 'native custom' – for example if customary compensation might be paid to the victim's family, as the Legal Secretary in 1930, Davidson, explained:

> Although it is essential that serious crime and particularly homicide must be tried by Major or Minor Courts and not by Chiefs' Courts, there is no objection in proper cases to the sentence being made to conform to native ideas of what is just. This is a matter in which generally speaking the Administrative Authorities on the spot are the best judges, and consequently in forwarding to the Chief Justice cases where 'compensation' has either been ordered or recommended the Governor should express his views.[4]

He added that this strategy of adjusting the sentence rather than the verdict 'has the advantage of not mixing up procedure under the Codes with native custom'; the letter of the law was not to be diluted or distorted by custom, though the latter might be taken into account in sentencing.[5]

Witchcraft cases and cultural 'reasonability'

This kind of strategic compromise by British judges thus represents a way of addressing customary and statutory law separately at different moments in the judicial process, rather than attempting to fuse incompatible laws. Similar strategies would be used in cases involving witchcraft, but here less obvious solutions were available to administrators and judges. The Sudan Government – unlike neighbouring colonial administrations – did not enact any specific legislation to deal with witchcraft, ensuring that courts had only the penal code with which to handle cases involving witchcraft accusations or suspicions. It was acknowledged that such cases were better left to the native courts, since chiefs had a better understanding of the cultures from which they emanated. Cases in which the defendants were accused of practising witchcraft were therefore generally heard by the chiefs' courts; while these courts understood and condemned the alleged offences, their limited penalties were of little efficacy in addressing the local demand for justice or protection. Where witchcraft was alleged to have caused death, cases might

---

4 Davidson, LS, commenting on *Sudan Government v. Tudringwa Bari*, 1930 (AC-CP-184-30 / MP-Maj.Ct-41.C-13-30), Sudan Archive Durham (SAD) Hayes Box 1 File 1.
5 Ibid.

be heard by DCs, whose demand for empirical evidence tended to discount the possibility of murder convictions. Chiefs and DCs who stuck to their judicial remit were thus able only to issue relatively light sentences upon those accused of witchcraft, because chiefs' sentencing powers were limited, and because DCs would at most convict the accused of criminal 'intent'.

> We cannot regard such death as homicide unless something more than magic has been employed or unless the victim has by being made aware of the employment of Magic been literally frightened out of his life; repression of magic without such additional features is probably best left to the Native Courts.[6]

As this suggests, the only way of translating death by witchcraft into colonial legalese was to propose that the accused had acted in such a way as to induce terror in the victim, who had then become ill or died purely through the belief that they had been bewitched. In one such case in 1927, however, an initial conviction along these lines was overturned by the Chief Justice and Legal Secretary, who argued that even if fear had indeed been the cause of death, there was no evidence that this fear was the result of a deliberate act by the accused.[7]

The colonial justice system thus offered little legal remedy for the problem of witchcraft with which many of its subjects were concerned. Instead it more often sought to prosecute those who harmed or killed alleged witches, whether by physical attack or by means of ordeal trials. In the highest appeal court records, witchcraft therefore appears not as an offence but only as a context and potential mitigating factor in cases of murder or serious harm. In the debates among British judges and officials over such cases, we can discern a much earlier equivalent of the attempt to distinguish culture from crime that Comaroff and Comaroff explore in contemporary South Africa. Colonial judges in Sudan similarly sought to determine whether culture and common belief represented a 'legitimate mitigation of crime', by constituting 'reasonable' behaviour (Comaroff and Comaroff 2004). If it could be established that any 'reasonable man' would have held the same beliefs and might therefore have acted in the same way, the act of murdering a suspected witch might be mitigated. It was thus necessary to ascertain and take into account common beliefs about witchcraft and public opinion as to the reputation of the alleged witch. Yet while this public opinion might demonstrate the perceived threat to society posed by witchcraft, the colonial government was even more concerned with the threat to public security – that is, to its own sovereignty – posed by non-state justice and killing of

---

6   Legal Secretary, cited in Governor Equatoria to DC Zande, 22 October 1938, South Sudan National Archives, Juba (SSNA) Equatoria Province (EP) 41.A.20.
7   *Sudan Government v. Mohammed Abdullah (Kugur)*, 1927 (AC-CP-190-27 / BNP-Maj.Ct-41.C-13-27), SAD Hayes Box 1 File 1.

witches. Commenting on one case involving the latter, Chief Justice Bennett asserted that

> Whatever sympathy one may feel for the accused in the difficult situation into which he was led by his superstitious background and the delusions he harboured, we cannot for one moment allow any impression that persons in this situation may take the law into their own hands. The accused's statement 'I was afraid of the Government' is ... significant on this point.[8]

Judges like Bennett were keen to issue deterrent sentences to enforce the state monopoly on juridical violence and to maintain a healthy fear of government. But they remained reluctant to criminalize culture in the form of witchcraft beliefs, as exemplified by an earlier Chief Justice, Owen, in 1934:

> [T]he people cannot be punished for or deterred from holding the belief that some of them possess supernatural powers for good or evil. It is a belief held throughout the world – civilized or uncivilized – in one form or another.[9]

In the same year, Owen issued 'A note on the trial of witchcraft cases' to all magistrates in Sudan, emphasizing that the complex and varied manifestations and ramifications of the widespread 'honest belief' in witchcraft made it 'impossible to lay down hard and fast rules to govern the manner in which such cases should be treated'.[10] His first priority was nevertheless to assert the sovereignty of the law:

> The law which should be applied is laid down in the Penal and Criminal Procedure Codes and their provisions must be followed strictly. All cases must be approached in the letter and spirit of those Codes. It would constitute a most dangerous departure from the settled policy of the Government if Courts and Magistrates were permitted to go outside the provisions of the law merely because the people concerned were primitive or held strange beliefs.[11]

This is where the legal notion of 'reasonability' ran up against questions of cultural relativism – could seemingly irrational beliefs define what was

---

8   Bennett, CJ, commenting on *Sudan Government v. Deng Diang*, 28 April 1945 (AC-CP-105-45 / UNP-Maj.Ct-41.C.2-45), SAD Hayes Box 2 File 4.
9   Owen, CJ, commenting on *Sudan Government v. Amin Karama and others*, 1934 (AC-CP-39-34 / DP-Maj.Ct-41.C.2-34), SAD Hayes Box 1 File 2.
10 Howell Owen, Chief Justice, 'A note on the trial of witchcraft cases', Khartoum, 5 May 1934, SSNA EP 41.A.20; duplicate in SAD 641/9/1-2.
11 Ibid.

considered reasonable behaviour in a particular cultural context? Owen cautiously suggested that they could:

> The fact, if it is a fact, that [the victim] was popularly attributed with supernatural powers for evil and that on that account he inspired fear and hatred amongst the people might be taken into consideration in mitigation of the offence of killing him, but the allegation must be proved and proved up to the hilt. Where such mitigating sircumstances [sic] are so proved, the court should then and only then make them the subject of a recommendation to the Confirming Authority.[12]

Again, then, the solution to the incompatibility of culture and law lay in the gap between finding and sentence, and between the court and the confirming authority. British judges and officials thus hoped to use the initial court verdict and death penalty to assert and publicize the state's monopoly over juridical killing, whilst subsequently commuting the sentence to demonstrate their cognizance of the cultural context.

Despite Owen's attempt to outline these 'broad principles' to 'help magistrates to overcome the doubts and difficulties inherent' in witchcraft cases, his guidance must have left considerable uncertainty as to whether and when witchcraft beliefs should mitigate witch-killing. We can only speculate as to how the strategy of reducing sentences at a later stage would have been understood by local people. Owen himself stressed that the government's object was 'not so much to eradicate a superstitious or mistaken belief as to deter the commission of wanton and cruel acts arising out of it'. The uncertainties and contradictions of colonial justice, if anything, opened up new arenas of debate and discussion of witchcraft, in the local courts as well as in official correspondence. Owen's note stressed the need for courts to gather 'all available material' to establish the role of witchcraft beliefs in cases:

> The nature and strength of the belief, the extent and incidence of its practices as carried out in the District or tribe, and the customs arising from it, should be proved by the evidence of chiefs, elders and other substantial witnesses, whose views should also be invited as to the heinousness of the offence before the Court. Regard too should be had to the question whether or not the witch-doctor, sorcerer, witch, wizard – (whatever name be applied to him) – is a normal figure in the social life of the people, and whether or not he is looked upon as a source of evil or good. Every local consideration, social, religious, and political, should find expression in the proceedings, for it is only then that the offence can be seen in its real perspective.[13]

---

12 Ibid.
13 Chief Justice, 'A note on the trial of witchcraft cases', 5 May 1934, SSNA EP 41.A.20.

The colonial state's attention to the cultural context thus encouraged rather than discouraged the discussion of witchcraft in the courts. The emphasis on public opinion ascertained via 'expert' witnesses like chiefs and elders, the question of 'good' and 'bad' forms of supernatural activity, and the demand for empirical evidence would all shape the nature of the emerging legal discourse around witchcraft in the local courts, as examples from south-central Equatoria will now demonstrate. The insistence of Owen and the rest of the government judiciary on adhering to the letter of the law and simultaneously mitigating on cultural grounds ensured that witchcraft and law remained separate and antithetical, producing considerable contradiction and confusion for magistrates and no doubt also for litigants. But this also ensured that any solutions to witchcraft cases would lie in the practice of justice and its translation into legal discourse, rather than in a hybrid law.

Demanding evidence: witchcraft cases in Equatoria Province

While the senior judges and legal secretaries in Khartoum sought to produce guidance on the handling of witchcraft cases in accordance with the law, British district and provincial administrators were faced with the often much more immediate challenge presented by witchcraft accusations on the ground.

> We tell the people we cannot countenance their old methods of dealing with the problem, that they can only give (milder) sentences on proof and not on suspicion, and we shall punish those who take the law into their own hands. The people being on the whole docile accept our rulings, they then quite rightly ask us for protection against the poisoners. The administrative problem that confronts us is how to afford that protection, and persuade the people that our methods will be effective.[14]

The demand for state protection from witchcraft thus represented an opportunity as well as a challenge for those officials engaged in developing state–society relations at the local level. Officials like this governor of Equatoria Province often stressed that witchcraft beliefs and the killing of witches had been prevalent even in recent European history, and emphasized 'the necessity for a sympathetic understanding of native mentality regarding this complex subject'.[15] While they stopped short of acknowledging any supernatural efficacy of witchcraft practices, they did frequently accept that certain people were *attempting* to cause harm by supernatural means. They were also keen to differentiate benevolent from malevolent practitioners of

---

14 Governor Parr of Equatoria to DC Latuka, 9 October 1937, SSNA EP 41.A.19.
15 Extract from Yei B Court and chiefs' meeting of June 1941, December 1941, SSNA EP 41.A.20.

magic and medicine, and, in engaging in such discourse around ideas of 'good' and 'bad' magic, they tended to put aside any questions of credulity. The colonial government thus took witchcraft seriously, enabling it to enter judicial and legal discourse.

In particular there were possibilities for translation and shared discourse around the notion of antisocial behaviour. Witchcraft was a fundamentally antisocial activity in indigenous understanding; likewise the attempt to practice it, whether to do harm or for material gain, was seen by colonial officials as a threat to the social order.

> There are undoubtedly cases where a man performs antisocial acts with the intention of causing hurt or death in circumstances in which both he and the community in which he lives believe that he has the power to cause such hurt or death. We may not believe it, but that is not necessarily relevant.[16]

The difficulty however was how to prove in court that anyone had practised – or sought to practice – witchcraft. This was not solely a colonial British concern; local people had also developed their own mechanisms for identifying suspects, beyond individual accusations. The use of oracles, ordeal trials or other methods of divination had been an important means of obtaining proof and of abstracting the conviction of witches, just as their punishment was often carried out collectively, to avoid individual responsibility. The chiefs continued to turn to diviners or other experts – 'smellers-out' as colonial officials termed them – to help them in witchcraft cases. Their findings were not considered admissible evidence by the colonial authorities, and in some cases their methods were condemned; but witch-finders were not suppressed altogether. One diviner's rod was even appropriated by the government to use in oath-taking in district courts; the government was willing to harness indigenous beliefs in the pursuit of justice and order.[17]

The only forms of evidence on which colonial officials and local courts could agree were witness statements (including expert witnesses testifying to public opinion), confessions by the accused, and material evidence of harmful substances (combined with witness testimony as to their use). The chiefs' court in Yei in 1941, for example, convicted people for using 'magic' on the grounds of their own admission; their possession of objects to be used for

---

16 Legal Secretary, cited in Governor Equatoria to DC Zande, 22 October 1938, SSNA EP 41.A.20.
17 There is sometimes a tendency to generalize about the colonial government suppression of all witchcraft detection practices (e.g. Gray 2001: 340; Fields 1985: 248; Crais 2002: 13). As Waller (2003) shows, there were more complex struggles to reconcile colonial law with administrative concerns, which variously sought to suppress occult activity, or to undermine the witch-finders, depending on which appeared the greatest threat or rival to the government.

magic; or for promising but failing to use magic to cure the sick. Another case of suspected killing by 'magic' was dismissed due to evidence of natural illness from the medical officer; the accused was nevertheless sentenced to six months imprisonment for 'threatening harm' by cursing the father of the deceased. The DC reported his cautionary advice to the court:

> Emphasis was laid on the necessity of proving facts in magic cases just as in any other case viz. motive, and evidence of definite incriminating speech, act or behaviour, it was not enough to quote common report or general knowledge or previous conviction for using magic. This was received without great enthusiasm – to the native mind what all the world knows and says is powerful evidence and public opinion has its weight in any native court.[18]

The government nevertheless invited public opinion to be taken into account in cases of witchcraft, as Chief Justice Owen's note in 1934 had advised. Considerable discretion was thus left to the chiefs' courts and DCs as to how this general opinion was to be ascertained and used. Like the gap between verdict and sentence, this represented another area of manoeuvre, in which individual courts could negotiate outcomes that were technically outside the criminal procedure code but were justified by treating public opinion as evidence of guilt. The district and province authorities were willing to allow such verdicts, provided the courts did not seek – as they often did – to exceed their sentencing powers.

Proof of poison: translating witchcraft cases into legalese in south-central Equatoria

In one particular type of case, the province government made explicit its willingness for public opinion to play a central role in convictions, together with material evidence. Accusations of 'poisoning' appeared to offer a greater potential for the intersection of witchcraft and criminal law, which perhaps explains in part why such cases are particularly conspicuous in the colonial record. These cases were largely confined to specific parts of south-central Equatoria, as Governor Parr explained:

> In Opari and Kajo-Kaji there is a strong tradition that (many) women practice poisoning as a pastime or as a means of exercising power over the community through fear. There is evidence that the claim to be able to poison is in some cases genuine.[19]

---

18 Extract from Yei B Court and chiefs' meeting of June 1941, December 1941, SSNA EP 41.A.20.
19 Governor Parr of Equatoria to DC Latuka, 9 October 1937, SSNA EP 41.A.19.

Causing harm or death by poisoning was of course an offence that could be heard under the penal code, and therefore appeared a more straightforward crime than witchcraft. However, indigenous and colonial definitions of poisoning were not quite as commensurable in reality. The local category of poison – known as *inyinya/enyanya* in the Madi and Lugbara languages, and as *kisum* in the Kuku language – in fact straddled supernatural and natural harm. It first came to government attention in the early 1920s, when a junior (northern Sudanese or Egyptian) government employee in Kajo-Kaji District 'uncovered' two cases in which women were accused of poisoning; one confessed and was sentenced to 'penal servitude'. A Syrian medical officer, El Yuzbashi Negib Yunis, employed as part of the colonial campaign against sleeping sickness in the area, subsequently wrote up a detailed account of poisoning in the Kuku tribe, published in the government ethnographic journal *Sudan Notes and Records* in 1924. According to Yunis (1924), poisoning was an exclusively female propensity, inherited through the female line; a daughter who refused to 'acquire and practice the art' from her mother would be doomed to sterility. He detailed the methods by which these women extracted the poison, or *kishum*, from snakes, and then hid it in gifts of food to their victims. But he also noted that the poison could be applied by touch or hidden in the victim's house, and could thus also cause, 'by some mysterious power', lightning strikes or attacks by wild animals. As a DC later emphasized, 'there is no clear dividing line between witchcraft and poison'.[20]

By the late 1930s, poison cases were being reported across the districts bordering Uganda, particularly Kajo-Kaji, Opari/Torit and Yei. Colonial officials were now also reporting alleged poisoning by men, but they were told by their local informants that this was a new phenomenon, and that male poisoners were purchasing their poison from 'outside sources', particularly in Uganda, where increasing numbers of Equatorian men were migrating to work for wages in the plantations.

> During a visit this month to Ch. Koshi Gumbiri I heard the old ex chief Gumbiri say (quite unsolicited) that this fear of poison had only been brought into the Sudan during the last 15 years from Uganda (clearly via the Madi who live in both countries). [DC] Capt. Cooke at once asked his English speaking Kuku servant from Kajo-Kaji when fear of poisoning had become prevalent at Kajo-Kaji. He replied that when he was servant to Major Stigand at Kajo-Kaji in 1917 there had been no such fear … I had thought hitherto that we were dealing with a very old and deep-rooted superstition.[21]

---

20 DC Latuka to Gov, Torit, 5 November 1937: 'Some notes on poison amongst the Madi of Opari', SSNA EP 41.A.19.
21 Gov Equatoria to Civsec, 27 March 1937; also DC Yei, Tracey, to Gov, 1 May 1939; Lilley, DC Torit, to Gov, 1 December 1937; DC Latuka to Gov, Torit, 5 November 1937; all SSNA EP 41.A.19.

The anthropologist John Middleton (1960: 245–246) later described similar categories and ideas of poisoning among the Lugbara over the border in Uganda:

> Witches affect their victims by mystical means, but sorcerers use material medicines. There are two main types of sorcerers, the 'people with poison' ('*ba enyanya beri*), and *elojua*. The former are usually women and are said to be traditional; the latter are men and are a recent introduction. Both are spoken of as 'poisoning people'.

According to Middleton's informants, male poisoning had been introduced by migrant labourers, who purchased poison for cash from other migrants, particularly those from Congo. Middleton (ibid.) asserted that it was 'an expression of the fear and resentment of the changes taking place in Lugbara society, changes such as those implied in labour migration, in a cash economy and a market system'. Both female and male poisoning were categories of occult activity associated with forces *outside* the patrilineal local community, and thus poison allegations provided a means of defining community boundaries and asserting lineage authority. At a time when the colonial economy was leading young men to travel far to earn wages, and when communities were being forcibly resettled away from lineage lands as part of the sleeping sickness campaigns, discourse about poison as a foreign import may have been a particularly salient expression of the need to define social and moral boundaries and to reassert patriarchal authority (Leonardi 2007; see also Allen and Storm 2011; Allen and Reid 2014).

The prevalence of poison cases in the courts by the 1930s perhaps reflected then an overall increase in suspicion and accusation due to wider social and economic change, which was seen to be widening this particular category of harmful occult activity. But the reported increase of poison cases was also related to the imposition of colonial justice. If people were bringing more of these cases to the chiefs' courts, police and government, this is likely to have been a consequence either of the government repression of alternative forms of justice, and/or of the receptiveness of the courts to allegations of poisoning.

Poison allegations initially led to some of the most dramatic confrontations between indigenous and state justice. In 1932, deaths attributed to poisoning in Kajo-Kaji prompted the Kuku chiefs to call a Madi expert to conduct a poison ordeal trial of two hundred women, in which five women died. The 'poisoner-hunter', Ajuko Oluwa,[22] was tried for murder but found guilty of manslaughter and imprisoned for life; the leading chief, Yenge, was fined for abetment. At a retrial by the acting governor, which confirmed the

---

22 The term *Ajwaka* (probably here 'Ajuko') is the Acholi word for 'diviner' used also by Madi (Allen and Storm 2011).

sentences, the opinion of Chief Wye Wye from Yei District was sought to confirm and explain that the women had voluntarily subjected themselves to the ordeal and therefore their deaths did not constitute murder: the court was reported to have paid 'great attention to the views of Chief Wye Wye as regards the thoughts, fears and reactions of the women concerned', reflecting the way in which trusted chiefs were treated as expert witnesses, even in relation to the opposite sex.[23]

In 1937, another crisis of suspected poisoning led several other chiefs to employ physical torture to try to obtain confessions of poisoning from over two hundred women, three of whom later died in hospital. The Province Diary declared that there was 'no doubt that the public panic has little foundation in direct evidence and probably little in fact', yet also revealed the uncertainty of government officials in the contradictory assertion that 'it is probably certain that some poisoning has been going on'.[24] A heavy collective fine was imposed on the community and Governor Parr visited Kajo-Kaji to address the chiefs and people. His speech emphasized that in future anyone convicted of causing death by torture would be hung, although in this case the government was showing mercy: 'I know that you were frightened when you did these things – unreasonably frightened like children frightened of the dark, and for that reason I am not going to have any of you hung.'[25] He stressed that anyone suspected of having been poisoned was to be taken to a doctor to determine the cause of illness or death. The suspected women poisoners had to be kept in protective custody, while the men accused of their torture were released from prison.[26] The DC later reported that the Governor's instructions to chiefs had been misunderstood or mistranslated, so that the chiefs thought they 'were to collect all "poisoners" and bring them to me', which produced a further 44 suspects.[27]

Clearly the government actions in this case would have done more to confirm than to reverse the public belief in the threat of poison and in the suspected women's guilt. This was perhaps not least because the district and provincial authorities were quite prepared to believe that some women were indeed practicing, or claiming to practice, poisoning: 'a certain number of

---

23 *Sudan Government v. Ajuko Oluwa and others*, 1932 (AC-CP-190-32 / MP-Maj.Ct.41.C.16-32), SAD Hayes Box 1 File 2; Mrs Selwyn, Annual Letter Kajo Kaji, August 1932, Church Missionary Society Archives, University of Birmingham Library (CMS) G3 AL; Winder, 'Fifty Years On': Service in Mongalla Province, 1930–33', (1979) SAD 541/7/1-32.
24 Equatoria Province Monthly Diaries, September–October 1937 and February–March 1938, NRO Civil Secretary 57/4/17 and 57/7/29.
25 'Speech made by Governor at Kajo Kaji on 20 September 1937 to Chiefs, accused and general public', enclosed in Governor Parr to DC Yei River District, Juba, 5 October 1937, SSNA EP 41.A.19.
26 Ibid.
27 A/DC Yei River District, Sullivan, 'Summary of poisoning cases at Kajo-Kaji', 25 October 1937, SSNA EP 41.A.19.

women do deal in substances which they aver is poison in order to "put it over" the people'.²⁸ Colonial officials sent off a number of samples of alleged poison to the government laboratories; while the results were largely negative, and certainly no snake venom was ever discovered, the government chemists did occasionally find Cantharides in the form of blister beetles, and vegetable poisons such as *Courbonia virgate*, both of which were commonly used to poison arrows for hunting.²⁹ Even if a poisonous substance could be identified, however, proof of possession and harmful use was still required:

> [W]e are at once up against the difficulty, as the people themselves are quick to point out, of proof of possession. Even the most enlightened Madi is quite unable to understand this fetish. 'But everyone *knows* she is a poisoner: what more proof do you want?'³⁰

The DC of Torit, Colonel Lilley, was sent to report on the poisoning problem in Kajo-Kaji and Opari; in the latter area too, the government responded credulously to popular concerns:

> Owing to complaints by the people to the DC regarding the prevalence of poison, chiefs were instructed to collect suspected poisoners, primarily in order to show that the Government wished to take steps to eradicate any widespread fear of poison in the District. All the suspects were interviewed by the DC and a very large number of them were released, a few being imprisoned on their own admission that they had dealt in what they believed to be poisonous substances.³¹

Lilley stressed the need to demonstrate 'that the Government is taking steps to eradicate this menace' but noted that such steps were difficult to prescribe due to 'the very flimsy nature of the evidence'.³² He proposed several measures: ordering people to take suspected poison cases to the dispensary or hospital; keeping chiefs' registers of deaths and their causes; arresting anyone possessing a substance which people believed to be harmful; and publicly hanging anyone who was actually convicted of poisoning by a Major Court.³³ The Yei DC was critical of the latter proposal as too 'barbaric'; the Latuka

---

28 Lilley, DC Torit, to Governor, 'Historical notes on "poison" in Kajo Kaji and Opari', 1 December 1937, SSNA EP 41.A.19.
29 Government Chemist to Senior Medical Inspector Juba, Khartoum, 14 October 1937; JG Myers, Economic Botanist, to Governor Equatoria, Kagelu, 30 November 1937, SSNA EP 41.A.19; Sudan Government (1947: 9–10).
30 DC Latuka to Governor, 'Some notes on poison amongst the Madi of Opari', Torit, 5 November 1937, SSNA EP 41.A.19.
31 Lilley, DC Torit, to Governor, 'Historical notes on "poison" in Kajo Kaji and Opari', 1 December 1937, SSNA EP 41.A.19.
32 Ibid.
33 Ibid.

DC noted that the Madi demanded permanent exile of poisoners, which was not 'practical': 'An alternative might be found in either short or long terms of imprisonment, coupled with periodical organized police searches of the houses of all suspects with a view to making things as unpleasant for them as possible.'[34]

As DCs shared their desire to take conspicuous measures against suspected poisoners, Governor Parr settled on the following guidance:

> If it is proved to the satisfaction of the native court that an accused person was in possession of what the court and she believed to be poison, then it would be right that accused should be sentenced by the native court. Obviously such possession is an offence by native law and custom. It is immaterial in my view whether the substance really is poison provided all parties think it is, or provided that the woman who keeps it knows it will be regarded as such (and keeps it with that knowledge).[35]

This was far from the letter of the law codes, however. The Chief Justice wrote to Governor Parr a few months later commenting on convictions for poisoning in the chiefs' courts, even though he had no direct oversight of the Native Courts: 'it is essential to prove that the substance is in fact poisonous ... I do not see how the mere possession of a harmless substance which others believe to be poison can be a crime'.[36] Parr disagreed:

> In native eyes the mere possession of a substance, definitely identifiable as a substance regarded by the people as poison, for the possession of which there is no excuse except that others regard it as poison, is an antisocial act which is forbidden by their law and custom under penalty. Such a point of view seems to me reasonable, and one that is not repugnant to humanity, equity or good conscience. I am referring this point again to the Chief Justice, because in its simplest terms the native view is 'You must not keep a substance in your house which everyone else regards as poison, and for which you have no other use except the fear of you which it inspires.'[37]

In a letter to the Civil Secretary, however, Parr emphasized that 'this is not fear of magic or witchcraft, but fear of actual poison'.[38] Yet the definition of 'actual poison' was to be determined by public opinion rather than by laboratory tests. His proposed policy seems to have been accepted and applied

---

34 DC Latuka to Governor, 'Some notes on poison amongst the Madi of Opari', Torit, 5 November 1937, SSNA EP 41.A.19.
35 Governor Parr to DC Yei River District, 9 October 1937, SSNA EP 41.A.19.
36 Chief Justice to Governor Equatoria, Khartoum, 12 January 1938, SSNA EP 41.A.19.
37 Governor to DC Torit, Juba, 2 February 1938, SSNA EP 41.A.19.
38 Governor Parr to Civil Secretary, Juba, 11 March 1938, SSNA EP 41.A.19.

throughout the province; it was still being followed in 1945 according to a Torit District report:

> The recurrence of poisoning cases was also discussed. The government's attitude was defined and the old rule was reaffirmed that possession of a root or other 'medicine' known or believed to be a poison which has no other use, combined with threats to use poison, is sufficient evidence to secure a conviction before the B Court. What usually happens is that an old woman threatens to use poison and is then found to have in her house various roots and concoctions. The old Madi plan was to make her drink them. The new rule is that (following her threats) she will be assumed to have possessed them to inspire fear unless she can show an innocent purpose for them.[39]

Province policy thus encouraged a focus on material substances, which neatly intersected with local definitions of poisoning, even though the latter incorporated supernatural as well as natural effects of such substances. The government even colluded with indigenous opinion in being prepared to disregard the scientific toxicity of the alleged poisons and instead accept local opinion as to their harmful potential. Yet the emerging legal discourse around poisoning may nevertheless have added a new layer of forensic science to indigenous ideas of occult materiality, as the government and medical authorities sent off samples for testing and conducted corporeal investigations to determine their effects.

Compromise and administrative expediency in 'a case of poison'

In 1939, another case emerged in Kajo-Kaji, which was eventually investigated and recorded in detail by a police sergeant from Yei, and then written up as a long, flowery narrative titled 'A case of poison' by the Yei DC, Tracey. This time the suspected poisoners were two men, one of whom, Karibbe, was accused of applying a poisonous substance provided by the other, a quasi-Muslim medical practitioner known as 'the Khalifa', to the body of his young wife, Gune, who subsequently died in childbirth. Tracey recounted with considerable sympathy the efforts of the local chiefs to find judicial remedies at various stages of the case to avoid attracting government attention, after the recent punishments for their handling of previous poison cases. 'The only chance of hushing the case up lay in a compromise', and so the chiefs had initially decided to wait and see if the poison had any effect before bringing the case to court: 'This compromise possessed great merit in that no one committed himself in a matter in which the inscrutable powers of darkness

---

39 Extract from Torit District Monthly Diary, October 1945, SSNA EP 41.A.19.

and poison were rife. Since no judgment had been given, nothing need be recorded.'[40]

When Gune's relatives assaulted Karibbe, the chiefs' court ignored the context of poison allegations and recorded the sentence as: 'These men have not done well and will go to prison each for four months.'[41] After Gune's death, however, one of Karibbe's accusers approached the British missionary in the district with the case, and finally the DC came to supervise the hearing of the case. Interestingly Tracey himself wrote that his speech in Arabic to the chiefs' court was 'transmogrified into Kuku by the sergeant', thus highlighting the problems of direct translation in such cases. He declared that this was *not* a case of poison, and that Gune had died naturally in childbirth. But he then adopted virtually the same language as the local chiefs in sentencing Karibbe and the Khalifa to prison:

> These men however had not done well. They had tampered with the powers of darkness. Thereby they had brought many foolish persons into a state of alarm; and they had imperilled the peace of the realm. Karibbe would go to prison for six months, because he had frightened his wife with a pretence of magic. The Khalifa would go to prison for three months; and should leave the country and go whence he had come. He had taken money from simple folk by his fraudulent talk of sorcery.[42]

Tracey interpreted the chiefs' reluctance to sentence the Khalifa as a sign of their fear of the latter; he therefore discerned an opportunity to insert the external judicial power of the state: 'he, the District Commissioner, would sign this [court] book without fear – the book was here signed with a flourish and held up for display to the public gaze – the responsibility for all such cases would thus be borne by him'.[43] Apparently quite consciously, the DC was thus attempting to take on the role previously played by expert diviners from outside the community, wielding the new mysterious powers of bureaucracy to combat the 'powers of darkness'. His verdict represented just as much of a compromise and contradiction as the chiefs' own efforts to find a safe legal language in which to record the case. Not doing 'well' was hardly a criminal offence; causing 'fright' was little better. But the DC 'departed satisfied that Justice and administrative expediency had both of them been well served'.[44]

Colonial administrators were thus more concerned to meet popular demand for government protection from poisoning and witchcraft, as well as

---

40 DC Tracey, 'A case of poison', Yei, 31 December 1939, Rhodes House Library, Oxford, MSS Perham 549/5 ff. 1–2.
41 Ibid.
42 Ibid.
43 Ibid.
44 Ibid.

to prevent extrajudicial killing or torture, than they were to adhere strictly to the legal codes. Even chiefs stressed popular demand for state justice in such cases: 'Chief Yengi openly stated that he would not have allowed the majority of cases to come; but he, like other chiefs, have been so beleaguered by their subjects demanding that the District Commissioner should see them that he permitted it.'[45] For colonial administrators on the ground, this popular demand represented not only a challenge but also an opportunity to establish the primacy of state justice and protection. They were therefore willing to find a compromise between indigenous and legal definitions of poisoning, which they did by focusing on the centrality of a material substance *perceived* to be harmful.

The use of the English term 'poison' created an impression of commensurability between indigenous and state legal discourse. Yet the forensic science of the state largely failed to support this impression, and instead administrators fell back on a shared discourse about the antisocial nature and effects of the practice of poisoning, and a shared acceptance of public opinion and witness statements as legal evidence. In a sense this compromise satisfied no one: the senior judiciary demanded medical evidence in any such cases that reached them and disapproved of the methods used to try poison cases in the chiefs' courts; and local opinion was not satisfied by the short prison terms that were generally the only remedy available to these courts. But, as administrators were well aware, it was nevertheless significant that poison cases were reaching the courts at all. As in other parts of colonial Africa, British responsiveness to local opinion and attempts to find judicial remedies for witchcraft fears ensured a discursive space for witchcraft and poison in the colonial judicial system.

Conclusion

We can only speculate as to any enduring effects of this colonial engagement on ideas of poison in central Equatoria. But the various strands of colonial strategies for handling poison cases are certainly still discernible in more recent cases in Kajo-Kaji and neighbouring counties. During both the Anyanya One (*c.*1963–1972) and Sudan People's Liberation Movement/Army (1983–2004) civil wars, the rebel armies are said to have carried out mass killings of suspected poisoners and witches. Subsequent efforts from the late 1990s to regulate these killings led to a new policy by the SPLM/A administration of Yei and Kajo-Kaji counties to overcome the problem of evidential proof in poison cases by demanding that accusers identify and produce the poisonous substance that they claimed defendants had used – a policy first urged by the colonial government, as we have seen. If litigants

---

45 A/DC Yei River District, Sullivan, 'Summary of poisoning cases at Kajo-Kaji', 25 October 1937, SSNA EP 41.A.19.

could do so, the defendants were now ordered to consume the poison to see how deadly it really was.[46] Many people accused of poisoning are said to have died after being forced to consume tins of insecticide or other chemical or poisonous substances allegedly found in their homes, in what were effectively ordeal trials. In early 2007, three elderly women near Yei were accused of putting poison in food and water, and were beaten until they reportedly produced the substance they had used, which was then administered to them, causing their deaths. According to the sub-chief, 'the ones who died said that they had bought the medicine during the exile from some Lugbaras'; the idea that poison was purchased in foreign markets has very much endured, and has only been exacerbated by refugee migrations and commodity trade between Uganda and Sudan.[47] In Kajo-Kaji, as increasing numbers of people returned from Uganda after 2005, several mob killings of suspected poisoners occurred, often involving beatings and burning. Some chiefs and other community leaders here advocated instead 'excommunication': the eviction of suspects from the community, which they claimed had sometimes been a practice in the refugee camps in Uganda.

The re-establishment of a formal court system, particularly since the 2005 peace agreement, made it increasingly difficult to convince magistrates and judges of evidential proof in poison cases, especially if the case concerned a more remote effect such as a lightning strike rather than the administration of a poisonous substance. In 2009, a means of identifying suspects was followed in Kajo-Kaji which had also reportedly been imported from the Ugandan camps – and which was already being practised across the border in Moyo District of Uganda (Allen and Reid 2014). After two boys were killed by lightning, community leaders, including teachers, parents, chiefs and local administrators, asked the boys' schoolmates and the wider community to vote by secret ballot to identify the culprit(s). A clear majority identified a particular woman and her children, and the 'election' was seen to have constituted evidential proof, a claim rejected by the county magistrates, police and commissioner, who were nevertheless forced to take the suspect family into protective custody (Leonardi et al. 2010: 56–58).

None of these recent attempts to find solutions to poison cases have succeeded in simultaneously satisfying *both* the government judges seeking to uphold legal procedure, and local concerns and fears about poisoning. But they demonstrate enduring tropes in the attempt by state actors – particularly at the local level – to translate these fears and concerns into judicial solutions and legalese discourse. The idea of 'elections' draws on discourses of modern democratic government in ways redolent of the 'vernacular Afromodernity' that Comaroff and Comaroff (2004) discern in the local handling of witchcraft cases in contemporary South Africa. But this chapter has demon-

---

46   Interview with elderly male retired local government officer, 16 August 2005, Yei.
47   Interview with male sub-chief (formerly a refugee camp block leader), 22 January 2007, near Yei.

strated a longer history to such translation; the elections in Kajo-Kaji might be seen as the latest manifestation of the colonial attention to and demand for evidence of public opinion. More generally, the transmogrification of indigenous ideas of *inyinya* and *kisum* into the legal category of 'poisoning' has supported and encouraged a focus on the materiality of witchcraft and the identification of harmful substances as a point of intersection between state and local legal cultures. In a sense this has produced an illusion of commensurability, just as the wider popular impression of 'the Law' applied in the local courts implies the existence of a hybrid law in South Sudan. But this is an impression conveyed by the skill of justice providers in compromising and translating their contingent practice of justice – often drawing on incommensurable and contradictory sources of law – into an apparently coherent discourse of legality.

Acknowledgements

I would like to thank the editors for convening the original conference panel and for their helpful comments on the paper from which this chapter is derived. Thanks also to W. J. Berridge for providing me with useful archival references, and to the staff of the Sudan Archive in Durham and the South Sudan National Archives in Juba for their assistance.

References

Allen, T. and Reid, K. 2014. Justice at the margins: witches, poisoners, and social accountability in northern Uganda. *Medical Anthropology* 34(2), 1–18.

Allen, T. and Storm, L. 2011. Quests for therapy in northern Uganda: healing at Laropi revisited. *Journal of Eastern African Studies* 6(1), 22–46.

Chanock, M. 1998. *Law, custom and social order: the colonial experience in Malawi and Zambia*. Portsmouth, NH: Heinemann.

Comaroff, J.L. and Comaroff, J. 2004. Criminal justice, cultural justice: the limits of liberalism and the pragmatics of difference in the new South Africa. *American Ethnologist* 31(2), 188–204.

Crais, C. 2002. *The politics of evil: magic, state power and the political imagination in South Africa*. Cambridge: Cambridge University Press.

Diwan, M.A. 2004. Conflict between state legal norms and norms underlying popular beliefs: witchcraft in Africa as a case study. *Duke Journal of Comparative and International Law* 14, 351–387.

Dupont, J. 2001. *The common law abroad: constitutional and legal legacy of the British Empire*. Littleton, CO: Fred B. Rothman & Co.

Fields, K.E. 1985. *Revival and rebellion in colonial Central Africa*. Princeton, NJ: Princeton University Press.

Fisiy, C.F. 1998. Containing occult practices: witchcraft trials in Cameroon. *African Studies Review* 41(3), 143–163.

Fisiy, C.F. and Geschiere, P. 1990. Judges and witches, or how is the state to deal with witchcraft? Examples from southeast Cameroon. *Cahiers d'Études Africaines* 30(118), 135–156.

Gray, N. 2001. Witches, oracles and colonial law: evolving anti-witchcraft practices in Ghana, 1927–1932. *International Journal of African Historical Studies* 34(2), 339–363.

Lambert, G. 2012. 'If the government were not here we would kill him' – continuity and change in response to the witchcraft ordinances in Nyanza, Kenya, c.1910–1960. *Journal of Eastern African Studies* 6(4), 613–630.

Leonardi, C. 2007. The poison in the ink bottle: poison cases and the moral economy of knowledge in 1930s Equatoria, Sudan. *Journal of Eastern African Studies* 1(1), 34–56.

Leonardi, C. 2013. *Dealing with government in South Sudan: histories of chiefship, community and state*. Woodbridge: James Currey.

Leonardi, C., Moro, L.N., Santschi, M. and Isser, D. 2010. *Local justice in southern Sudan*. Washington, DC: Rift Valley Institute and United States Institute of Peace.

Luongo, K. 2011. *Witchcraft and colonial rule in Kenya, 1900–1955*. Cambridge: Cambridge University Press.

Mann, K. and Roberts, R. (eds). 1991. *Law in colonial Africa*. London: James Currey.

Middleton, J. 1960. *Lugbara religion: ritual and authority among an East African people*. London: Holt.

Nalder, L.F. 1936. *Equatorial Province handbook, vol. 1: Mongalla*. Khartoum: McCorquodale.

Nalder, L.F. (ed.). 1937. *A tribal survey of Mongalla Province, by members of the Province staff and Church Missionary Society*. London: Oxford University Press.

Sudan Government. 1947. *Wellcome Chemical Laboratories, Sudan Medical Service, Khartoum: report of the government analyst for the year 1947*. Khartoum: McCorquodale.

Waller, R.D. 2003. Witchcraft and colonial law in Kenya. *Past and Present* 180(1), 241–275.

Yunis, Y.N. 1924. Notes on the Kuku and other minor tribes. *Sudan Notes and Records* 7(1), 1–41.

5 When the state is forced to deal with local law

Approaches of and challenges for state actors in emerging South Sudan

Katrin Seidel

Introduction

In dealing with hybrid legal realities in which different intertwined normative orders[1] co-exist, state actors pursue different approaches. In this respect, the Republic of South Sudan[2] presents an interesting case since statehood itself, in particular a 'permanent' constitution, is still under negotiation. The emergence of the new state poses a huge legal challenge in regard to maintaining internal cohesion and negotiating the idea of the 'modern' state,[3] particularly in light of the highly segmented South Sudanese society with approximately seventy ethnic local communities,[4] many of which adhere to their own normative orders (Jok et al. 2004: 17; Danne 2004: 201). 'Customary laws', respectively local laws – with various perceptions of loyalty, authority, and approaches to conflict settlement – are the predominant normative tools to regulate social interactions shaped by dynamic multiple group identities. Even though statutory laws have been in use throughout the area especially since the Anglo-Egyptian condominium (1899–1956), in the legal reality they have been subordinated to local legal values.

In order to deal with the plural legal reality of South Sudan, the current Transitional Constitution of the Republic of South Sudan, 2011 (TCRSS)

---

1   A normative order may be defined as 'a body of interrelated norms, or of rules and principles' (Woodman 2011: 10).
2   South Sudan declared its independence on 9 July 2011, following a referendum that had taken place from 9 to 15 January 2011. On 14 July 2011 the General Assembly of the United Nations approved a resolution (S/RES/1999 (2011)) which had been adopted by the UN Security Council on 13 July 2011 admitting the Republic of South Sudan as the 193rd member of the United Nations.
3   The idea of the 'modern' or territorial state belongs to 'a fundamental ontology of political thought' (Schlichte 2004), which was, according to the legal philosopher Georg Jellinek's, characterized by three elements of statehood: territoriality, sovereignty and nation (Jellinek 1929 [1900]: 180–190; see also Eckert 2011). The idea of the state has been attributed with different meanings, but the notions of territoriality (borders), internal and external sovereignty and the state as a body of administrative institutions seem to prevail (Schlichte 2004: 150–151).
4   See www.ethnologue.com/country/SS.

and previously The Interim Constitution for Southern Sudan, 2005 (ICSS)[5] vaguely acknowledge 'traditional authority' and 'customary law' including its dispute resolution mechanisms (Art. 173ff ICSS; Art. 166ff TCRSS).

This chapter focuses on state actors' attempts to constitutionally recognize and to integrate local law and authority into a South Sudanese judiciary. However, one has to keep in mind that in contexts where state actors are not able (or willing) to impose their rules on other local actors, the question arises, 'how much scope non-state legal orders leave for recognition of other legal orders (including that of the state) and governance authorities' (Benda-Beckmann et al. 2009: 8). The assumption is that a constitutional recognition of existing local laws and authorities might grant – despite inherent and visible normative collisions – space and forum for continuous negotiation processes between various social actors. Nevertheless, claims of state actors to reach so called national unity or internal cohesion by merely formal recognition of legal plurality appear to be futile. My study on state-recognized legal pluralism in Ethiopia shows that due to the norm conflicts inherent to the system this coexistence of different normative orders has created negotiation spaces. However, as long as these spaces are just used to negotiate situational solutions for specific (normative) conflicts and not to identify and formulate mutual values in light of and respect for different moralities, the project 'national unity' lies dormant (Seidel 2012: 237).

The South Sudanese judicial reality shows that the overall majority of arising legal disputes are settled through employing local law mainly on the basis of reconciliation applied by both 'customary courts', also called 'chiefs courts', as well as statutory courts in urban areas (Jok et al. 2004: 6; Pimentel 2010: 13; Hinz 2010: 141–142). The dynamic notion of local judicial orders might be described as an 'amalgamation of multiple forms of law and judicial procedure' (Leonardi et al. 2011: 113). Even though statutory law is part of the whole legal picture it can be considered as just a minor factor that influences the decision-making, actions, and relationships of people. It is just one variant among many normative orders, which are generated and preserved by multiple institutions and authorities with different bases of legitimacy. However, as will be demonstrated by means of the judicial constellations in South Sudan, the manner in which state law *de jure* defines its relationship towards other normative orders is not necessarily reflected in the legal reality. The legal reality, in which the majority of legal disputes is adjudicated in local courts, leaves the evolving state with the demanding task of formulating a common legal frame including and respecting local normative orders and values. This is also part of negotiating the idea of the South Sudanese state among the manifold social actors in order to

---

5   The constitution-making process of the ICSS was externally influenced and needs to be viewed in the context of the Comprehensive Peace Agreement 2005 (CPA). The CPA determined the procedural and substantial framework for the constitution-making process (see Dann and Al-Ali 2006: 442–449).

achieve popular acceptance (of the state) and to promote the idea of a South Sudanese identity. In an interview, the former Chief Justice of Southern Sudan, Ambrose Riiny Thiik, regarded local law as:

> a manifestation of our customs, social norms, beliefs and practices. It embodies much of what we have fought for these past twenty years. It is self-evident that customary law will underpin our society, its legal institutions and laws for the future.
>
> (Jok et al. 2004: 7)

This statement may shed some light on the efforts of South Sudanese governmental actors and international agencies to construct a South Sudanese identity. The emerging state South Sudan currently appears to be only slightly more than a geographical factum since the 'historical unity was one of convenience not of conviction'. Clearly, nations don't just happen, 'they have to be planned, forged and crafted' (Jok 2012: 58). The nation building project consists, among other things, of 'identifying a political class as building blocks, inventing national symbols such as flag, currency, national anthem, utilizing material culture as well as telling a narrative of South Sudanese journey to nationhood' (ibid.: 58–59). In Benedict Anderson's (2005 [1983]: 49) words: '[A]ll communities larger than primordial villages of face-to-face contact (and perhaps even these) are imagined. [Thus, a nation] is an imagined political community – and imagined as both inherently limited and sovereign.'

Local law and its dispute resolution mechanisms have been asserted by governmental actors as a crucial element within a *unity in diversity* approach[6] (Leonardi et al. 2011: 112). The concept of *unity in diversity* and claims for cultural identity by former socio-political minority communities of Southern Sudan emerged as a counter-strategy to dominant concepts of *unity in conformity* promoted by Northern Sudanese political elites, already during the struggle for sovereign self-determination (El-Battahani 2007: 37, 50–51; Frahm 2012: 22–24). Aggressive 'nation-building' policies, including confrontational juridification of Islamic normativity were forced upon the people in the south of Sudan by northern Sudanese political elites. In response to perceived political and socio-economic marginalization, the Southern Sudanese political elite mobilized the dimension of 'cultural identity' in order to claim access to political and socio-economic resources. The notion of *unity in diversity* appears to have been adapted to the new South Sudanese political contexts[7] in processes of negotiating and redrawing socio-political boundaries. An adapted *unity and diversity* claim becomes officially the

---

6   This approach is regarded to take into account South Sudanese various ways of lives and cultures which need to be reflected and celebrated in the 'nation' (Jok 2013).

7   'We may be Zande, Kakwa, Nuer, Toposa, Dinka, Lotuko, Anyuak, Bari and Shiluk, but remember you are South Sudanese first' (Kiir Mayadit 2011).

foundation of the construction of the South Sudanese state. State actors' claims to sovereignty create for themselves privileged roles for negotiating political spaces. Moreover, they attempt to define the conditions of this imagined sovereignty by claiming *unity and diversity*. Local law becomes a bargaining tool in negotiating and controlling access to resources, collective identities, space and power. Thus, in order to better understand why and how state actors attempt to mobilize legal categories of 'customary law' or 'traditional authority' in the course of negotiating the idea of the state and their position within, one has to take into account that those recognizing strategies and techniques are embedded and deeply intertwined with shifting power relations and political concepts such as nation building and *unity and/in diversity*.

Before focusing on state actors' different attempts of recognizing local law within the broader concept of *unity and diversity*, the central categories 'customary law' and 'ethnicity', utilized by South Sudanese state legislation, need to be briefly conceptualized in order to lay bare the origin and underlying assumption of these widely used terms.

The contentious legal category of 'customary law' and 'ethnicity'

'Non-state' forms of social ordering have been originally labelled 'customary law' in the context of colonial rule. To distinguish existing pre-colonial from colonial law, judicial systems were constructed as 'bipolar scheme[s]' (Mamdani 1996: 109; see also Williams 2003: 333–336). In the legal sphere of colonialism, 'customary law' became a 'blanket racial category' (Mamdani 1996: 111), related to ethnic identity. 'The notion of the ethnically defined customary law ... grounded racial exclusion in a cultural inclusion' (ibid.: 112). The primary unwritten local rules, derived from sources outside of the colonial state, were partially *de jure* acknowledged or accepted. They were used as guidelines for colonial jurisdiction, at least to the extent to which they were consistent with the colonial interests and corresponding ideologies (Snyder 1981: 49, 76–77; Merry 1988: 875; Mamdani 1996: 115–116).

In its 'evolution', contemporary customary law 'must be recognized as a composite colonial construction' (Moore 2001: 98) shaped by 'resistance, struggles among colonizers, and forms of accommodation by colonized elites' (Merry 2003: 569). Regarding their identity, the various societies were characterized by mobility, overlapping networks and multiple group memberships as well as by contextual boundaries and border crossings (Schlee et al. 2009). Only in response to the European project of categorizing colonized people into 'tribes'[8] for the sake of colonial bureaucracy, ethnic group

---

8   Eckert used the German phrase '*Denken in Stämmen*'.

ideologies developed out of the multitude of dynamic collective identities (Eckert 2000: 2–5).

Also in the (South) Sudanese context ethnicized discussions of law have been on-going since the colonial era. Currently, so-called 'tribal identities' and differences have been also mobilized in debates on the South Sudanese political and institutional design (see Mabor 2013: 4; Lupai 2012: 9; Ateny 2012: 7, 15; Tor 2012a: 7). The emphasis on differences becomes apparent during the constitution-making process, especially in discussions on decentralization, and 'ethnic' or regional federalism versus centralized government (Kuol 2013: 4; Tor 2012b:7). In order to avoid loading the concept with an ideological overtone, I use the term local law as one of the various forms of 'local knowledge' (Geertz 1983) to refer to the different normative orders of the local communities co-existing in South Sudan.

The introduction of statutory law: colonial state attempts to de jure acknowledge legal reality

In the Sudanese context the state recognition of local normative orders is derived from different statutory laws originally formulated under Anglo-Egyptian indirect rule. According to Johnson (1986: 67–68), two aspects of indirect rule need to be considered:

1 It was intended to keep costs down and administrative organization simple by allowing the Sudanese to get on with 'non-essentials'.
2 It had an evolutionary aim to develop native institutions through 'the inevitability of gradualness', shedding what was 'evil and barbarous', but nurturing those aspects which administrators deemed locally valuable. In this system courts were to provide both cathartic entertainment and justice in order to improve public security.

Under colonial rule, local law was formally addressed in the Civil Justice Ordinance (CJO) of 1900. The CJO set up procedural mechanisms for settling civil disputes. This legal document provided for the recognition of local law, as far as applicable and not repugnant to 'good conscience', e.g., in matters of succession. It emphasized an administration of 'justice, equity and good conscience' (see §§3 and 4 CJO). This latter phrase had stereotyped custom in colonized areas and filled up the interstices with principles of English common law (Guttmann 1957: 404). Guttmann, after having analysed the reception of the common law in Sudan, remarked critically: 'But it is not the law of England which is applied in Sudan. The law of England has only persuasive authority in Sudan' (ibid.: 414). The above-mentioned sections of the CJO had been re-enacted in 1929 in §§5 and 9. Section 5 of the Civil Justice Ordinance 1929 was later literally adopted in the Civil Justice Act 1983. This §5 provided:

> Where in any suit or other proceeding in a civil court any question arises regarding succession, inheritance, wills, legacies, gifts, marriage, divorce, family relations or the constitution of wakfs, the rule of the decision shall be any custom applicable to the parties concerned, which is not contrary to justice, equity and good conscience, [...] and has not been declared void by the decision of a competent Court.

The determination of the imported legal categories 'justice, equity and good conscience' was very much related to colonial actors' steering efforts and ideas of obtaining 'interpretational sovereignty'. These concepts were being 'equated with the English law by the English judges' (Makec 1986: 7).

In addition, according to the Chiefs' Courts Ordinance 1931 (CCO): '[t]he Chiefs' Court shall administer native law and custom prevailing in the area or among the tribe over which the court exercises jurisdiction provided that the same is not contrary to justice, morality or order' (§7). The CCO of 1931, applied in three southern provinces, provided for establishment by authorization of three tiers of courts under the hand of chiefs' adjudication. The jurisdiction of their courts dealt with civil as well as criminal matters. Analysing the future significance of the Chiefs' courts, Khalil (1971: 641) incorrectly anticipated:

> [...] the importance of these courts is bound to diminish more and more with the improvement of the system of communication, the extension of educational facilities and other services, the change of social and economic conditions and the availability of sufficient numbers of qualified professional lawyers with a common background of education and outlook, all of which are factors which are likely to promote cohesion and homogeneity.

This legal positivist approach is typical for the thinking of elites in the first decades after independence (Sudan achieved independence in 1956), influenced by ideas of modernization and progress as well as 'nation-building'. Deng (1966–1967: 41) criticized the ethnocentric mind-set of 'lawyers both African and non-African':

> Consciously or unconsciously, customary law is still viewed largely as a temporary system which may only be tolerated because of momentum of the population adhering to it [...] For some people customary law must go, and the sooner the better.

The above-mentioned Chiefs' Courts Ordinance 1931 was repealed by the People's Local Courts Act 1977 (revised 1981). Section 13 of this Act provided: 'A peoples' local court shall administer the custom prevailing within the local limits of its jurisdiction provided that it is not contrary to justice, morals, and public order'. Currently, the interfaces between local laws and statutory laws are formally codified in §5 of the Civil Procedure Act 2003 which almost literally adopted §5 of the repealed Civil Justice Act 1983. Furthermore, §6(2) of the Penal Code Act 2008 provides: 'In the application of this Act, Courts may consider the existing customary laws and practices prevailing in the specific areas'. Both of these sections might be viewed as key mechanisms constituting the 'crux of customary-statutory interface' (Danne 2004: 212).

As the legal reality shows after decades of efforts of legal transplanting and of striving for legal uniformity, local laws and their dispute resolution mechanisms are still prevalent in South Sudan. Moreover, clear boundaries between local and statutory law as well as between local courts and state courts do not exist (Leonardi et al. 2011: 113). Local laws have been shaped in the colonial era by interactions between colonial administration, local chiefs and elders[9] in processes of 'inventing traditions'.[10] Leonardi (2013: 218–220) found that chief courts have proven to be the most resilient and vital of local state institutions in the South Sudanese setting. Furthermore, 'the intensified wartime pressures led not to the destruction of "traditional authority", but rather to the intensification of debates and discourses around chiefly legitimacy' (ibid.: 179). During the war, chiefs succeeded in refracting their institutional character away from military authority with whom they worked very closely. State and community were and are being made through both dialectic imagining, and mutual recognition of chiefships (ibid.: 179–180). Thus, specific interests of local communities and governmental as well as international actors have shaped the local courts, resulting in a hybrid set of judicial practices. Accordingly, contradicting visions of tradition and modernity have endured in governmental discourses since colonial days and become visible in current strategies of harmonizing local with statutory law. The aim of harmonization strategies is considered as

> to marry 'customary law' with 'modern' law. Customary laws need to be sensitized on issues such as gender and Human rights. We advocate for marrying the two legal systems in order to create a sound statutory system that is reflective or accommodating our values, customs and norms.
>
> (Mijak 2013)

Whether this strategy is likely to be successful will be discussed below.

9   Juba Archives, file no. EP/39.C.3, LND/48.A.2.
10 According to Hobsbawm, the term of 'invented tradition' refers to 'a set of practices, normally governed by overtly or tacitly accepted rules and of a ritual or symbolic nature, which seek to inculcate certain values and norms of behavior by repetition, which automatically implies continuity with a [suitable historic] past. It is] essentially a process of formalization and ritualization, characterized by reference to the past' (Hobsbawm 1999: 1; see also Ranger 1999).

Constitutional recognition of local law

Constitution making has become a key element in political transition. It is regarded to be of utmost importance for political stability since a constitutional system provides a framework for the political decision-making process. Establishing a constitution is not only the setting of 'rules of the political game', outlining fundamental principles and institutions of governance in a country, but also developing statements about fundamental values, meta-rules and the nature of the political community. Simeon (2011: 242) mentions that 'constitutional-making is in large part about making bets about the future' (i.e. particular institutions and rules are expected to have the desired effects). The different actors involved often contest these bets since they lead to crucial questions about values and distribution of power. Integrating local law and 'traditional authority' in the constitution is a matter of great concern in the South Sudanese context.

The Interim Constitution of Southern Sudan 2005 (Art. 5(c) ICSS) already acknowledged 'customs and traditions of the people' as sources of legislation which remained in the Transitional Constitution of the Republic of South Sudan 2011 (TCRSS). Thus, constitutionally recognized are 'traditional authority' as well as 'local law' as sources of legislation including the dispute resolution mechanisms, which shall be considered at federal as well as at state levels (Art. 5(c), 166f TCRSS). According to Art. 166 TCRSS:

1   The institution, status and role of Traditional Authority, according to customary law, are recognized under this Constitution.
2   Traditional Authority shall function in accordance with this Constitution, the state constitutions and the law.
3   The courts shall apply customary law subject to this Constitution and the law.

In regard to the role of 'traditional authority', Art. 167 TCRSS provides:

1   Legislation of the states shall provide for the role of Traditional Authority as an institution at local government level on matters affecting local communities.
2   Legislation at the National and state levels shall provide for the establishment, composition, functions and duties of councils for Traditional Authority leaders.

The constitutional frame enhances 'decentralization' and encourages diffusion of powers by recognizing 'traditional authority'. However, it does not distinguish the roles and status of the 'traditional authority' on one side and local government on the other yet. This is one of the issues left to the ongoing negotiations towards the so-called permanent constitution.

Besides, the TCRSS mandates the establishment of the judiciary of South Sudan as an independent decentralized institution which shall be structured as follows: It comprises the Supreme Court of South Sudan, Courts of Appeal, High Courts, County Courts and other courts (Art. 122 II, 123, 124 TCRSS). Judicial power shall be exercised by the courts in accordance with the customs, values, norms and aspirations of the people and in conformity with the constitution and the law (Art. 122 I TCRSS). In adjudicating cases of civil and criminal matters, the TCRSS states that 'adequate compensation shall be awarded to victims of wrongs and voluntary reconciliation agreements between parties shall be recognized and enforced' (Art 122 V (c, d) TCRSS). The principles of reconciliation between the wronged and wrongdoer and the importance of compensation or restitution are followed by the overall majority of local legal orders (Deng 2006: 21).

Thus, the constitution frames two forms of recognition of local law, which can be described in Woodman's (2011: 21) terms as normative recognition and institutional recognition. South Sudanese state actors attempt to acknowledge rules and principles of local law as valid norms of the state (normative recognition) and treat acts of 'traditional authority' such as dispute processing decisions as having valid effect in state law (institutional recognition).

However, given these constitutional provisions the question arises how the *de jure* state-recognized legal pluralist arrangement can be implemented in the legal reality where the state is negotiating its legitimacy for co-regulation. The basis for the incorporation of 'traditional authority' as well as the 'customary court system' is provided by the Local Government Act of 2009 (Art. 101ff, 9,15f LGA). The operationalization of the Work Plan for the Implementation of the Local Government Act 2009 will take decades, since the training of local government actors alone is expected to take between five and ten years (De Klerk and Kuon 2009: 10). According to the LGA the Customary Law Courts shall be of a three-tiered structure: Customary courts of the County, Regional courts and Chiefs Courts. Additionally, Town Bench Courts can be established (Art. 97 LGA). Thus, the South Sudanese statutory law has structured the judicial institutions in the hierarchal dualistic manner shown in Table 5.1.

The table shows that neat hierarchies of both, local courts and governmental courts, are constructed. This *de jure* arrangement does not reflect the judicial reality since the two judicial systems only in theory do exist separate from each other. In practice, they are part of a (semi-parallel) single system, especially at lower levels (Mennen 2007: 5–6). Specifically, the position of the 'customary courts' within the legal system seems to be unclear. Chief courts did not get *de jure* warrants of establishment yet. The two statutory laws relevant for establishing them – The Judiciary Act 2008 and the Local Government Act 2009 – are not consistent with regard to 'defining the roles of the actors involved in the establishment, supervision and management of

Table 5.1 South Sudanese judicial institutions.

Governmental Administrative Unit	Local Government Act 2009: 'Customary Courts'	Judiciary Act 2008: 'Judiciary Courts'
National		Supreme Court SoSu
State		Court of Appeal
State		High Court
County	C court: county paramount chief Appeals from B courts and to county judge (supervised by county commissioner)	County Judges (first and second grade)
Payam	B (regional court): head chief (town and rural benches) Original jurisdiction + Appeals from A courts and to C courts (supervised by paramount chief)	Payam judge (statut. legally trained)
Boma	A (Chief) court: executive chief (town and rural benches) Appeals to the B court (supervised by head chief)	

the customary courts as well as the implementation of the LGA regarding the functions and structures of the "customary law courts"' (GoSS 2012: 1).

The question of distribution of fields of competencies is one of the contentious jurisdictional issues. According to the South Sudanese statutory law, the Customary Law Courts shall have the competence 'to adjudicate on customary disputes according to customs, norms and ethics of the communities, [but they] shall not have the competence to adjudicate on criminal cases except those criminal cases with a customary interface referred to it by a competent Statutory Court' (Art. 98 I, II LGA). Since they shall have only exceptional competence to adjudicate criminal cases, the statutory law obviously distinguishes between criminal and civil law, a distinction that is rather alien to local law. Enquiry at the 'customary courts' shows that they adjudicate disputes in all areas of law, i.e., family, criminal, contract, land and property. Reconciliation through compromise and reparation for wrongs committed are core principles, which shape local legal practice. Social balance appears to be the main aim of local law. Regarding the local law of the Nuer for example, Johnson (1986: 59–60) emphasized that the system of arbitration was neither designed to pronounce on guilt and innocence, nor to enforce deterrent punishments. Their concepts of justice were based on principles of social obligation and a spiritually sanctioned moral order, where moral and social obligations are often combined (see also Evans-Pritchard 1940: 150–176).

The local law of the Dinka follows a similar rationale since restoring social equilibrium through payment of damages is desired (Makec 1988: 198). 'Litigation among the Dinka is designed more to reconcile the adversaries than it is to find a right and wrong side. Unless people succeed in this, the conflict is not adequately resolved' (Deng 1972: 113). Due to the emphasis on restitution rather than punishment, a dichotomy between crime and civil wrong does not appear to fit the legal reality. Yet it has to be mentioned that continuous interactions of local and statutory normative values have led to a combination of both restorative and retributive judicial practices. This has resulted in varying applications of procedures and punishments between and within courts (Mennen 2010: 242–243). Generally, local law procedure follows a kind of investigatory approach with chiefs or judges actively engaging the dispute parties during the decision-making process. One can argue that in a local normative order a chief or an elder is prosecutor, judge and police in personal union. 'Every detail is examined, every chief and elder who wishes to be heard is heard, and a general dialogue of persuasion continues until the alleged wrong is revealed to the party at fault and the party concur' (Deng 1972: 113). This differs fundamentally from English-common law adversarial systems according to which the judges act as 'detached' observers and, later on, decision maker (Jok et al. 2004: 16).

The above-mentioned *de jure* South Sudanese court hierarchy lays out a comprehensive system of appeal (see Table 5.1), originally introduced under Anglo-Egyptian rule (Guttmann 1957: 404–405). Currently, an appeal from the lowest Chiefs Courts can be heard at the Regional Courts and then up to the Customary Law Court of the County. Decisions of Customary Law Courts shall be appealed against at the level of the County (statutory) Court Judge (Art. 99–102 LGA). Appeals above that level go to the High Courts and finally to the Courts of Appeal (see Table 5.1). The Supreme Court of South Sudan, as the final judicial instance, has jurisdiction in respect of any litigation or prosecution under national law, including local law.

The appeal competence of the statutory courts from county level upwards raises the question on which legal basis decisions of the County Customary Courts shall be reviewed. Defining the sources of law in South Sudan appears to be challenging in light of the numerous local laws. The appeal courts appear to become a judicial arena where the legal conflicts between local and statutory law will be negotiated. Much will depend on the opinions and decisions of judges presiding over cases at the customary-statutory interface at the level of appeal court. In cases of local law which are referred upwards to the higher courts upon which those courts rule on the appeal, a judge's decision sets a precedent, which, in effect, sets law in form of judicial circulars issued by the chief justice. This process may affect local law since it may challenge the particular local law and its authorities to adapt in order to avoid revision in the future.

However, South Sudanese state actors negotiate their legitimacy by utilizing different legal techniques to propose dispute resolution mechanisms to contemporary legal conflicts. To illuminate those techniques, legal disputes on paternity will serve as an example. In cases where the biological father once refused to marry the impregnated woman and did not even acknowledge the impregnation by paying cows according to Dinka law, the relatives of the impregnated woman have the power to retain the child into their custody until the woman marries another man. In former Lakes State of South Sudan with its capital city Rumbek[11] the still applied Re-Statement of Bahr El Ghazal Region Customary Law (Amended) Act No. 1, 1984, §10 provides: 'If the father intends to obtain the child he shall pay to the woman's relatives a specific number of cows for the child'. The South Sudanese judicial practice shows that paternity disputes do especially arise in contexts of marriage and dowry negotiations. Biological fathers, who did not acknowledge paternity, in particular not during the more than two decades lasting armed conflicts, increasingly wish to get involved in the exchange of marriage gifts and therefore start claiming rights of fatherhood (Thiik 2013). This is a strategy of gaining access to resources and social security networks.

State actors' attempts to manoeuver the issue of the rejection of impregnated women/girls is shown in §33 of Lakes State Customary Law Act 2010: 'whoever rejected or jilts impregnated a girl/lady commits an offence of destruction and upon conviction, shall pay three cows for the damage and seven cows for the redemption'. Accordingly, a rejection of impregnation of a woman/girl is *de jure* considered as a crime. In order to 'compensate' those 'offences of destruction', statutory law refers to dispute settlement under local law. However, the local laws of the Dinka of the Bahr El-Ghazal Regions had not formulated a time limit for claiming paternity of a child born out of wedlock. When once a biological father claimed fatherhood after 15 years of absence, the judges at appeal court level in Rumbek decided for a cut-off point. They actively offered a solution by negotiating the concept of fairness. After ten year of absence of a biological father, the child is considered to belong to the 'family' who *de facto* brought up the child (Thiik 2013; Mijak 2013). This judicial in(ter)vention shows an attempt to deal with those conflicts by, on the one hand, trying to intervene legislatively and criminating such behaviour. On the other hand, state judicial actors promoting a resolution for increasingly arising socio-legal challenges hope that these 'offers' will be accepted and taken into account by the local judiciary for preventing or solving future conflicts. It can be assumed that by doing so, state actors expect to improve their positions as relevant actors in the legal and judicial arena.

11   Lakes – a part of the Bahr El-Ghazal regions – was one of the former ten (federal) states of South Sudan. The number of states has been increased from 10 to 28 by a Presidential Decree (PD 36/2015) in October 2015. In January 2017 President Salva Kiir issued another PD that increased the number of (federal) states from 28 to 32. Rumbek is currently the capital of Western Lake state.

However, beside those techniques, state actors have to deal with another 'old' problem: How to deal with the often conflicting plural normativity? How to institutionalize a functioning appeal system in light of migration movements within the country, that have brought people with different legal perceptions in closer contact? How to deal, on the one hand, with the lack of legitimacy of statutory law, and on the other hand with rarely written local laws? Since local laws reflect values, aspirations, practices, and beliefs of a local community, codification efforts risk a less flexible social space of negotiations. Unwritten laws may be more susceptible to misinterpretation and bias at appellate judicial levels. In particular, for chiefs and judges at appeal level knowledge of the respective *local laws* being applied appears to be essential.[12]

The appeal system constructed under statutory law has been questioned since it 'deprive[s] local communities of ownership of and control over their law' (Pimentel 2010: 1). Pimentel asserted that the appellate body inevitably applies different law or is left to second-guess the interpretation and application of customary law, which may lead to a loss of public confidence in judicial decision making (ibid.: 22–23). The statutory law-trained judges of the appeal courts set up by the government usually do not have knowledge on local law being applied. Thus, these judges are not qualified to second-guess the 'correctness' of the lower court decisions.

With regard to the challenges of establishing comprehensive appeal and cassation systems, the situation in neighbouring Ethiopia can serve as example: In Ethiopia, the power to review final judicial decisions rests with the cassation divisions of the federal and regional supreme courts. However, the judges of the regular supreme courts have pronounced themselves unqualified to judge on substantive error of law with regard to reviewing local or religious law, especially in light of primarily unwritten applied laws. The cassation practice in Ethiopia shows only a reviewing on errors of *procedural* law applied since all judicial forums are supposed to follow the Ethiopian Civil Procedure Code (CPC) as minimum requirement (Seidel 2012: 235). However, this procedural approach has its challenges since each normative order has developed its respective procedural regulations, which are not necessarily in line with the legal ideas of the CPC. The case study Ethiopia demonstrates that Kadis of the Federal Sharia courts apply the statutory CPC – besides substantive Islamic law – merely to the extent they became familiar with it in the course of their work. Sometimes they rely rather on Islamic rules for procedure matters. When comparing the CPC with Islamic law procedures differences become obvious, for example regarding the law of evidence. These contradictions challenge the working system of the Sharia courts and leave them with a dilemma regarding the application of procedural rules (ibid.: 227–229). In practice, state-reviewing

---

12 Makec (1986: 19) has criticized the lack of knowledge of state court judges 'who have neither experience nor training in either the nature or in substance of the customary law' (see also Mijak 2013; Jada 2013).

of local and religious court substantive decisions becomes obsolete and it remains a cassation on procedural defaults. The question addressed in the following section is: which are the strategies of the South Sudanese government to deal with the above mentioned complex challenges of state recognized legal pluralism.

Efforts of 'harmonizing' local laws with state and international laws

South Sudanese state actors' approaches to local law and regarding its relationship to statutory law tend to focus on 'harmonizing' local normative values with principles enshrined in the Transitional Constitution as well as establishing clear boundaries between different normative orders. The strategy is proficiently summarized by Leonardi et al. (2011: 112):

> Policy interventions increasingly are focused on the idea of customary law ascertainment, culminating in a GoSS-UNDP strategy proposal whereby the customary law ... would be identified and recorded in written form by the communities themselves, a process termed 'self-statement'. These statements would then become the basis for the direct application, harmonisation, and modification of customary law, towards a unified system meant to comply with modern standards of equality and human rights.

According to Art. 142 TCRSS, a South Sudan Law Reform (Review) Commission (SSLRC), an independent constitutional body, has been de jure established and is expected to serve as a negotiation forum. Its aim is to be responsive to the *status quo* and the *status quo ante* of legal reality. Besides other tasks, the SSLRC shall 'seek to harmonize the traditions and social values of the people [...] as expressed in their various customary law regimes, with the statutory laws of South Sudan and the constitutionally enshrined principles of international law' (GoSS 2011a). It has to be agreed that utilizing terms such as 'harmonizing' tend to mask in the end the 'hegemonic project of state legal and judicial control' (Leonardi et al. 2011:117). This project attempts to balance two contradicting goals: *unity and diversity*. On the one hand, 'rule of law' reform efforts shall strive for greater consistency, certainty, and predictability of judicial outcomes fitting to (inter-)national human right laws. On the other hand, 'cultural rights' and legal diversity shall be protected (Hinz 2010: 139, 145; Mijak 2013). In order to deal with the contradicting goals, the government of South Sudan, in cooperation with international agencies such as the United Nations Development Programme (UNDP)[13] and legal experts, has developed a Customary Law Strategy (see

---

13 'The ascertainment of customary law is an integral element of the access to justice support by UNDP to MOJ [Ministry of Justice]' (Olenasha et al. 2012: 7).

Hinz 2009, 2010). This strategy comprises the following approach to the so-called customary law reform:

- ascertainment of the customary laws of south Sudanese communities;
- establishment of an institutional focal point to facilitate and coordinate customary law reform;
- engaging with communities to promote grass-root dialogue and momentum for customary law reform;
- creating a legal framework to harmonize customary and statutory laws; and
- conducting further research on customary law (UNDP 2012, undated).

In order to facilitate and coordinate this strategy, a National Customary Law Centre (CLC) was officially established on 30 August 2012 as an institutional focal point under South Sudan's Ministry of Justice. The CLC is expected to facilitate coordination between different governmental levels and actors of the local law system.[14] Further tasks outlined in the Customary Law Strategy include: 'conducting research and creating public awareness; advising national, state and local governments on customary law issues and training customary and statutory actors and key stakeholders' (Sudan Tribune 2012).

The chosen strategy seeks to balance the above mentioned contradiction by empowering the local communities to contribute to harmonizing local law even though this approach redefines the nature of local judicial administration. Furthermore, the questions arise who will speak for the respective local communities and who will structurally direct the process since certain chiefs or traditional authorities already have a privileged position in the judicial system. State-recognized chiefs are in a dilemma since they already have to fulfil a 'dual mandate' by supporting the state through conducting part of its functions at the local level, and at the same time satisfying the needs of their local constituencies (Hoehne 2008: 3). This situation is probable to create changes in the ways in which authority can be exercised, especially in cases where chiefs depend rather on the approval of state officials than on that of their constituency (Woodman 2011: 23). Otherwise state-recognized local authorities need to justify their position in order to not lose their popular legitimacy or to reach popular acceptance during day-to-day judicial practice. In order to avoid this dilemma, ascertainment of local law shall be conducted by ascertainment assistants who consult focus groups of identified local communities comprising chiefs, elders, representatives of women, youths and others, who will speak for the respective communities (Mijak 2013).

---

14 The NCLC had not started operating at the time of the author's last fieldworks in South Sudan (as of 5 May 2013, as of 25 May 2015 and as of May 2017).

Another critical point is the judicial structure that constructs a hierarchy among the chiefs of the different judicial levels. A historical perspective demonstrates that, particularly among 'acephalous' societies residing in southern Sudan such as Nuer and Dinka, chiefs and 'customary law' were created during the colonial period. The hierarchy of Paramount chiefs, head chiefs, chiefs and sub-chiefs, elders etc. is somewhat artificial and an expression of the contact between local groups and external (state) powers (Hoehne 2008: 19). Thus, questions of hierarchy appear to have a high potential for conflict between 'traditional' and governmental authorities. Conflicts among local authorities might run the risk of politicization and manipulation of the positions of authority and may be contested among locals.

Being in a hybrid position the Councils of Traditional Authority Leaders is considered to provide a dialogue forum with all levels of government on matters of local law and offer advice to the government (Art. 120f LGA). The highest local law authority in a county is the Customary Law Council (CLC) comprising the County Paramount chief of the highest local court, all Head Chiefs of the 'B' Courts or Regional Courts of the County as well as three community elders, three women and one youth representative (Art. 93–95 LGA). The CLC shall ensure women participation by at least twenty five per cent of the membership. The Council shall be further responsible for selecting, recruiting, and training of Customary Courts staff as well as ensuring the upholding of the constitutional rights at customary courts (Art. 96 LGA). Particularly, ensuring the principle of equality in customary law courts seems to be challenging in the light of decisive normative and conceptual differences. By reflecting societal structures and representing certain local interests, decisions of customary courts may infringe on equal rights of all citizens, 'since those who are predominantly subject to traditional authorities and customary law in fact enjoy only conditional citizenship' (Hoehne 2008: 3) with rights nominally granted under statutory law but effectively subject to qualifications and limitations by traditional authorities and the customary law they administer.

In order to deal with normative conflicts, the Government of South Sudan (GoSS) has focused on ascertainment of local law. Three different ways to ascertain may be identified: codification, re-statement and self-statement (Hinz 2009: 134–135). The legal reality has shown that previous codification efforts of local law run the risk of non-recognition by the people whom it was supposed to serve since codifications imply the existence of conformity (Bennett and Vermeulen 1980: 218–219). Restatement approaches to local law[15] led for instance to the above-mentioned Re-Statement of Bahr

---

15 A Restatement of African Law Project (RALP 1959–1977) set up at School of Oriental and African Studies of the University of London (SOAS) was initiated by Antony Allott. Its object was 'to facilitate, undertake, assist in the recording of customary laws in Commonwealth African countries in a systematic legal fashion' (Cotran 1987: 15).

El Ghazal Customary Law (Amend) Act 1984, which has rather fixed and homogenized the 'living laws' of the Dinka, the Luo and the Ferit. Currently, governmental actors follow the third strategy, which is 'self-statement' of local law. This is considered to be produced by local communities themselves in order to preserve more flexibility and negotiability. According to Hinz (2009: 135),

> [s]elf-stating customary law refers to a process of ascertaining customary law by the owners of the law to be ascertained, the people, the community, the traditional leaders as the custodians of customary law. [...] Self-statements come close to codification, codification not by the state, but by organs of the traditional communities themselves.

Those self-statements are considered to provide principles granting 'certainty' and consistency as well guaranteeing 'local ownership' of customary law (Leonardi et al. 2011: 118–119). They might as well help to bridge the knowledge gap of applied local law at appeal level. However, ascertainment efforts usually face huge legal challenges, which arise from the salient features of local laws. These characteristics comprise, e.g., continuous changes in the content and varying degrees of mandatory force. Local laws are rarely 'fixed' and have been objects of controversy at any particular time (Woodman 2011: 23–24).

The involved hybrid institutions of 'traditional authority' and chiefs already have a privileged position within the judicial system and have to fulfil a dual mandate as state-recognized local authorities. Moreover, 'once it is written, customary adjudicators can be subjected to second-guessing on the substantive law they apply' (Pimentel 2010: 20). In practice the available written documents may be viewed by chiefs and judges rather as codes of law. On the other hand, even these documents are probably to be absorbed into and adapted by dynamic local practices. This approach has been criticized since it:

> [...] tends to essentialize legal orders into a customary-state dichotomy, or seeks to shoehorn 'living law' into fixed forms, rather than engaging with the more complex, hybrid and fluid system that prevails... and can be used to mask or obscure the political motives and consequences of restructuring the legal order, and of shifting power from local, often semi-autonomous, actors to state institutions.
> (Leonardi et al. 2011: 136)

Taking the above-mentioned challenges into account, an alternative approach to appeal systems calls for establishing mechanisms of 'collateral review' of customary court decisions (Pimentel 2010: 23–28). The reviewing shall not be on the decision's merits but rather on procedural matters and outcomes. This means, the statutory courts would review decisions only against external principles reflected and guaranteed in the respective national constitution. The customary courts should be left to render the final judgement since ascertainment may threaten the 'ownership' of local law and its flexibility (always reacting to changing socioeconomic conditions), which are local law's major strengths. The procedural approach pursues a far more limited review than a general right of appeal since 'the procedure leaves the customary court to determine what its law is and how it should be applied, with the statutory court reviewing those decisions only against external standards' (ibid.: 23). It 'may maximize the autonomy of customary courts, which may be maintaining the relevance and effectiveness of those institutions' (Pimentel 2010: 20; see also Mennen 2007). It seeks to prevent the dilemma which a hierarchical appeal system between local courts and statutory courts may create. In this respect, a 'collateral review' of local court decisions for guaranteeing the application of constitutional principles could be a less intervening strategy (on the side of the state) and may avoid the contentious issue of reviewing a decision of a local court by a statutory court since this concerns the autonomy of the *de jure* established local courts and their constitutional status.

The on-going bumpy constitution-drafting process: Lessons learned

As I have mentioned before, the Transitional Constitution of the Republic of South Sudan just vaguely acknowledges traditional authority and local law including its dispute resolution mechanisms (Art. 173ff ICSS; Art. 166ff TCRSS). The negotiations and formulation of a specific arrangement have been deferred to the drafting of the so called 'permanent' constitution. The Transitional Constitution lays out the design for the making of the 'permanent' constitution which is supposed to derive 'its authority from the will of the people', implying the existence of a certain societal consensus. The adoption of the TCRSS by the parliament was pushed through only three days before South Sudan's independence (in July 2011) to ensure that this document could serve as a preliminary normative frame for the new state. The South Sudanese public took up the TCRSS with mixed feelings. It was quite evident that the draft had been thrown together quickly without the participation of many actors and without addressing many of the concerns raised beforehand (An-Na'im 2011; Adiebo 2011; Lubang 2011). Criticisms were, for instance, directed towards the lack of popular consultations during the drafting process as well as towards the appointing procedure resulted in a two third dominance of the ruling party Sudan People's Liberation Movement (SPLM) (Seidel and Moritz 2011: 92–93) within the Technical Committee to Review the Interim Constitution of Southern Sudan. According to opposition parties, the committee's composition constitutes a unilateral breach of the consensus that had been reached at the All Southern Sudan Political Parties' Conference in October 2010 (International Crisis Group 2011: 15).

One result of this conference was the establishment of a National Constitution Review Commission (NCRC), consisting of an 'all-party constitutional conference'.[16] On the side of the SPLM, it has been argued that only technical amendments to the ICSS should be made in the first phase of the constitution drafting process.[17] Based on the results of the Technical Committee, an extended participation of all political actors should take place during the making of the 'permanent' constitution. Accordingly, a comprehensive participation has been constitutionally guaranteed through the established National Constitutional Review Commission (Art. 202 TCRSS) and subsequent through appointing the National Constitutional Conference.[18] However, the objectives during the first period of drafting the TCRSS were not only 'technical' amendments. Negotiations actually concerned fundamental issues such as government structure, distribution of state functions between the legislative, executive and judiciary, the distribution of powers between federal and state governments as well as the duration of the transitional period (GoSS 2011b: 7). The scope of the Technical Committee's work was to 'evaluate and identify provisions in the ICSS that may need immediate modification or amendment to ensure effective governance, and present recommendations for such modifications [...]' (GoSS/PD/J/002/2011, 3.1.4). Due to public and political pressure, a few members from other Southern Sudanese political parties, from civil society actors as well as from faith-based groups were appointed to the Technical Committee (GoSS/PD/J/08/2011; GoSS/PD/J/09/2011). However, the ruling SPLM party clearly dominated the Technical Committee which proved to be convenient as a two-third quorum was required for the adoption of the draft of the TCRSS according to the Internal Rules and Procedures of the Technical Committee (GoSS 2011b: 8). The remaining third of the committee's members perceived their participation as being reduced to 'rubber stamps' (Aciek 2013). The composition of the Technical Committee might at least partly have been due to the imminent pressure of time, since the Technical Committee had just three months after its establishment on 21 January 2011 to present a first draft document (GoSS/PD/J/002/2011, 3.1.6)

16 Final Communiqué of the All Southern Sudanese Political Parties Conference, 17 October 2010.
17 Art. 208 (7) ICSS: 'If the outcome of the referendum on self-determination favours secession, this Constitution shall remain in force as the Constitution of a sovereign and independent Southern Sudan, and the parts, chapters, articles, sub-articles and schedules of this Constitution that provide for national institutions, representation, rights and obligations shall be deemed to have been duly repealed.'
18 According to Art. 203 (1) TRCSS 'upon the presentation of the Draft Constitutional Text and Explanatory Report by the Commission, the President of the Republic shall, after consultation with relevant stakeholders, constitute and convene a National Constitutional Conference comprising delegates representing the following categories: (a) Political parties; (b) Civil society organizations; (c) Women organizations; (d) Youth organizations; (e) Faith-based organizations; (f) People with special needs; (g) Traditional leaders etc.'

Yet a closer look at the composition of the since 2012 mandated NCRC unveils a similar picture. After the South Sudan Civil Society Alliance, an umbrella organization of more than two hundred of South Sudan's Civil Society organizations, had successfully fought for getting a voice in the NCRC, a few representatives of CSOs were appointed as well, all serving as part-time members (RSS/PD/J/36/2012; Lorna 2013; Swaka 2013; Tier 2013b: 1–2). However, political parties represent the overall majority (43) of the 54 commissioners,[19] whereby 26 party members are members of the ruling SPLM (RSS/PD/J/03/2012). Similar to the drafting process of the TCRSS, the dominant actors of the SPLM carved out for themselves a privileged position for negotiating the political leeway necessary to assert control over the constitution-making process. This has happened through procedures such as incorporation, regulation, exclusion or marginalization of communities, organizations, or other kinds of socio-political orders presented in the environment of the state (Kapferer and Taylor 2012: 5). This led to the 'politicization' of the process, especially when party interests become dominant (Akol 2013). The former view of the late NCRC chairperson that 'a constitution is an agreement between political parties' (Tier 2013a) had been already fundamentally challenged in 2013 during a public lecture on constitution making held at Juba University (Adigo 2013). Many conference participants disagreed with this view and referred to Art. 202(6) TCRSS, which states that 'the commission [NCRC] shall review the Transitional Constitution and collect views and suggestions from all the stakeholders on any changes that may need to be introduced to the current system of governance'. The commission is further mandated to reconcile traditions, social values and different customary laws with the legal laws of South Sudan and the accepted principles of international law (Kulluel 2012).

Already at the end of the year 2012 the late NCRC chairperson Akolda Maan Tier (2012) admitted that the commission 'is in a state of coma due to a dearth of key resources such as financial means and appropriate locations'. Accordingly, the NCRC requested an extension of its mandate (Jok 2013: 3). Subsequently, the National Legislative Assembly (NLA) extended the NCRC's mandate until the end of 2014 (Art. 202(4) TCRSS amend. 2013). By mid-2013, only the commission's structure and rules of procedure, an Action Plan 2013–2014 as well as six sub-committees[20] had been established with the support of international actors (Tier 2013a, 2013b: 2). Following the Action Plan, the NCRC launched a civic education

---

19 Besides the dominant SPLM, these are, among others, the National Democratic Front (NDF), United Democratic Front (UDF), Sudan African National Union (SANU), NJMP, National Congress Party (NCP), Popular Congress Party (PCP), Communist Party (CP), and the National United Democratic Front (NUDF).
20 Five of these groups are working on specific constitutional issues enshrined in the TCRSS and the remaining one sub-committee on civic education and supposed to work on a Training Manual which is near completion.

programme in mid-2013 to involve the public in the ten states of South Sudan in the constitution making. Due to a continuous lack of funding, the campaign was doomed to failure. Moreover, the still ongoing disastrous political crisis erupting in December 2013[21] 'increased such lack of funding, limited the availability of technical support and has restricted the NCRC's ability to continue implementing its civic education and public participation campaign due to security concerns' (IDEA 2014). In 2015, the former NCRC-chairperson emphasized the significance of civic engagement and questioned the chosen design of constitution making, which did not fulfil the proclaimed idea of a 'peoples driven constitution'. He wondered whether it would be more conducive to start with a National Constitutional Conference (NCC) to agree first on constitutive blocks of a South Sudanese constitution (Tier 2015).

Due to the disastrous continuation of the political and military re-negotiations, which severely limited the NCRC's ability to continue its work (NCRC 2014), the former NCRC chairperson strongly recommended that the NLA should extend the commission's mandate 'for a period not less than three years subject for review when a permanent peace is realised in the country' (NCRC 2015). Accordingly, the parliament extended the tenure of the NCRC once more, this time until 2018 (Art. 202(4) TCRSS amend. 2015). Despite all efforts to bring the warring political and military factions back to the negotiating table, the implementation of the latest Agreement on the Resolution of the Conflict in the Republic of South Sudan (ARCRSS) – which was negotiated and signed by the warring factions in August 2015 under pressure from the East African Community (EAC), the Intergovernmental Authority on Development (IGAD) and the international community – is completely void due to the ongoing military re-negotiation throughout the country. The ARCRSS has modified the constitution-making approach that had been agreed upon earlier. In the amended roadmap, local ownership and comprehensive popular participation are expected to be the guiding principles (see Ch. VI ARCRSS 2015). Thus, currently it is not clear how a new constitution-making roadmap will look like. According to the TCRSS, it was envisioned that, after the NCRC completed the draft for the constitution, a National Constitutional Conference (NCC) will, within six months, deliberate on the text and gather public opinions (Art. 203IIIe TCRSS). The NCC shall be composed of representatives of professional associations, war widows, veterans, business leaders, traditional leaders, trade unions, the academia, other groups and members of the NCRC (Tier 2013b: 3). Subsequently, 'the President shall, upon receipt of the Draft Constitutional

---

21 The major violent conflict began end of 2013 and, until 2017, cost more than 10,000 lives; around two million people have been displaced. It began as a power struggle within the SPLM, which focused on constitution-making. The main contenders are President Salva Kiir and his (then) Vice-President Riek Machar with their respective followers. They are not the only protagonists in light of the fragmented armed forces.

Text, cause the same to be tabled before the National Legislature, at least one year before the end of the Transitional Period, for deliberation and adoption within three months' (Art. 203 VII TCRSS). However, in reality, this chosen design for constitution making prevents involvement of South Sudanese citizens; rather, the governmental actors debate among themselves. Whatever input the citizens will give during the NCC, the decision will afterwards be taken by the politicians in the NLA, who mainly belong to the SPLM. Several of these politicians have also been appointed by President Kiir in recent years; this influences their loyalty considerably.

With respect to the issue of public participation, empirical studies have shown that it serves as a process of integration through which the feeling or perception to have a say is increased. While this does not necessarily lead to the incorporation of new legal ideas, it still can enhance the sustainability of the outcome (Klug 2011: 70–71; Saati 2015). Symbolic participation may stimulate 'talks' and discussions among the people on the constitution (and constitution making) whereby a certain legitimacy is produced through the feeling of participation and through processes of 'naturalization'.

Being relegated to a second tier of negotiations, civil society actors created various citizens' constitution-making forums with the hope and desire of participating in the official state-making process. They have already collated views and recommendations for inclusion in the upcoming constitution in almost all regional states in 2012. About 1200 citizens were consulted via so-called focus groups comprising representatives of traditional authorities, women's groups, youth groups, civil society, state assemblies, religious groups, members of parliament and local government actors. The general findings were subsequently passed on to the NCRC. It was hoped that the actors at the official NCRC negotiation table will consider and integrate the outcomes and suggestions of the various CSO forums into the constitution-making process (Seidel and Sureau 2015).

It is not yet clear how the on-going conflict dynamics are influencing the continuation of the work of the NCRC. The commission's work depends much on the commitment of its members and the necessary political will. It is the responsibility of governmental actors in South Sudan to demonstrate their openness and readiness for an inclusive political dialogue, in order to create confidence among the population for governance and the social visions of the political elites. The president's announcement of a National Dialogue in December 2016 (Kiir Mayadit 2016) and the establishment of the National Dialogue Steering Committee in April 2017 (PD RSS/RO/J/08/2017) could be a new step towards a more inclusive approach, if not the same exclusion dynamics happen as one could notice over the previous six years. If an inclusive public consultation process is again postponed, it is doubtful whether a so produced 'national consensus' will gain public legitimacy. It may only serve to increase tensions and even violent conflicts as many actors with different normative claims would feel continuously excluded despite all their efforts to gain a place at the negotiation table. It remains to be seen whether a South Sudanese constitution gets a chance to be developed out of a comprehensive 'national dialogue' and thereby become 'the Constitution of Zol Meskin' (Juba Arabic for 'common person'), or not. At least the first is the vision that was announced by South Sudanese civil society actors on huge billboards at two main roads in Juba, visible to all who enter or leave the capital city when I was conducting fieldwork in 2013.

Concluding remarks

In South Sudan, the internal legitimacy of the state actors is still negotiated. In order to progress with regard to state formation and to gain internal and external recognition, it is important to establish normative and institutional frameworks. Generally, the process of constitution making provides spaces for negotiation in which different actors are putting their own normative ideas on the table. Negotiation spaces are necessary to ensure a continuous (re-)structuring of power relations. Under negotiation are still the definition of the spaces of action and the identification of participating actors. However, governmental actors, though claims to sovereignty, have already created for themselves privileged roles for negotiating political spaces. This becomes visible in the constitution making where some actors of the emerging state party SPLM attempt to control the process via forums and institutions.

Constitutional recognition of local normative orders appears to be a legal and a political tool for dealing with the *de facto* only marginal influence of state law. South Sudanese state actors are aware that the constitutionally granted space needs to be utilized to improve their position of co-regulating. They utilize the negotiation spaces for promoting a South Sudanese identity, hoping to increase their influence and popular acceptance as relevant political actors within the existing power relations.

With regard to South Sudan's constitution-making efforts, even though quite pluralistic approaches have found their way into the TCRSS, it is still not clear how the legal plurality will be dealt with if already at the formation stage of the new state, along with the notion of safeguarding unity and stability, centralist tendencies of the ruling party become visible. Since the negotiation of a federal-pluralistic arrangement leads over a bumpy road, it will be essential for the future constitution of South Sudan to originate from an open discussion incorporating all relevant actors and promoting a public debate throughout the country. It is only then that the document can represent the 'will of the people' (Art. 1 TCRSS), has a chance to be considered the 'supreme law of the land' (Art. 3 TCRSS), and generate public legitimacy for the authority of the institutions laid down in it.

A constitution as law organizing the state is related to a defined polity. The power struggle within the highly segmented South Sudanese political and military elites, which erupted violently in December 2013 and is still on-going, has proven once again that no consensus on the polity's extent has yet been reached. The process of South Sudan's 'becoming of a state', which has sorely already led to more than 50,000 human losses, about 1.5 million displaced people, and a situation in which almost two-thirds of the population depends on external food aid (see UNHCR 2017; Weber 2016), 'has radically politicised ethnic allegiance and ideological preferences' (Mamdani 2014). These dynamics clearly demonstrate that the South Sudanese governmental actors have very little time left to position themselves as relevant players in the political and legal arena and to promote the idea of a South Sudanese state. Public patience is wearing thin as people's high expectations for the emerging state remain unfulfilled.

It does not appear to be constructive that the same political actors, that are partly responsible for the on-going political crisis, sit in the institutionalized forums to negotiate among themselves made-up models of a 'permanent' constitution. Deng et al. (2014) have rightly observed, '[v]iewing the crisis as a problem that can be solved by the political and military class alone would repeat the same mistake that has been made in past negotiations'.

References

Aciek, G.N. 2013. Interview by K. Seidel, Juba University, Juba, 14 April.
Adiebo, K.A. 2011. Interview by K. Seidel and J. Moritz, Juba University, Juba, 6 April.
Adigo, O. 2013. Building the Constitution in South Sudan, Juba Lecture Series 2013, University of Juba, 6 March.
Akol, Z.D. 2013. Building the Constitution in South Sudan, Juba Lecture Series 2013, University of Juba, 6 March.
Anderson, B. 2005 [1983]. Imagined communities, in *Nation and nationalism: a reader*, edited by P. Spencer and H. Wollman. Edinburgh: Edinburgh University Press, 48–60.
An-Na'im, B. 2011. Interview by K. Seidel and J. Moritz, Juba University, Khartoum, 3 April.
Ateny, A.W. 2012. Tribe county, clan county, sub-clan county, and finally extended family – are we build the nation? *The Citizen Newspaper*, 12–13 July.
Benda-Beckmann, F. et al. 2009. Rules of law and laws of ruling: law and governance between past and future, in *Rules of law and laws of ruling: on the governance of law*, edited by F. Benda-Beckmann et al. Farnham: Ashgate Publishing, 1–30.
Bennett, T.W. and Vermeulen, T. 1980. Codification if customary law. *Journal of African Law* 24(2), 206–219.
Chiefs' Courts Ordinance No. 10. 1931. Anglo-Egyptian Sudan.
Cotran, E. 1987. Tony Allott, pioneer of the study of African law: a personal memoir. *Journal of African Law* 31(1–2), 15–17.
Dann, P. and Al-Ali, Z. 2006. The internationalized *pouvoir constituent*: constitution-making under external influence in Iraq, Sudan and East Timor, in *Max Planck Yearbook of United Nations Law*, 1, edited by Bogdandy, von et al. Koninklijke: Brill, 423–463.

Danne, A. 2004. Customary and indigenous law in transitional post-conflict states: a South Sudanese case study. *Monash University Law Review* 30(3), 199–228.
De Klerk, M. and Kuon, J. 2009. A scan of the current state of affairs of local government in Southern Sudan. CBTF-Study. Retrieved 15 November 2012 from www.cbtf-southsudan.org/resource/529.
Deng, F.M. 1966–1967. The family and the law of torts in African customary law. *Houston Law Review* 4(1), 1-45.
Deng, F.M. 1972. *The Dinka of the Sudan*. New York: Holt, Rinehart & Winston.
Deng, F.M. 2006. Customary law in the cross-fire of Sudan's war of identity. Retrieved 14 February 2011 from http://s4rsa.wikispaces.com/Administration+of+Justice+information.
Deng, F.M. 2010. *Customary law in the modern world: the crossfire of Sudan's war of identities*. New York: Routledge.
Deng, D. and Deng, E. 2014. South Sudan talks must make provision for justice and reconciliation. *African Arguments*, 8 January. Retrieved 12 January 2014 from http://africanarguments.org/2014/01/08/an-integrated-response-to-justice-and-reconciliation-in-south-sudan-by-david-deng-and-elizabeth-deng.
DNIS. 2012. National constitution review commission conducts a conference on constitutional challenges. Retrieved 20 August 2012 from www.sudanradio.org/national-constitution-review-commission-conducts-conference-constitutional-challenges.
Doki, C. 2012. Constitutional commission calls for extension of its mandate. *The Niles*, 16 November. Retrieved 16 November 2012 from http://theniles.org/articles/?id=1571.
Eckert, A. 2000. Tradition – Ethnizität – Nationsbildung. Zur Konstruktion von politischen Identitäten in Afrika im 20. Jahrhundert. *Archiv für Sozialgeschichte* 40, 1–27.
Eckert, A. 2011. Nation, Staat und Ethnizität in Afrika im 20. Jahrhundert, in *Afrika im 20. Jahrhundert. Geschichte und Gesellschaft*, Edition Weltregionen, 21, edited by A. Sonderegger et al. Vienna: Promedia, 40–59.
El-Battahani, A.H. 2007. Tunnel vision or kaleidoscope: competing concepts on Sudan identity and national integration. *African Journal on Conflict Resolution* 7(2), 37–61.
Ethnologue. 2013. Languages of the world: languages of Sudan, 2009. Retrieved 28 September 2015 from www.ethnologue.com/country/SS.
Evans-Pritchard, E.E. 1968 [1940]. *The Nuer: a description of the modes of livelihood and political institutions of a Nilotic people*. Oxford: Clarendon Press.
Final Communiqué of the All Southern Sudanese Political Parties Conference. 2010. Retrieved 4 March 2011 from www.southsudannewsagency.com/news-a-events/press-releases/all-southern-sudanese-political-parties-conference--final-communique.
Frahm, O. 2012. Defining the nation: national identity in South Sudanese media course, *Africa Spectrum* 47(1), 21–49.
Geertz, C. 1983. *Local knowledge: further essays in interpretive anthropology*, New York: Basic Books.
GoSS. 2011a. South Sudan Law Reform (Review) Commission (SSLRC). Retrieved November 2011 from www.goss-online.org/magnoliaPublic/en/Independant-Commissions-and-Chambers/South-Sudan- Law-Review-Commission.html.

GoSS. 2011b. Report of the Technical Committee to Review the Interim Constitution of Southern Su*dan, 2005* (confidential working draft). Retrieved 15 November 2012 from www.gurtong.net/LinkClick.aspx?fileticket=55kyBBH4y U8%3D.

GoSS. 2012. *Recommendations of the workshop to 'Harmonize customary law and statutory law systems' given by South Sudanese Judiciary, Ministry of Justice and Local Government Board* (13–15 November), Juba: Government of South Sudan.

Guttmann, E. 1957. The reception of the common law in the Sudan. *The International and Comparative Law Quarterly* 6(3), 401–417.

Hinz, M.O. 2009. The ascertainment of customary law: what is it and what is it for? In *Customary justice and legal pluralism in post-conflict and fragile societies: conference packet*, edited by USIP & World Bank. Washington, DC: United States Institute of Peace, George Washington University & World Bank, 133–138.

Hinz, M.O. 2010. A new Sudan: precondition of peace at the Horn of Africa? *Namibia Law Journal* 2(2), 135–145. Retrieved 10 November 2011 from www.kas.de/upload/auslandshomepages/namibia/Namibia_Law_Journal/10-2/NLJ_section_8.pdf.

Hobsbawn, E. 1999. Introduction: inventing traditions, in *The invention of tradition*, edited by E. Hobsbawn and T. Ranger. Cambridge: Cambridge University Press, 1–14.

Hoehne, M.V. 2008. *Traditional authority and local government in southern Sudan*, Working Paper on ESW 'Southern Sudan: strengthening good governance for development outcomes in a post-conflict setting. Retrieved 12 September 2015 from www.eth.mpg.de/cms/en/people/d/mhoehne/pdf/consultancyReport.pdf.

IDEA. 2014. *Amid conflict and crisis, what future for the South Sudan's permanent constitution project?* Stockholm: International Institute for Democracy and Electoral Assistance.

Interim Constitution of Southern Sudan, 2005 (ICSS). Retrieved 21 February 2012 from www.unhcr.org/refworld/docid/4ba74c4a2.html.

International Crisis Group. 2011. *Politics and transition in the new South Sudan*, Africa Report No. 172, 4 April. Retrieved 21 February 2012 from www.crisisgroup.org/en/regions/africa/horn-of-africa/sudan/172-politics-and-transition-in-the-new-south-sudan.aspx.

Jada, A.M. 2013. Interview by K. Seidel, Court of Appeal for greater Bahr el Ghazal, Rumbek, 24 April.

Jellinek, G. 1929 [1900]. *Allgemeine Staatslehre*. Berlin: Springer.

Johnson, D.H. 1986. Judicial regulation and administrative control: customary law and the Nuer, 1898–1965. *The Journal of African History* 27(1), 59–78.

Jok. J.L. 2013. The TCRSS 2011, (Amendment) Act 2013, Legislative Explanatory Note. Juba.

Jok, J.M. 2014. South Sudan and the prospects for peace amidst violent political wrangling. *Pambazuka News*, 8 January. Retrieved 26 January 2014 from http://pambazuka.org/en/category/features/90076.

Jok, J.M. 2012. South Sudan: building a diverse nation, in *Sudan after separation: new approaches to a new region*, edited by T. Weis. Berlin: Heinrich Böll Stiftung, 58–67.

Jok, A.A. et al. 2004. A study of customary law in contemporary Southern Sudan. Retrieved 28 July 2012 from www.gurtong.net/LinkClick.aspx?fileticket=VjBn4P%2FhMio%3D&tabid=343.

Kapferer, B. and Taylor, C.C. 2012. Forces in the production of the state, in *Contesting the state: the dynamics of resistance and* control, edited by A. Hobart et al. Wantage: Sean Kingston Publishing, 1–20.

Khalil, M.I. 1971. The Legal System of the Sudan. *The International and Comparative Law Quarterly* 20(4), 624–644.

Kiir Mayadit, S. 2011. H.E. General Salva Kiir Mayadit, President of the Republic of South Sudan's Maiden Speech. On the Occasion of the Proclamation of Independence, Juba, 9 July. Retrieved 15 November 2011 from www.gurtong.net/ECM/Editorial/tabid/124/ctl/ArticleView/mid/519/articleId/5440/President-Kiirs-Independence-Speech-In-Full.aspx.

Kiir Mayadit, S. 2016. Speech of His Excellency the President announcing the commencement of national dialogue, Juba, 14 December.

Klug, H. 2011. South Africa's experience in constitution-building, in *Reconstituting the constitution*, edited by C. Morris et al. Heidelberg: Springer, 51–81.

Kramer, J. and Schneider, H.P. 1997. Das Fundament des Regenbogens. Ein Zeugnis der Verständigung – die Verfassung des neuen Südafrikas. *Kritische Justiz* 4, 475–490.

Kulluel, A. 2012. Kiir names constitution review team. *The New Nation*, 12 January. Retrieved 12 January 2012 from www.thenewnation.net/news/34-news/293-kiir-names-constitutional-review-team.html.

Kuol, S.P. 2013. Peril of ethnic federalism in South Sudan. *Juba Monitor*, 18–19 April, 4.

Leonardi, C. 2013. *Dealing with government in South Sudan: histories of chiefship, community and state*. Oxford: James Currey.

Leonardi, C. et al. 2011. Politics of customary law ascertainment in South Sudan. *Journal of Legal Pluralism* 63, 111–142.

Local Government Act of 2009 of Southern Sudan (LGA), Juba: GoSS.

Lorna, M. 2013. Interview by K. Seidel, SSuDEMOP, Juba, 1 May.

Lubang, S.M. 2011. Interview by K. Seidel and J. Moritz, Juba: 6 April.

Lupai, J.K. 2012. One best way of fighting tribalism in South Sudan, *The Citizen Newspaper*, 21 July, 9.

Mabor, B. G. 2013. Lack of national identity is a cry of the owl for South Sudan. *Juba Monitor*, 27 March, 4.

Makec, J.W. 1986. *The customary law of the Dinka (Jieng). A comparative analysis of an African legal system*. Khartoum: St George Printing Press.

Makec, J.W. 1988. *The customary law of the Dinka people of Sudan*. London: Afroworld Publishing.

Mamdani, M. 1996. *Citizen and subject: contemporary Africa and the legacy of late colonialism*. Princeton, NJ: Princeton University Press.

Mamdani, M. 2014. South Sudan: the way forward for South Sudan. *Al Jazeera*, 6 January. Retrieved 6 January 2014 from www.aljazeera.com/indepth/opinion/2014/01/way-forward-south-sudan-20141565251473808.html.

Manyuon, P.G. 2013. Interview by K. Seidel, SLS, Juba, 3 April.

Mennen, T. 2007. Legal pluralism in Southern Sudan: can the rest of Africa show the way? *Africa Policy Journal* 3, 49–73.

Mennen, T. 2010. Lessons from Yambio: legal pluralism and customary justice reform in Southern Sudan. *Hague Journal on the Rule of Law* 2(2), 218–252.

Merry, S.E. 1988. Legal pluralism. *Law and Society* 22(5), 869–896.

Merry, S.E. 2003. From law and colonialism to law and globalization. *Law and Social Inquiry* 28(2), 569–590.

Mijak, D.B. 2013. Interview by K. Seidel, Public Grievances Chamber, Juba, 10 April.

Ministry of Legal Affairs and Constitutional Development Organization Act, 2008, Juba: GoSS.

Moore, S.F. 2001. Certainties undone: fifty turbulent years of legal anthropology, 1949–1999. *Journal of Royal Anthropology Institute* 7, 95–116.

NCRC. 2014. *Action Plan 2013–2014.* 3rd Draft, 28 March, Juba: National Constitutional Review Commission.

NCRC. 2015. *Timelines for constitutional review entities in other countries*, 23 March, Juba: National Constitutional Review Commission.

Olenasha, W.T. et al. 2012. *In search of a working system of justice for a new nation : the ascertainment of customary law in 15 communities of South Sudan (the customary law of the Toposa, Lopit, Lango, Baka, Bongo, Ahu-Kumbo, Lotuko, Azande, Jurbel, Avukaya, Moru, Ndogo, Mundari, Wadi, Balanda)*. A Consultancy Report submitted to UNDP/Ministry of Justice, GoSS, 2/15/2012.

Penal Code Act, 2008, *The Southern Sudan Gazette* 1(1), 10 February 2009, Juba: GoSS.

Pimentel, D. 2010. Rule of law reform without cultural imperialism? Reinforcing customary justice through collateral review in Southern Sudan. *Hague Journal on the Rule of Law* 2(1), 1–28.

Presidential Decree GOSS/PD/J/002/2011, 21 January 2011, Juba: GoSS. Retrieved 21 March 2012 from www.goss-online.org/magnoliaPublic/en/president/documents/2011/mainColumnParagraphs/0/content_files/file6/Decree02-110001.pdf.

Presidential Decree GoSS/PD/J/08/2011, 17 February 2011, Juba: GoSS. Retrieved 21 March 2012 from www.goss-online.org/magnoliaPublic/en/president/documents/2011/mainColumnParagraphs/0/content_files/file12/Decree08-110001.pdf.

Presidential Decree GOSS/PD/J/09/2011, 18 February 2011, Juba: GoSS. Retrieved 21 March 2012 from www.goss-online.org/magnoliaPublic/en/president/documents/2011/mainColumnParagraphs/0/content_files/file13/Decree09-110001.pdf.

Presidential Decree GOSS/PD/J/10/2011, 21 February 2011, Juba: GoSS. Retrieved 21 March 2012 from www.goss-online.org/magnoliaPublic/en/president/documents/2011/mainColumnParagraphs/0/content_files/file13/Decree09-110001.pdf.

Presidential Decree RSS/PD/J/03/2012, 9 January 2012, Juba: GoSS. Retrieved 20 May 2013 from www.constitutionnet.org/files/constitution_commission_decree.pdf.

Ranger, T. 1999. The invention of tradition in colonial Africa, in *The invention of tradition*, edited by E. Hobsbawn and T. Ranger. Cambridge: Cambridge University Press, 211–262.

Saati, A. 2015. The participation myth. outcomes of participatory constitution building processes on democracy. Unpublished dissertation, Umeå Universitet, Umeå.

Schlee, G. and Watson, E.E. (eds). 2009. *Changing identifications and alliances in north-east Africa: volume II, Sudan, Uganda and the Ethiopia-Sudan borderlands*. New York: Berghahn Books.

Schlichte, K. 2004. Staatlichkeit als Ideologie: Zur politischen Soziologie der Weltgesellschaft, in *Ideologien in der Weltpolitik*, edited by K.-G. Giesen. Wiesbaden: VS Verl. fur Sozialwissenschaften, 149–166.

Seidel, K. 2012. Secularism and state-recognized legal pluralism in Ethiopia: relationship between Islamic family law and state law. *Law in Africa* 2, 223–237.

Seidel, K. and Moritz, J. 2011. The Transitional Constitution of the Republic of South Sudan: Ein kontroverses Dokument des jüngsten Mitglieds der Staatengemeinschaft, *GAIR-Mitteilungen*, 2 November. Retrieved 4 April 2012 from www.gair.de/wp-content/uploads/2011/10GAIR-Mitteilungen-2011.pdf.

Seidel, K. and Sureau, T. (eds). 2015. Introduction: peace and constitution making in emerging South Sudan on and beyond the negotiation tables. Special collection: Emerging South Sudan: Negotiating Statehood. *Journal of Eastern African Studies* 9(4), 612–633.

Simeon, R. 2009. Constitutional design and change in federal systems: issues and questions. *The Journal of Federalism* 39(2), 241–261.

Snyder, F.G. 1981. Colonialism and legal form: the creation of 'customary law' in Senegal. *Journal of Legal Pluralism*, 49–90.

SSHURSA. 2012. Rights group calls for extension of constitutional commission time. *South Sudan News Agency*, 16 November. Retrieved 16 November 2012 from www.southsudannewsagency.com/news/press-releases/rights-group-calls-for-extension-of- constitutional-commission-time.

Sudan Tribune. 2012. Lakes state gets new customary law centre. *Sudan Tribune*, 8 September. Retrieved 10 September 2012 from www.sudantribune.com/spip.php?article43850.

Swaka, H. 2013. Interview by K. Seidel, Handicap International, Juba, 10 April.

Thiik, A.R. 2013. Interview by K. Seidel, Nyakulan Cultural Center, Juba, 8 April.

Tier, A.M. 2012. *A note on the present state of the NCRC*, 2 August. Juba: NCRC.

Tier, A.M. 2013a. Building the Constitution in South Sudan, Juba Lecture Series 2013, University of Juba, 6 March.

Tier, A.M. 2013b. Constitutional review in South Sudan: from the constitutional commission and beyond, Juba: NCRC, 20 April.

Tier, A.M. 2013c. Interview by K. Seidel, NCRC, Juba, 3 April, 3 May.

Tier, A.M. 2015. Interview by K. Seidel, NCRC, Juba, 14 May.

Tor, W.S. 2012a. It is our constitution duty to pay allegiance to our nation and not to our tribes, *The Citizen Newspaper*, 20–27 October, 7.

Tor, W.S. 2012b. Federalism and protection of the citizenship rights. *The Citizen*, 19 September, 7.

Transitional Constitution of South Sudan 2011 (TCRSS), Juba: GoSS.

Transitional Constitution of South Sudan 2011 (Amendment) Act, 2013, Juba: GoSS.

Transitional Constitution of South Sudan 2011 (Amendment) Act, 2015, Juba: GoSS.

UNDP. 2012. Customary law in South Sudan. Retrieved 5 October 2012 from www.undp.org/content/dam/southsudan/library/Documents/2011-AWPs/DG/UNDP-SS-customary-law-08-12.pdf.

UNDP. Undated. National customary law centre opens in Rumbek. Retrieved 15 September 2012 from www.ss.undp.org/content/south_sudan/en/home/presscenter/articles/2012/09/07/national-customary-law-centre-opens-in-rumbek.

UNHCR. 2017. Number of refugees fleeing South Sudan tops 1.5 million. Retrieved 20 February 2017 from www.unhcr.org/news/stories/2017/2/589dba9f4/number-refugees-fleeing-south-sudan-tops-15-million.html.

Weber, A. 2016. Wieder zurück auf Los. Der Konflikt im Südsudan flammt wieder auf. Retrieved 30 July 2016 from www.swp-berlin.org/fileadmin/contents/products/aktuell/2016A46_web.pdf.

Williams, J.M. 2003. Law, in *Colonialism: an international social, cultural and political encyclopedia*, edited by M.E. Page et al. Santa Barbara, CA: ABC-CLIO, 333–336.

Woodman, G.R. 2011. A survey of customary laws in Africa in search of lessons for the future, in *The future of African customary law*, edited by J. Fenrich et al. Cambridge: Cambridge University Press, 10–30.

Work Plan for the Implementation of the Local Government Act 2009. Retrieved 25 April 2012 from www.cbtfsouthsudan.org/sites/default/files/work_plan_for_implementation_of_the_local_government_act_2009.pdf.

6 Co-opted, abolished, democratized

The Guinean state's strategies to manage local elders

Anita Schroven

Introduction

Customary law does not live in and of itself. In rural African settings it is often embodied by elders. Just as they are a heterogeneous group with varying positions, the customary law they represent and dispense is highly variable. This flexibility seems to oppose the state. Ideally, the state should be a coherent actor but in practice it is very amorphous and can therefore be more appropriately studied by its practices than by its laws and formal institutions.

Guinea's state institutions have, formally speaking, fundamentally changed over the last 60 years. The elders who make up the political elite in rural Guinea, have not followed such substantial ideological and instructional changes. They represent a seeming constant in rural governance despite the fact that customary law, their bases of authority, and their own position in local governance is in itself not officially recognized by the state. This has become a challenge to those state officials who have to work with the elders and are expected to guide them through new state regulations of local government. It is here that the negotiations between the Guinean state's policies and the realities of rural life take place. It is where this chapter investigates strategies with which the contemporary state is approaching the resilience of elders' authority.

For analytical reasons I separate two spheres with regard to state. One is the idea of state conveyed in its official history, ideals, constitution and laws. The other sphere that is central here is the practice of state by those people who represent and implement it: state officials, public servants, elected representatives and other persons who make reference to state and act in its name. It is these women and (in Guinea mostly) men who are the face of state towards the general population. They interpret constitution and laws, act in the name of the state and they do so in interaction with the wider population. These interactions reveal how political actors position themselves between the normative perspective of the law and the practice in the political arena which is highly localized due to the relevance of the other, localized actors. Thereby, the Guinean state becomes just as localized through public servants as the elders are.

Drawing on the government-led decentralization programme and analysing it as a local governance reform project, I explore how ideas that are part of a global discourse on participatory democracy are institutionally translated into the local arena. The ethnographic material in this paper foregrounds state officials, elected councillors and elders who are descendants of (pre-) colonial chiefs. They all live and work in the regional centre of the Prefecture Forécariah, situated in Western Guinea. The way these actors perceive, debate and implement established norms and new ideas of political authority reveals how impulses coming from the state may be incorporated into the local arena, and how adaptations can become an integral part of state agents' long-term dealings with elders.

Changing relations between different actors in the local arena lie at the heart of this paper, both considering historic dimensions and contemporary power shifts. The evolution of Guinean state institutions from the colonial to the post-socialist era will give an insight into the institutional (and legal) pluralism that needs to be taken into account when considering the complexities of the decentralization programme and the debates on political authority and control over land in rural Guinea.

After debating approaches to continuity and change in the local arena, policy debates of decentralization will highlight its inherent legacies of popular participation and representation. Decentralization is but one contemporary reform process, yet one that addresses many contested spheres of life in rural Guinea. It becomes a lens for the investigation of changes that cut across ties and effect diverse spheres of political or public life. It touches on individual and collective identities and social relations often mediated through seemingly established categories such as landlord-stranger relations,[1] title of village elder or the position in the state hierarchy. These issues find expression in contemporary debates of legitimate rule. They are the normative 'by-products' of decentralization that find their way into debates on (traditional and contemporary) authority.

Two case studies[2] will introduce the intricacies state agents face working with elders on decentralization-related issues. The first case presents state agents as representatives of change that is mirrored by elders engaging with new forms of political authority introduced by the state. The second case

---

1   Landlords are called *lasiri* in the local language Susu and also hold spiritual access to land which is secured by their first-comer status – they are regarded as the founders of ancient and current settlements in the area. Classificatory strangers are late-comers and therefore in a client-position to their landowning hosts (cf. Crowley 2000; Rodney 1970).
2   Ethnographic fieldwork was conducted in Forécariah Prefecture in Guinea 2006–2007, and in 2016–2017 with the Max Planck Institute for Social Anthropology, Germany. Fieldwork included (non-/semi-) structured interviews with local elders, state agents, public servants and political brokers as well as participant observation at formal and informal (administrative) meetings, NGO proceedings and workshops as well as family meetings of landlords and strangers. Archival documents were gathered in the Guinean National Archive in Conakry and the Archive of the Prefecture Forécariah.

study sheds light on state agents' top-down engagement with elders, supposedly incorporating local history and oral tradition, while in actual fact igniting established antagonisms in the course of their actions.

Taken together, these examples reveal how intricately interwoven contemporary and past institutions are, represented and engaged with today by both elders and state agents. The empirical material shows that the two portrayed parties are less opposed than they seem and that today's state agents take recourse to the past in order to engage with elders and the authority they represent in rural Guinea.

Political figurations: conceptualizing continuity and change in Guinea

Looking at governance in Guinea many different institutions co-exist today due to the varying political regimes of the past leaving their legacies behind that can be captured in competing ideologies but also in governing institutions. These are equipped with infrastructure and personnel and do not fade away with a change in governance systems or official ideology. Some may be explicitly terminated, others outlast the changes, leading to an accumulation of governing bodies which are not isolated from each other but interact, counteract, promote and obstruct each other. Today's actors include official parts of state administration and remnants from previous political regimes such as families of first-comers, colonial chiefs' descendants, socialist-inspired neighbourhood committees and elected members of town councils.[3]

Different institutions do not simply 'accumulate' with time but are characterized by complex interactions that the actors in the local arena employ to pursue their individual goals and ambitions. They may do so by blurring the boundaries between the old and new, formal and informal, resulting in what Lund called 'twilight institutions' (Lund 2006). Beyond this flexible and creative employment of the different possibilities open to actors I argue that institutions, termed old and new, formal and informal, official and unofficial by different authors, shape people's behaviour by providing cognitive scripts that are indispensable for action. Without them actors could not find orientation for their own actions nor could they interpret the action of others:

> When they act as a social convention specifies, individuals simultaneously constitute themselves as social actors, in the sense of engaging in socially meaningful acts, and reinforce the convention to which they are adhering [...] The relationship between the individual and the

---

3 This phenomenon has been investigated in the African context from various perspectives and with different theoretical approaches, see Bierschenk (1998), Lewis and Mosse (2006), Magid (1976), Trotha and Rösel (1999), and van Bakel, Hagesteijn and van de Velde (1986).

institution, then, is built on a kind of 'practical reasoning' whereby the individual works with and reworks the available institutional templates to devise a course of action.

(Hall and Taylor 1996: 15–16)

Institutions in this understanding can shape what actors regard as possible and as socially appropriate. Along these lines it becomes interesting how actors engage with new institutions and combine them with those they are already used to act in or interact with. Research has shown actors' skill at forging links between old and new institutions, to construct continuities and to merge titles from older into new institutional realms (cf. Klinken 2008; Moore 1986; Root 1994). The present chapter investigates such strategies for the changing arrangements of state actors towards local elders. Each case study foregrounds two particular groups of actors to show how, speaking with Hall and Taylor, individuals 'work and rework institutional templates' (1996). By using established templates, actors not only reify them but by merging them in creative ways, they blur the institutions' boundaries.

Together, the two case studies show how recently introduced notions of representative democracy and popular political participation enter the local discourses and may challenge what has so far been regarded as legitimate decision-making processes. In these debates state actors and local elders fuse discourses from different historic periods to forge their claims to authority in a legitimate and socially appropriate way. These debates effect the construction of identities and at the same time reveal the importance of being 'modern', i.e. being an active participant in the local arena who is ready to engage with changes, beyond merely accommodating them.

Elias's notion of figurations conceptualizes the tension between continuity and change (Elias and Scotson 1994). It highlights how individuals are immersed in multiple, yet highly specific and potentially discrete figurations or social relations that are so much established that the figuration itself becomes independent of the individuals themselves. In this capacity it can serve as a resource for actors' negotiations of power in the local arena. Here, the notion of figuration is employed to conceptualize institutions that are carried through time by a diversity of individuals, and thus guide people in their thinking and their employment of the institutions or figurations.

Adaptations of the figuration itself may not have been Elias' focus whereas they will be in this chapter. To this end, the theoretical concept of Strauss' arena will be combined with comparative works on administrative reforms in Francophone West Africa (cf. Bierschenk 1998; Olivier de Sardan 2004) as well with studies addressing decentralization by Ribot and many others (Ribot 1996; cf. Trotha and Rösel 1999). This body of literature will form the background upon which the Guinean decentralization programme and particular events following the government-led introduction of local government in Forécariah can be better understood. The presented case studies will highlight that figurations such as landlord-stranger-relations, (colonial) chieftaincy or public service are carried throughout time into other (ideological) contexts and are simultaneously perpetuated in this process while the individuals who carry these figurations/institutions also accommodate new elements brought into the arena.

Policy-talk of 'social cohesion' and 'authentic rule' with an interest to combine a presumed local sense of power with formal processes of Western-style democracy has emerged in many documents discussing decentralization. The idea of combining traditional norms of rule with contemporary ideas such as elections and representative democracy is raised for the Guinean case, too. Legitimacy to rule in practice therefore has to be examined in various contexts to understand whether – and if so – how this combination is achieved.

In this chapter I argue that legitimacy 'is not an all-or-nothing affair' (Beetham 1991: 19–20). Questions of legitimacy and capability to rule come together when for example councillors and communal secretaries negotiate the correct proceedings of meetings, elections or tax collection. Each party comes with different capacities and desires and potentially all of them are operating on shaky legal grounds as well as, outside the legal realm, varying degrees of legitimacy that the population is assigning or affording them. Therefore, questions of personal and formal qualifications as well as the individual's ancestors become relevant when trying to gain legitimacy.

Policy debates: decentralization and political participation

Major inter-governmental bodies such as the World Bank Group conceived decentralization as a tool to reform overburdened government bodies and public service delivery and attached normative ideas such as democratization and a more efficient development of civil society to the concept of subsidiary government systems. Ribot (2007: 43) has termed these (more or less intended) side-effects 'decentralization dividends'. Decentralization is thus not merely a project in its own right but a means to other ends. The programme itself backgrounds the intricate intertwining of neoliberal market logics and international policy interventions while foregrounding notions of good governance and democracy. These were enabled by a global shift of attention that was brought about with the end of the Cold War. With the shift of official governance mechanisms that was termed the 'third wave of democratization' (Huntington 1991),[4] some authors have argued that democracy in Africa was impossible unless adapted to local conditions. These conditions were also being associated with notions such as indigeneity, autochthony, a *longue-durée* approach to history and, related to these ideas, local understandings of political legitimacy. Such considerations were translated into demands to integrate so-called traditional authorities, often short-termed as

4   For a critique of this concept see Diamond (1996), Huntington (1997), and Rose and Shin (2001).

'elders' or 'chiefs', into local governance. This was for example postulated by powerful policy actors such as the World Bank Group under the title 'Promoting partnership with traditional authorities' (Berry 2006: 261; World Bank 2000: 79). The role of chiefs in local governance is sometimes linked to a so-called domestication of democracy. Reports from such projects in Ghana, South Africa or Burkina Faso often depict these rural institutions to be not unproblematic but essentially intact and widely accepted (Lentz 2006; Ouédraogo 2004; van Rouveroy van Nieuwaal 1999).

This view is contrasted by other authors who argue that decentralization reforms today are not a new phenomenon at all. They present (pre-) colonial empires in Africa as organized in a decentralized fashion and therefore preceding contemporary global reform movement. Electing local government would thus not pose such a challenge as historically the population had gained experience in governing itself (cf. Condé 2003). Decentralization attempts are identified in previous governance phases, for example the thirteenth century Mali Empire that often serves as a cultural and political reference for governments in Guinea and Mali today. Olowu argues with a different example that these ideas reach back into the colonial era, attempting to turn local administration from 'mere population control' into local governance. Nevertheless, these efforts were pushed to the background by national independences and later economic crises. Only much later did governments approach the subject again, with structural adjustment programmes forcing attention to a leaner and more efficient public sector (Olowu 2001: 6–8).

Beyond questions of efficacy of public services, efficacy of democratic institutions has been linked to decentralization as well. Along these lines, some authors claim that chieftaincy has to be 'domesticated' by and integrated into governance systems if African countries aspired to practice a form of democracy that was open for popular participation (van Dijk and van Rouveroy van Nieuwaal 1999). However, popular participation which has become a key term in policy debates on decentralization is not unproblematic in itself. When 'village chiefs and the rural councils of local state governance structures are [...] taken to represent rural populations [...] representation without participation' (Ribot 1996: 1) may be the inadvertent result. In other words, participation can become 'a modern reproduction of indirect rule [...] Like colonial rule, it can also strengthen and legitimate the non-representative, unaccountable governance forms it relies on' (ibid.: 7).

Participation as an instrument for broader change, by some authors termed 'the new tyranny' of international cooperation (Cooke and Kothari 2001), may thus lead to reifications of established authorities and processes of decision making that were actually intended to be changed. Critical analyses show that people participating are more likely reasserting the existing powers and by a participation-based consensus even reify and legitimate norms by the participatory process itself. Transferred to the realm of political decentralization, this invokes a subtler, yet pervasive integration of people into the state, rendering criticism of or resistance against it more difficult (Kothari 2001: 141, 144).

These considerations of political participation – theoretically leading to people's integration into political structures – do not necessarily affect the everyday workings of power in a localized setting. Here, inequalities may persist due to perceptions of normality or legitimacy of the status quo. Under such conditions Trotha projects a shift from 'administrative chieftaincy', where chiefs are directly co-opted to become the executives of central governments, towards 'civil chieftaincy', by granting more autonomy to any given local governance structures, these inadvertently turned the chiefly office into a 'parastatal agency' (Trotha 1996: 103).

Taken together, including so-called traditional authorities or councils of elders into governance processes may neither lead to more authentic and thus more legitimate ways of governance, nor to the 'domestication' of supposedly traditional authorities into more democratic modes of governance. Postulations such as the above-cited imply that 'domestication' was indeed necessary due to systemic neglect or side-lining of the aforementioned elders. More importantly, these policy documents, or those of the World Bank mentioned above, imply an inherent antagonism between good governance, decentralization and democracy on the one hand and the institution of chieftaincy on the other. That such oversimplified oppositions do not exist in reality is not difficult to imagine as neither are state reforms and changes of governance new, nor have those termed traditional been frozen in time. Further below I will discuss how the actual relations between Guinean state officials and elders play out.

Considering the brief policy review, in these debates it is often not explicated what is exactly meant by terms such as decentralization or democracy. It is obvious that such terms are often employed in both policy/theory discourses and also found in empirical contexts, (political) practitioners employing them in potentially very different ways. These terms seemingly lead double lives. In this chapter, the latter context shall be examined, more precisely the efforts state agents and elders make in translating and effecting decentralization policies imposed by the central government and circulated by transnational donor agencies (Merry 2006: 41–43).

In his publication on Guinea's decentralization process, the minister for the interior and decentralization, Mr Condé links the degree of solidarity, that the Guinean people are supposed to naturally possess, to shared ancestry, believes and historic experiences. These should come to the forefront with the reinstitution of local decision-making processes deemed 'natural' and 'culturally appropriate' for the supposed descendants of the Mali empire of thirteenth century (Condé 2003: 51–52).[5] It is in this vain that a council of elders has, according to official state laws, been reinstated

---

5   Looking closely, sources such as Condé (2003) conflate the public administration's deconcentration in the sense of subsidiarity with today's notion of decentralization of political power.

within rural communities, allegedly continuing a cultural trait essential to 'social cohesion' and the 'authentic ruling' of the Guinean people (ibid.: 59–60). The term commonly employed in this context is *sages* [elders]; this term does not necessarily indicate the descent of today's elders from (pre-)colonial chiefs but effectively addresses members of a family of first-comers, village founders and thus landlords, the *lasiri*. It is the same families that have presented from among their midst chiefs during colonial rule. Contemporary public discourse does not address the question of colonial collaboration and abuse of office by many chiefs. In 1956 this had the reason for chieftaincy being abolished as part of French colonial administration. They were again targeted during the so-called 'demystification campaigns' of the socialist regime's nation-building efforts in the 1950s and 1960s. It is curious that although elders' councils are included in Guinean official decentralization documents and state rhetoric, they do not feature in the country's current constitution (Rey 2007: 55) and therefore formally exist and operate in a legal 'grey zone'.

The theoretical considerations above notwithstanding, today's governments and state agencies are faced with the challenge to negotiate the perceived need of fulfilling international donor agencies' decentralization guidelines in policy making as well as implementing ideas of democratic participation. These negotiations become vital in the current context of the Guinean decentralization programme. Government-led initiatives and NGO-executed workshops about the formal process of decentralization will form the empirical backdrop for the investigation of potentially shifting notions of legitimate rule and the meaning of political participation in Guinea.

Institutional evolution and contemporary reform in Guinea

Before entering into detailed considerations of decentralization and people's engagement with it, the institutional history of the region shall be introduced. The area of Forécariah has been exposed to migration processes for centuries. Migrants from the northeastern region of today's Guinea had brought along Mandé-linked political organization into a predominantly Susu-inhabited area in the eighteenth century and founded principalities. Trade and migration networks made for an early presence of imperial influences from the theocratic Fouta Empire to the northeast and Europeans and Krios from Freetown to the south. A slow French conquest of the region began along the coast during the nineteenth century. With the final agreement of the border between Guinea and Sierra Leone (Brot 1994) the internal delimitations of the new Guinean colony could begin. The Cercle de Méllacorée[6] was formally established around 1875. Around 1905 the French

---

6 *Cercle* was the basic unit of territorial administration headed by French colonial officers; it roughly corresponds to the British colonial district.

headquarter was moved from coastal Benty to inland Forécariah, renaming the area Cercle de Forécariah.

Indigenous participation in governance was officially based on village chiefs (*alkaly*) with their deliberating councils and *canton* chiefs (*almamy*) who were to supervise them and mediate between them and the French colonial staff at the *cercle* level (see Table 6.1 below). Throughout approximately 60 years of colonial rule the *cercle* of Forécariah had gone through several phases of realignment of internal borders, with cantons being dissolved, divided and newly created. As various documents of the Prefectural Archive of Forécariah reveal, these changes had various causes. Official records include a decrease in taxable population in one *canton*, making expensive salaries for *canton* chiefs unnecessary by joining two *canton*s together. Internal conflicts of ruling families or between competing families rendered the continued governance by the chiefs in place too complicated for the French administrator so sometimes one *canton* was divided into two. The motives nevertheless were similar: creating boundaries and choosing individuals as chiefs who would increase the population's (social) cohesion to make the area governable with less local involvement of French officials (cf. Goerg 2011). In other words, individuals were chosen as new *alkalies* or *almamies* who could 'deliver' the required services. These came from the ranks of pre-colonial chiefs and their families, who are also the settlement's founding families, a concept that is up until today vital for the legitimation of power in the whole region.

After strong resistance against colonial politics, particularly tax payments and forced labour during World War II, France introduced the *loi cadre*, which introduced representative democracy via elections to the colonial

Table 6.1 History of administrative units and contemporary self-governing bodies.

Administrative unites over time			Self-governing bodies today	
French Colony (*Local Leader*)	1. Republic	2. Republic	Rural Setting (*Local Leader*)	Urban Setting (*Local Leader*)
–	Province	Région	–	–
Cercle	Arrondissement	Préfecture	–	–
Canton (*Almamy*)	–	Sous-Préfecture	Communauté Rural de Développement (*Président*)	Commune Urbaine (*Maire*)
Village (*Alkaly*)	Pouvoir Révolutionnaire Local	District	Conseil du District (*Chef du District*)	Conseil du Cartier (*Chef du Cartier*)

Note: Territorial entities and administrative hierarchies are represented schematically.

subjects in 1956. Territorial assemblies were created in the colonies and their jurisdiction expanded over time. Simultaneously, the number of elected representatives from former colonies, now called 'overseas' territories' increased significantly in the national assembly in Paris.

This slow reform movement towards political inclusion of the wider population was abrogated in Guinea. Starting within the political party *Rassemblement Démocratique Africain* (RDA) that spread over all French West African colonies, the Guinean leadership under Sékou Touré quickly became a vanguard to demand more political rights for colonial subjects and even full independence from war-weakened France. The mass mobilization, protests and strikes organized by RDA's Guinean party section were to become parts of the founding myth of the First Republic that gained independence in 1958. One cause of the population's support of this party was their quite radical call for – and by 1956 achievement of – the abolishment of colonial chieftaincy and therefore of the system of French indirect rule in Guinea (Schmidt 2005, 2007).

The abolition of colonial chieftaincy was merely the beginning of a larger political enterprise. What has later become known as 'Demystification campaigns' formed part of a much larger reform project of the government intended to create 'new' Guinean citizens. Campaigns were waged against old land-tenure and agricultural practices ambitiously aiming at industrialized farming. Religious and spiritual practices in the countryside were attacked: secret artefacts were exposed and destroyed and representatives of these 'old believes' such as chiefs/landlords and leaders of secret societies were attacked and chased away (Højbjerg 2007; Sarró 2009). While many chiefs left for a period of time, most extended families remained in their established area of rule and continued to lead the rural communities, albeit under the title of village elders or in new legal forms.

After independence in 1958 the government introduced different modernization policies and soon became an influential force to promote pan-African socialism to liberate the population of the old bonds of gerontocratic control in order to build a modern and enlightened nation-state (Camara 1996; Dumbuya 1974). The binding of people to the new nation-state was to be facilitated by their integration into the one-party-state by the newly establishing bureaucracy that was strongly tied to the ruling party. On the level of villages and districts, party and governing bodies were closely intertwined and overlapped in individuals holding several party- and government- or administrative offices simultaneously. These people were not necessarily the colonial chiefs personally but often close relatives. In Forécariah, the younger brother of the last *canton* chief, new head of the town's founding family and biggest landholder in the region became head of the regional party chapter within a decade after independence (Schroven 2010: 165). In Elias's terms the figurations from the (pre-)colonial era were carried into a new phase of governance that seemed to be opposed to their personal and ideological origins.

Interestingly, the internal delimitations of Guinea were not changed with independence, only their names were changed from *cercle* to *arrondissement*. Already before the end of First Republic that came about with the death of President Touré in 1984, the mode of governance in rural Guinea was being criticized. With the spirit of change in the advent of the Second Republic (1984–2008),[7] territorial administration was again reformed. *Arrondissements* were renamed into prefectures, provinces into regions.

Effectively, today's public institutions in rural Guinea are part of the wider system of governance inherited from the centralized colonial and later independent socialist state. The basic hierarchy of Guinean administration starts with the president, goes to governors of the eight regions, the prefects of the 33 prefectures and then down to the sub-prefects. To all these levels staff from line ministries (such as health, education, and agriculture) are assigned to provide public services. Together with police, gendarmerie and military these have been the governing institutions until 1991, when the introduction of elected local-level government began.

In the local context, as well as on the central government level, the question has to be asked whether administrative reforms really amounted to changes in the political and ideological reference systems. Part of the continuity is the direct government representation on the prefectural level. Following the decree 081/PRG/SGG/87 the prefect is the direct representative of the president, cabinet and all other government to the prefecture. He is chosen by the president among the highest-ranking public servants or senior officers of the army to safeguard the execution of decrees and uphold the law. He is assisted by two secretaries, one responsible for the every-day administrative processes, the other for the so-called 'decentralized communities' (Rey 2007: 41) or self-governing bodies. These bodies include from top to bottom the *communautés rurales de développement* (CRD)[8] or *communes urbaines* (CU) that are in turn made up of *district ruraux* and *quartiers urbains* respectively (see Table 6.1). These councils elect from their midst the president of the rural CRD or the mayor of the town respectively. This happens in rural districts and urban neighbourhoods where the elected are usually referred to as chief.

It is on this level that a separate council of family and village elders is envisioned by official local government documents to 'share the authority over the district' with the elected council (Condé 2003: 59). Formally, this aims to accommodate rural realities by affording elders space in decision making processes, albeit keeping them separate from the elected councillors.

---

7   While the Second Republic ended with President Conté's death in 2008, the newly elected government of 2010 has not made changes in domestic administration and governance reform strategies.

8   By 2017, the CRDs have been renamed in 'communauté rural' (CR), leaving behind the nominal task of bringing about rural development. For reasons of clarity, I retain the initial nomenclature of CRD.

In practice, there is little separation. The CRD and CU councils and their presidents in Forécariah Prefecture have been predominantly elected from the leading members of the founding families/*lasiri* and (direct) descendants of (pre-)colonial *alkalies* and *almamies*, formally re-instating those elites that have been officially abolished before independence and spiritually 'demystified', thus hypothetically disempowered by the First Republic's state officials. In practice, it is the same elite who ruled the countryside in (pre-) colonial periods – so what has the decentralization programme changed?

While elections do not produce democracy per se, they are nevertheless a prominent part of legitimation rhetoric, both within the international discourse on governance (Schatzberg 2001: 209) and locally in Forécariah. Councillors recount with pride how many votes they received and how relevant this was to claim a strong position in the council and within the local community at large. For example, Mr Barry, member of Forécariah's municipal council and descendant of a family termed *santigi*, traditional advisors to the *almamy* of Moria, used his electoral votes to press his authority in negotiations of marital or neighbourhood conflicts. In other cases he was referring to his *santigi* family background to claim legitimacy to do the same.

In contrast to this seeming continuity, there is a group of people who become newly inserted into the local arena. Public servants from the line ministries are working together with the prefect and sub-prefect respectively to provide so-called technical services like health and education. The councils are currently under the 'tutorship' of the prefect and his staff. To assist in the everyday bureaucratic work, each council receives the services of a communal secretary, assigned by the central Ministry of Interior and Territorial Administration. These public servants are specialized in the laws guiding the decentralization process as well as the management of the CRDs' (paper-)-work. The management role of the secretaries is often questioned locally but from the government side defended by councillors' low (French) literacy rates (Rey 2007: 46). Part of this administrative duty regards financial oversight as the CRDs and CUs are supposed to collect a local development tax to enable them to work towards their raison d'être: local self-development (Condé 2003: 84–87).

Management tasks or possibilities reach even further. People like the communal secretaries or sub-prefects influence election choices by giving information on candidates' eligibility. High-ranking state officials may even intervene more directly. For example, the prefect had been rumoured to select a CRD president from within the elected council after the predecessor had passed away, rather than holding elections. Such proceeding of effectively running the CRDs rings familiar: French colonial officers used to appoint and manage chiefs with the interest of efficacy as well.

The local councils' responsibilities include provision of infrastructure like streets, health centres, schools and markets. Management of natural resources is also part of their charge, just as the keeping of public records

(092/PRG/SGG/90 of 1990). To this end they are also supposed to collaborate with the respective departments of public service. Therefore, the work of CRDs and CUs nominally intersects processes of public service deconcentration and political decentralization. Some argue that despite diverse such efforts rural Guinea has experienced no effective change in public service delivery or self-governance (Observatoire de la Décentralisation 2003: 221; Rey 2007: 44). Aside from effective power and access to resources, this reality can formally be justified by a decree passed after the decentralization decree itself: prefects and sub-prefects are entitled to suspend all decisions taken by CRDs and municipal councils if they contradict any law or proceedings that do not 'correspond with the official fashion' (040/PRG/SGG/92, article 55 of 1992). With this move, state representatives retain control over their ward – even formally. The problematic implications of this theoretically guardianship-oriented relationship shall be explored more closely in the following sections. The ethnographic material will reveal that while the rhetoric mastery of decentralization talk is decisive for all actors, the establishment of links to landowning families is even more relevant – for councillors. State officials are not endowed with such family ties as they are usually not posted in their area of origin. Therefore their position has to be bolstered by the power of the state – which may be effective and successful, or it may not.

Considering the different phases of reforming rural governance, the following examples will highlight how figurations are carried through time and how they manage to incorporate new elements without necessarily opposing already established practices. As a result, state officials still have to negotiate with new and old forms of customary law.

Case study 1: New 'men in the middle' – strangers as agents of change?

The following section highlights changing relations between rural-based councillor, so-called traditional elders and the communal secretaries. These men are the most local-level agents of the state and for large parts of the rural population they are the 'face of the state'. Their task of translating government law into local practice makes them 'men in the middle' (Merry 2006: 39) who are not locally embedded. In the current example of Kaliah council (see Map 6.1), seven councillors are descendants of (pre-colonial) chiefs. Only the president of the CRD and one other man, who is also district chief, are not part of a traditional landholding family. The elders-turned-councillors participate in the blurring of boundaries between the envisaged elected council and the deliberating group of elders. In their varying use of vocabulary and arguments they are brokering; they are presenting different (more or less legitimate) institutions with the respective notions of authority attached (James 2011: 334). Speaking with Elias, these elders-councillors perform seemingly different figurations that are, as is being argued here,

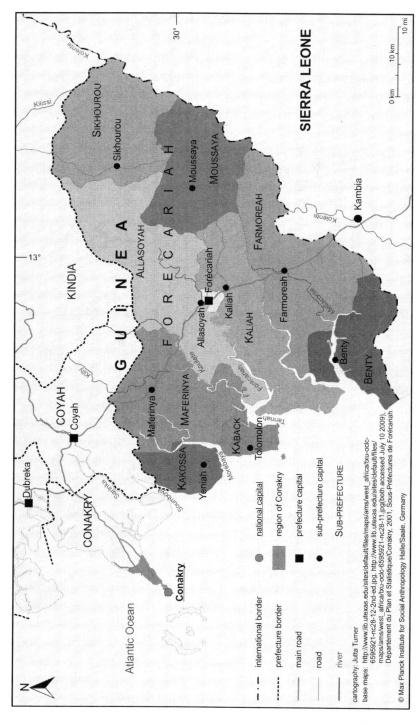

Map 6.1 Forécariah prefecture with its sub-prefectures.
Source: Schroven (2010: 31)

actually adaptations and interpretations of older figurations that have been changing for some time.

As every previous administrative reform process in Guinea, decentralization has brought in its wake demands to re-draw certain delimitations of villages that have now also become constituencies (CRDs or CUs). These debates are trigged by question of who is in effective control of land and who is legitimately entitled to its control. Notions of autochthony as a historic perspective and contemporary ideas of legitimate rule are intricately interwoven with this question. Different episodes of local history are used in all these concepts. Details such as cross-generational family ties, historic individuals' migration stories as well as old family feuds are brought forward in order to serve one's arguments. These may be accentuated by the assortment of actors who become involved in a particular case and represent *lasiri* families or to the other extreme, communal secretaries and other state agents who try to impose formal arrangements.

Some of these claims are recognized by state agents, others remain informal practice on the local level. For example, two new neighbourhoods in Forécariah town have been established by the municipal council. They are employed as basis for elections and tax collection without the relevant central ministry acknowledging their existence. Formal recognition of shifting boundaries however was achieved for the village Arabompa in the CRD of Allasoyah in 2002. Situated to the North of Forécariah river, it had been 'reclaimed' by elders and *lasiri* of the village and thus implicitly CRD of Kaliah. The village of Kaliah lies to the South of the river, but with the establishment of CRDs elders managed to successfully campaign for Arabompa to be brought under the self-governance of the area's landlords while at the same time remaining in the state administration/sub-prefecture of the Allasoyah.

The elders-turned-councillors managed to re-incorporate an old settlement of client-status, previously part of another sub-prefecture and hence CRD. While testimony of settlement history and founding family relations bolstered popular support, an important weekly market held in that village now also came to profit the CRD of Kaliah.

At another occasion the idea of local self-administration led to the splitting of a district into two parts after years of struggles for the recognition of their mutual independence. The communal secretary and the president of Kaliah's CRD together with some councillors embarked on a three-day journey to 'identify' two new district chiefs. 'Identification' was the term used in these accounts. Village elders would vote for the district chiefs rather than the whole population, but only after closed negotiations would ensure a unanimous vote. The former district-chief-elected-councillor of the area was member of the official delegation from Kaliah. He worried this division would upset the seemingly well-ordered situation within the CRD council:

> Currently we have a council member from every district. But now we will have two instead of one, so 10 districts. But the [communal] secretary tells us we are not allowed to have 10 councillors. This is odd. Now that there is rural councils again just like under Sékou [Touré], everyone should be represented, all the districts.
>
> (16 January 2007)

The communal secretary had previously commented with some pride that each district of the CRD had its representative on the council. He also hinted that achieving this had not been easy as 'some people just would not understand the idea of representation' and wished to vote for a person who happened to be from another district which was now a constituency that should not vote for its *lasiri* living in a different district (interview with communal secretary, 10 January 2007).

With the air of wanting to do everything to the letter, he and the above-cited councillor seemed to merge ideas of direct representation of the socialist era model with representative democracy of the kind envisioned in the current local governance act. Both men represent a contemporary model of governance in the context of a previous one, without acknowledging differences in ideology that stand behind the various forms of direct representation and participation. Accordingly, the communal secretary complained that decentralization would be used by some to reframe local grievances or personal interests in a supposedly more accepted way:

> People use decentralization for anything. They don't think what it is about, but participation sounds good. So they use it to justify why everyone can now decide everything. There is no order anymore, just personal interest. They say that the government has brought liberty [liberté] but we have debauchery [*libertinage*] in the capital. Now we have it here as well because people use decentralization and participation to be political about anything. Any personal query or argument with the neighbour becomes a question of rights to participate in politics [...] and there is no one we can turn to in order to set things right. Me and my colleagues are left alone.
>
> (23 January 2007)

Comments such as this are frequently made by state agents when asked about their personal opinion on decentralization or their relation to councillors they work with. The institutional chaos and government's indifference to outcomes of the official decentralization process leaves 'men in the middle' like the communal secretary to deal with the every-day effects and unintended consequences of new policies. Such leeway may also be used for personal gains. Forécariah rumour has it that most of the communal secretaries were making a lot of income aside from their rather meagre salary. An elder-turned-councillor lamented:

The town should be happy that they don't have a communal secretary. In the CRDs they twist and turn the laws and orders sent from the prefect and from Conakry so that they can eat parts of the money being moved around. Sometimes I think they become people who eat with both hands as well. They are not landlords [...] They can do as they please as they have no responsibilities to no one.

(27 November 2006)

The idioms used here are very strong. People accused of eating with both hands are usually regarded as those overstretching the accepted level of embezzlement their position is given leeway for. In the councillor's argumentation such activities would be very well possible because the actors concerned were not integrated into a larger body of 'accountability' that could regulate this over-consumption. According to this argument elders and landlords would be related to a 'moral community' (Le Meur 2006) whereas the secretaries have no local family ties and are therefore not accountable to the wider community.

Suffice it to say that the communal secretary, the district chief and the CRD president form a group apart from the other elders-turned-councillors in the CRD of Kaliah. All the councillors mentioned participate in blurring the boundaries between traditional elders and elected councillors. They employ the pluri-legal setting to find legitimate ways of framing and resolving conflicts. It should be noted that the aforementioned district chief and the CRD president are classificatory strangers within the dominant landlord-stranger-paradigm and therefore cannot be regarded as 'traditional' elders. It was the district chief who was temporarily ostracized and publicly shamed during the negotiations about the new districts – something a landlord-elder would not have to go through. Similarly, the communal secretary stands aside. He is not imbued with executive powers of a higher-ranking state official such as the prefect. Together, these individuals are examples of new 'men in the middle' created by the decentralization programme. The secretary in particular signifies the inaptitude of state to deal with elders whose basis of authority not fully understood in the formalistic proceedings of state management. Hence, the laws and regulations are ill-equipped for the secretary or non-local councillors to fulfil their task. The rhetorical turn to formalistic-legal vocabulary to perform as secretary, district chiefs or CRD presidents and to justify their actions and legitimize themselves is necessary and contributes to a vocabulary of change. This strategy stands in contrast to that of elders-turned-councillors who can employ both this state-offered rhetoric and the established *lasiri* rhetoric which the state agents have no access to.

Case study 2: The state employing history for local development

Aware of the differences in political rhetoric that hold authority state agents try to co-opt particular notions deemed historical and traditional in order to make contemporary reforms work. The following example illustrates that due to a formal institutional perspective these government actors aim at working with young decentralized institutions without taking their position in the overall, historically embedded arena into account.

The empirical material presented here is linked to a project aiming at economic self-development of rural communities, which is officially a major aim of the decentralization programme. It was initiated by the prefect who had visited CRDs in the Eastern part of the country that had pooled resources for local infrastructure projects with a UN-funded initiative. Shortly after plans were presented to the biannual administrative meeting of prefecture, sub-prefecture and CRD staff, on how the success story could be replicated. One of the prefect's closest collaborators, the secretary for decentralized communities, explained at length how the future 'development poles' would regroup certain CRDs that shared a common history, implying shared solidarity and trust that would facilitate cooperation.

The ensuing meetings were spent with people designing future collaborations for the development poles that would regroup the CRDs from political self-administrating entities into development partners. In this project the municipality of Forécariah and the CRDs Allasoyah and Moussayah were regrouped as *Moria*, the (pre-) colonial name for the area. The other poles bear names of former colonial *canton*s: Kimambourou, Benna and Méllacorée.

The regrouping and naming of development poles was highly intentional, as the prefect's staff explained:

> We want to emphasize the social cohesion based on shared ancestry. This historical experience will help the people to collaborate for their own development. I do not foresee any problems with this, except for Moria. The [landowning] Touré fight so much. They think that they have everything so they destroy every chance to change things. So the two CRDs might not cooperate with people in town. Finally they have their independence from town with decentralization, and then they should work together again.
>
> (26 December 2006)

While these comments expressed doubts about the feasibility of the prefect's idea, they highlight the ideas that have been expressed within the international discourse of democratic decentralization. In policy documents, shared history in rural settings is often said to ensure solidarity and thus heighten chances for collective action in the future. The origin of the development poles' names was a mixture of pre-colonial principalities (Moria, Benna) and colonial (Méllacorée, Kimambourou) political entities. Méllacorée was the name of a river and of the first French *cercle* in the region. The *cercle* was later enlarged and renamed into Forécariah. Kimambourou is the name of a

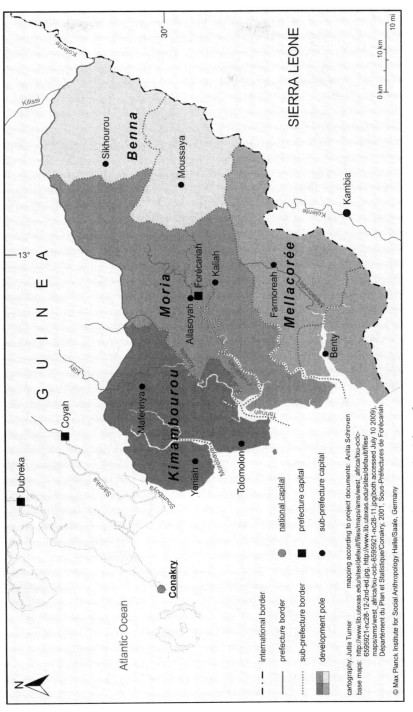

Map 6.2 Envisioned Development poles in Forécariah préfecture.
Source: Schroven (2010: 122)

canton that existed only for a couple of years in the first decade of the twentieth century. The names Kimambourou and Méllacorée are not commonly used any more, but the others can be heard in everyday conversations designating contemporary regional identities. The depth of historic reference is therefore very different in the four envisioned poles. As the prefect's staff member hinted above, a strong historic reference and shared (historic) identity may not always be helpful. It may even be counterproductive for the kind of solidarity and trust the development-pole project would imply.

This idea initiated a series of activities in Forécariah. A national NGO collaborated with the prefect's staff to organize workshops that would unite CRD councillors according to the envisioned poles. These workshops were to enforce councillors' capacities as elected representatives and encourage their cooperation in future projects. Following the prefect's wishes, this initiative was to further local solidarity and democratic understanding:

> I want to make a point here for progress, for development, for modernity. Democratic elections, representative democracy, these are new things for people here. How are the councillors supposed to know? But local solidarity, that has been here all throughout, so this is where we are going to start and turn it into something contemporary […] I want to leave a trace of modernity, to show that I moved things, that the Guinean countryside can evolve and lift itself out of darkness [*endroit sinistré*].
>
> (26 November 2006)

While the project contained many historical references, it was those recourses to the past that caused considerable problems in its execution. For example, the pole of Moria did not develop an intended project but stopped the proceedings after the initial NGO-sponsored workshop. In the ensuing discussions old accusations were aired about the town-people being 'lazy and privileged' and 'not ready to work'. The CRD councils of Allasoyah and Kaliah found many ways not to attend further workshops or not to reach decisions. In short, the project died quietly. The historic domination of the proposed pole that had been both principality and colonial *canton* before raised suspicions that it would be the rural surroundings again that needed to provide the manual labour for the benefit of the town-based elite. Instead of the intended solidarity and trust the shared memory led to mistrust and suspicion against the heirs of former rulers. As a consequence the state agents' experiment with elected councillors did not succeed; all the while they had tried to appropriate local history and those representing it for their project.

Conclusions

In the course of the twentieth century the state in Guinea has tried different ways of integrating traditional chiefs and make them work in its governance system. Under French colonial rule they were co-opted into the administrative and executive processes in the form of indirect rule. Chieftaincy was formally abolished and later 'demystified' on a spiritual level with independence. Chiefs and their heirs remained political leaders in the Guinean countryside throughout the First Republic when they became officials of the one-party-state. The contemporary state-run decentralization programme inadvertently led to the renewed formalization of elders as political leaders, formally resulting in a democratization of chiefly rule.

Integrating titles of authority and constructing continuities carried through time appears to be more easily done in retrospect than during a phase when new ideas of legitimate rule are being introduces, with negotiations and contestations dominating the local arena. This is a phase that local governance bodies currently find themselves in. Elders, councillors and state agents are well aware of the figurations; the rules of re-negotiating borders, projects and workshops are respected and the vocabulary of democracy and popular participation is employed. The words may receive their own, potentially new interpretation while becoming part of the local figurations. As a consequence, debates on legitimate rule become more complex. The authority of one decision-making body (local elders) has been challenged by the introduction of councils that in turn have a limited range of activity due to the presence of communal secretaries and are further curtailed by the tutor-position of state representatives.

Considering the different sources of legitimacy and authority that come to play in the local arena, Guinea's pluri-legal context becomes obvious – a fact that is neither publically debated or officially recognized. In light of the sometimes incommensurable laws, regulations and reform programmes, established figurations facilitate the translation process of the current decentralization programme into local governance practice – for all actors involved. Specific to the situation, they manage to negotiate the pertinent figurations and involve the relevant persons so as the bridge the apparent paradox.

During the different phases that the state in Guinea tried to co-opted, abolish or integrate elders' authority, political ideologies have fundamentally changed. The current democratization-phase is ideologically opposed to the previous abolition of chieftaincy under late colonial rule as well as the demystification campaigns and ensuing prosecution of chiefs after independence.

By constructing continuities in the figurations of local governance, these contradictions in state ideology do not present major problems in the everyday, neither to state officials, to the elders nor to the wider population. Elders in their comparatively recent position as councillors have maintained their influence on the formal and informal dealings of the state in rural settings. Traditional authority – whether with regard to access to land and resources, matters of family and community life – has not only lingered on but becomes formalized today in ways that after independence seemed unimaginable: people holding traditional forms of authority that the post-independence state had battled now formally wield power again. State officials either in particular projects like the development poles or in their everyday work as communal secretaries have to take these dynamics into account if they want to make the state work. Therefore it is these local levels and political practices of the everyday that make incommensurable laws, policies – and in the end the very state work.

References

Beetham, D. 1991. *The legitimation of power.* Atlantic Highlands, NJ: Humanities Press International.

Berry, S. 2006. Privatization and the politics of belonging in West Africa, in *Land and the Politics of Belonging in West Africa*, edited by R. Kuba and C. Lentz. Leiden: Koninklijke Brill, 241–263.

Bierschenk, T. 1998. *Les pouvoirs au village: le Bénin rural entre démocratisation et décentralisation.* Paris: Karthala.

Brot, M. 1994. Les regions frontalières Guinée Sierre Léone du début du vingtième siècle aux Indépendances. PhD, Université de Provence, France.

Camara, M.S. 1996. His master's voice: mass communication and politics in Guinea under Sékou Touré (1957–1984). Doctoral dissertation, Northwestern University, Evanston, IL.

Condé, A. 2003. *La décentralisation en Guinée: une expérience réussie.* Paris: L Harmattan.

Cooke, B. and Kothari, U. (eds). 2001. *Participation: the new tyranny?* London: Zed Books.

Crowley, E.L. 2000. Institutions, identities and the incorporation of immigrants within local frontiers of the upper Guinea Coast, in *Migrations anciennes et peuplement actuel des cotes Guinéennes*, edited by G. Gaillard. Paris: L Harmattan, 115–137.

Diamond, L. 1996. Is the third wave over? *Journal of Democracy* 7(3), 20–37.

Dumbuya, A.R. 1974. National integration in Guinea and Sierra Leone: a comparative analysis of the integrative capacities of single- and dominant-party regimes. PhD, University of Washington, Seattle, WA.

Elias, N. and Scotson, J.L. 1994. *The established and the outsiders: a sociological enquiry into community problems*, 2nd edition. London: Sage Publications.

Goerg, O. 2011. Couper la Guinée en quatre ou comment la colonisation a imaginé l'Afrique. *Vingtième Siècle: Revue d'histoire* 3(111), 73–88.

Hall, P.A. and Taylor, R.C.R. 1996. *Political science and the three new institutionalisms.* MPIFG Discussion Paper 96/6. Köln: Max-Planck-Institut für Gesellschaftsforschung.

Højbjerg, C.K. 2007. *Resisting state iconoclasm among the Loma of Guinea.* Durham, NC: Carolina Academic Press.

Huntington, S.P. 1991. *The third wave: democratization on the late twentieth century.* Julian J. Rothbaum Distinguished Lecture Series. Norman, OK: University of Oklahoma Press.

Huntington, S.P. 1997. After twenty years: the future of the third wave. *Journal of Democracy* 8(4), 3–12.

James, D. 2011. The return of the broker: consensus, hierarchy, and choice in South African land reform. *Journal of the Royal Anthropological Institute* 17(2), 318–338.

Klinken, G. v. 2008. Return of the sultans: the communitarian turn in local politics, in *The revival of tradition in Indonesia: the politics of Adat from colonialism to indigenism*, edited by J. Davidson and D. Henley. London: Routledge, 149–169.

Kothari, U. 2001. Power, knowledge and social control in participatory development, in *Participation: the new tyranny*, edited by B. Cooke and U. Kothari. London: Zed Books, 139–152.

Le Meur, P.-Y. 2006. State making and the politics of the frontier in central Benin. *Development and Change* 37(4), 871–900.

Lentz, C. 2006. Decentralization, the state and conflicts over local boundaries in northern Ghana. *Development and Change* 37(4), 901–919.

Lewis, D. and Mosse, D. 2006. *Development brokers and translators: the ethnography of aid and agencies*. Bloomfield, CT: Kumarian Press.

Lund, C. 2006. Twilight Institutions: An Introduction. *Development and Change* 37(4), 673–684.

Magid, A. 1976. *Men in the middle: leadership and role conflict in a Nigerian society*. Manchester: Manchester University Press et al.

Merry, S.E. 2006. Transnational human rights and local activism: mapping the middle. *American Anthropologist* 108(1), 38–51.

Moore, S.F. 1986. *Social facts and fabrications: 'customary' law on Kilimanjaro, 1880–1980*. Cambridge: Cambridge University Press.

Olivier de Sardan, J.-P. 2004. État, bureaucratie et gouvernance en Afrique de l'ouest francophone: un diagnostic empirique, une perspective historique. *Politique Africaine* 96, 139–162.

Olowu, D. 2001. *Decentralisation policies and practices under structural adjustment and democratization in Africa*. UNRISD 4.

Observatoire de la Décentralisation. 2003. *Etat de la décentralisation en Afrique*. Paris: Karthala.

Ouédraogo, H.M.G. 2004. Décentralisation et pouvoir traditionnel: le paradoxe des légitimités locales. Paper presented at workshop on 'Decentralisation in practice: Power, livelihoods and cultural meaning in West Africa', 4–6 May, Uppsala.

Rey, P. 2007. Le sage et l'état: Pouvoir, territoire et developpement en Guinée Maritime. PhD dissertation, Université de Bordeaux III – Michel de Montaigne, Bordeaux, France.

Ribot, J.C. 1996. Participation without representation: chiefs, councils and forestry law in the West African Sahel. *Cultural Survival Quarterly* 20(1), 40–44.

Ribot, J.C. 2007. Representation, citizenship and the public domain in democratic decentralization. *Development*, 50, 43-49.

Rodney, W. 1970. *A history of the upper Guinea coast, 1545 to 1800*. New York: Monthly Review Press.

Root, H. 1994. *Fountain of privilege*. Berkeley, CA: University of California Press.

Rose, R. and Shin, D.C. 2001. Democratization backwards: the problem of third-wave democracies. *British Journal of Political Science* 31(2), 331–354.

Sarró, R. 2009. *The politics of religious change on the Upper Guinea Coast: iconoclasm done and undone. International African Library*. Edinburgh: Edinburgh University Press.

Schatzberg, M.G. 2001. *Political legitimacy in middle Africa: father, family, food*. Bloomington, IL: Indiana University Press.

Schmidt, E. 2005. *Mobilizing the masses: gender, ethnicity, and class in the nationalist movement in Guinea, 1939–1958*. Portsmouth: Heinemann.

Schmidt, E. 2007. *Cold War and decolonization in Guinea, 1946-1958*. Athens, OH: Ohio University Press.

Schroven, A. 2010. Integration through marginality: local politics and oral tradition in Guinea. PhD thesis, Martin Luther University of Halle-Wittenberg, Germany.

Trotha, T. v. 1996. From adminsitrative to civil chieftaincy: some problems and prospects of African chieftaincy. *Journal of Legal Pluralism and Unofficial Law* 37–38, 79–108.

Trotha, T. v. and Rösel, J. 1999. Nous n'avons pas besoin d'état: Dezentralisierung und Demokratisierung zwischen neoliberaler Modernisierungsforderung, Parastaatlichkeit und politischem Diskurs, in *Dezentralisierung, Demokratisierung und die lokale Repräsentation des Staates*, edited by J. Rösel and T. v. Trotha. Köln: Rüdiger Köppe Verlag, 7–34.

Van Bakel, M.A., Hagesteijn, R.R. and van de Velde, P. 1986. *Private politics: a multi-disciplinary approach to 'big-man' systems*. Leiden: Brill.

Van Dijk, R. and van Rouveroy van Nieuwaal, E.A.B. 1999. Introduction: the domestication of chieftaincy: the imposed and the imagined, in *African chieftaincy in a new socio-political landscape*, edited by E. A. B. van Rouveroy van Nieuwaal and R. v. Dijk. Leiden: African Studies Centre and Lit, 1–20.

Van Rouveroy van Nieuwaal, E.A.B. 1999. *African chieftaincy in a new socio-political landscape*. Leiden: African Studies Centre and Lit.

World Bank. 2000. *Can Africa claim the 21st century?* Washington: World Bank.

Legislation

Loi-cadre, so-called *Loi n° 56-619 1956* or *Loi-cadre Defferre*, Paris: French National Assembly.

N°081/PRG/SGG/87 *Décret déterminant les conditions de nomination et les attributions des Préfets, des Secrétaires Généraux de Préfecture, des Sous-Préfets et des Sous-Préfets Adjoints 1987*, Conakry: President of the Republic of Guinea.

N°092/PRG/SGG/90 *Ordonnance portant organisation et fonctionnement des communautés rurals de développement en République de Guinée 1990*, Conakry: General Secretary of the Government of the Republic of Guinea.

N°040/PRG/SGG/92 *Décret portant tutelle des communautés rurals de développement en République de Guinée 1992* (article 55), Conakry: President of the Republic of Guinea.

7 State-orchestrated access to land dispute settlement in Africa
Land conflicts and new-wave land reform in Tanzania

Rasmus Hundsbæk Pedersen

Introduction

Land conflicts are rampant in sub-Saharan Africa. A new wave of land reforms has swept across the continent in the last couple of decades to address the problem. By recognizing existing rights to land – customary rights included – and decentralizing responsibility for land administration and land dispute settlement, states have aimed at setting up new institutions and establishing more formal systems for resolving such disputes. These systems also involve customary institutions, in particular in settling disputes (Quan 2000: 33; Wily 2003: 66; Deininger 2003; Boone 2007: 558; Lipton, 2009: 126–127; Knight 2010: 4). However, despite their novelty, the new-wave land reforms have become part of a decade-long debate over land reform. This chapter argues that, if we wish to acquire a better understanding of their institutional impact on land dispute settlement at the local level, we should not always equate the new-wave land reforms with the reform experiences of the past.

Previous, state-centric land reforms promoted the replacement of customary forms of land administration with new centralized institutions. State representatives and scholars from the property rights tradition found that customary systems were inefficient because they did not provide the infrastructure for land transactions (Platteau 1993).

A modernized, highly influential version of this formalization agenda has been provided by the economist Hernando de Soto, who argues that the reason why the West has grown rich whereas the rest has not can be found in their different property systems. A Western, formal property system with individualized land ownership and title deeds makes it possible to borrow money using land as collateral. In developing countries, these systems are inaccessible to the poor (de Soto 2000). De Soto and likeminded scholars therefore focus on getting the administrative techniques and the legal frameworks right. With their focus on technicalities and land titling, they tend to take land dispute settlement for granted.

Conversely, critical scholars, typically historians and anthropologists studying access to land and natural resources (Berry 1994; Peters 2004), have criticized state-led reform efforts. Based on experiences of reform in the 1970s and 1980s, they identify the formal systems' ineffectiveness and inability to deliver decisive decisions. Land dispute settlement is depicted as a site of competition between state institutions and customary and informal practices. Consequently, legal pluralism and forum shopping prevail, rights to land remain negotiable and are decided through local politics, and insecurity of tenure persists, as conflict resolution is depicted as problematic or downright impossible (Comaroff 1981; Benda-Beckmann 1981; Moore 2000; Nyamu-Musembi 2007: 1457; Lund 2008; Mwangi 2010: 728).

Typically, these critical scholars have used the concept of access to identify the persistence of customary institutions and informal practices mediating access to land at the local level. Access has been defined as the right to enter a defined physical area (Ostrom 2001: 134) and as the ability to benefit from resources, sometimes involving access to an authority (Ribot and Peluso 2003). Particularly in Africa, these critics have pointed out, having access to land differs from having rights to land. People may have the right to own a plot without having the ability to use or sell it and vice versa. According to Sara Berry (1993) there is something African in the negotiable and communal character of land rights that undermines reform. Social relations, she writes, have 'continued to provide significant channels for negotiating access to resources, even after African countries gained independence from colonial rule' (ibid.: 16–17).

Even when, more recently, like-minded scholars have acknowledged the state's important potential role in increasing security of tenure, they tend to emphasize the persistence of institutional competition (see, for instance, Evers et al. 2005: 5; Odgaard 2005: 247; Sikor and Müller 2009: 1308; Berry 2009; Joireman 2011: 153). In other words, despite innovations like decentralization and more localized governance of access to land, scholars tend to evaluate the new wave of land reforms in similar terms to past reforms.

The proponents of formalization and the critical access scholars thus share a focus on the unresolved, problematic relationship between the state and customary and informal institutions, but they disagree over what to do about it. Formalization proponents take the continued negotiability of rights to land to be a pretext for reform. Their critics argue that the state should not interfere too much in local-level land administration since this will only increase institutional competition.

I would argue that these two bodies of literature are debating within a 'competition paradigm'. Whereas this paradigm has provided priceless insights into the complexity of land dispute settlement in the past, it does not pay much attention to the impact of the recent new wave of land reforms. People's choice of institutions to settle land disputes appear opportunistic and haphazard when institutional competition is made an analytical a priori.

This chapter argues that, if a reform corresponds to people's demand for land dispute settlement services at the local level, as is the implicit ambition of most new-wave land reforms, competition may not be the best lens through which the reform should be analysed. Based on empirical research in mainland Tanzania, the chapter identifies a new-wave land reform's systemic impact on local-level land dispute settlement. In this, it is in line with Catherine Boone (2014), who recently classified Tanzania's land tenure regime as 'statist', arguing that this has come about due to shifting governments' choices over a long time period.

Tanzania's land reform came about with the introduction of two Land Acts in 1999 and a Land Court Act in 2002. Responsibility for administering land and for settling land disputes in rural areas has been devolved to local-level bodies, appointed by elected local governments and accepted by village assemblies. Customary laws and rights are recognized, and attempts are being made to incorporate customary authorities into the state-backed institutions for land dispute settlement.

Inspired by implementation studies – a distinct discipline within the social sciences – the chapter stresses the processual character of land reform implementation. Through analyses of access to land dispute settlement, it shows that Tanzania's state-backed land dispute settlement institutions have been strengthened despite ambiguous evidence and slow and uneven implementation (see also Knight 2010: 211; Pedersen 2012).

The chapter does not claim that customary, informal or downright irregular practices have ceased to exist. They are, however, increasingly influenced by the state's laws and institutions. Although Moore (2000: 29) has described these 'other reglementary organisations and arenas' as 'untameable', and although their unwritten character has been stressed (North 1990: 36), the evidence from Tanzania suggests that even these institutions increasingly adhere to the laws and procedures prescribed by the state and produce written evidence accordingly, as they are being incorporated into a state-backed land dispute settlement system. Rather than a paradox, the changes denote the mutual transformation of state and customary institutions. The chapter sheds light on these gradual changes and intermediate institutional forms.

In other words, a systemic reconfiguration of institutions is taking place due to reform. The more formal institutions, characterized by regularity and operating with the backing of the state (Hart 2008; Leftwich and Sen 2011: 322; Carey 2000), are being strengthened as the loci for land dispute settlement. Thus, a focus on gradual changes in the relationship between more or less formal institutions is suggested as a better alternative to a narrow focusing on institutional competition and the pros and cons of full-scale formalization. Whereas the chapter claims that access to the more formal institutions is becoming more important, it does thus not claim that all land in Tanzania has been formalized.

The chapter focuses on the topic of land dispute settlement, which is often overshadowed by the land titling debate. Nonetheless, access to land dispute settlement may be more important for most people's security of tenure. Titling is primarily mentioned when it affects the implementation of the land dispute settlement component or affects people's access to land dispute settlement institutions in other ways.

The focus is on small-scale disputes at the local or family level (Derman, Odgaard and Sjaastad 2007: 19). Throughout the chapter, particular attention is paid to the relationship between the classification of conflicts and the choice of institution for dispute settlement. What matters is Benda-Beckmann's (1981: 118) dictum that 'the jurisdiction of a forum depends in principle on the nature of the dispute'.

For didactic reasons, I use the term 'land conflicts' to describe competing *claims* to land and 'land dispute settlement' to designate *attempts* to settle these conflicts. Claims may vary on a continuum from mere access to an area to state-backed ownership rights with the accompanying ability to exclude others but also to transfer rights to others (Ostrom 2001: 134). It is particularly the claims to ownership rights and the accompanying dispute settlement machinery that are the focus of the chapter.

The decision to look at claims reflects a wish to include conflicts that are often not registered with the state-backed land dispute settlement institutions in the analysis. For instance, women's conflicts over land tend to be classified as family conflicts, and settlement is typically sought through the involvement of customary institutions. The same is often true of intra-ethnic land conflicts, that is, conflicts between parties from the same ethnic group.

The institutional changes described in this chapter – the strengthening of the state-backed institutions – affect people differently. The introduction of land use plans, spurred by a reformed Land Use Planning Act in 2007, turned conflicts which would previously have been settled through informal negotiations into cases of criminal trespass that increasingly fall within the jurisdiction of formal village institutions and the court system, often to the disadvantage of pastoralists. Changes thus render access to land dispute settlement unequal in new and unforeseen ways. Whereas these developments will be analysed in the light of the reconfiguration of institutions at the local level, I hardly touch upon questions of morality and justice in the complex land conflict cases.

The chapter combines a literature review of new-wave land reform experiences with ten months of fieldwork, carried out as comparative case studies of reform implementation in two villages in the northeastern part of mainland Tanzania in 2009–2012. Through comparative case studies of two villages, it analyses the effects of the reform's implementation. The registration of cases with the more formal land court institutions in the two villages and districts and testimonies from elders who are still engaged in land administration and land dispute settlement provided important entry points into the local contexts. Around a hundred structured, qualitative, in-depth interviews with villagers, elders, local leaders, district officials, court representatives, NGO representatives and ministry officials were conducted.

Overall, the interviews focused on people's past and present practices in securing rights and their choice of institution to settle conflicts. A special effort was made to trace women experiencing problems related to land.

For comparative purposes, evidence was collected for year 2000, that is, some years before the enactment of the Tanzanian Land Acts in 2001 and the Courts (Land Disputes Settlements) Act in 2004, and for year 2009, some years later. Furthermore, villages in which interventions to implement the legislation had been carried out were chosen for in-depth field studies to ensure that reform had had a fair chance to make an impact. One village in Handeni District and one in Kiteto District were chosen.

The two cases thus also represent two different types of intervention: an NGO-driven, rights-based approach, and state-backed intervention aimed at titling. The choice of villages that had been subject to targeted interventions also means that the findings are preliminary, pointing to more general institutional changes that are likely to be found elsewhere as reform implementation gathers speed. This point, which is aggravated by the changing jurisdictions of courts over the period, makes comparisons a daunting task. Differences apart, the chapter therefore pays equal attention to the similarities between the two cases. Indeed, the similarities were greater than the differences.

Land reform and land dispute settlement in Tanzania

Tanzania's new-wave land reform has been termed a 'land law reform' because it does not aim to redistribute land or introduce new categories of tenure (Fimbo 2004). It could also be called a 'land administration' and a 'land court' reform to describe its two main reform components. It had long been under way when it was introduced by the Land Act and the Village Land Act of 1999 and the Courts (Land Disputes Settlements) Act of 2002.

With its recognition of existing rights to land, customary rights included, the reform represented a break with the past, when the colonial and earlier post-colonial governments frequently alienated rural land for development purposes without proper compensation (Sundet 1997). In contrast, the Village Land Act, governing land in rural areas, states that land can only be transferred with the approval of the village council and upon agreement over the level of compensation. If no agreement can be made, the case is to be referred to the high court.

The reform was a response to the increased number of land conflicts caused by the opening up of private land ownership. A Presidential Commission of Inquiry into Land Matters had been set up in 1990–1991 to investigate the causes of land conflicts, and it found that 'in practice there is no known and clear machinery for settling disputes'. Back then, the primary courts were the key institutions in the judicial system that dealt with land disputes (GOT 1994: 101). However, the Commission concluded that 'the dispute settling machinery is inaccessible to the large majority' and that, due to the inaccessibility of the court system, administrative bodies and ruling party representatives were handling the majority of land conflict cases (ibid.: 103–105). The lower-level ward tribunals could not deal with disputes over land ownership (GOT 1985: part 3, §9).

The 1999 made it clear that the village authorities were responsible for land administration and land dispute settlement. The reform prescribed the establishment of a new decentralized system for land dispute settlement, starting with village land councils and ward tribunals. A more professionalized body – the district land and housing tribunal – was prescribed at the district level with the possibility of appeal to the High Court (Land Division) and the Court of Appeal at the national level. More controversially, village institutions were also made important in issuing title deeds – Certificates of Customary Ownership (CCROs) – in the villages.

A contentious element of the 1999 reform was its recognition of customary laws and customary authorities. It explicitly recognized customary laws and provided room for customary authorities to participate in dispute settlement (Knight 2010: 187). Generally, customary law applies mainly in civil matters and is important for succession, inheritance and family matters. However, the reform was ambiguous in several ways.

First, it lacked a precise definition of customary law (Fimbo 2004: 21). A Customary Law Order had been introduced in 1963 to regulate marriage and succession that restricted women from inheriting or owning land in patrilineal areas, but the codification of customary laws was only carried out in a small number of districts before it was abandoned. Though still applicable, the Law Order does not seem to be used much (Yngstrom 2002). Furthermore, a number of landmark High Court rulings have strengthened the position of women over the years. A High Court judgment in 1990 rejected a plaintiff's reference to the Customary Law Order and emphasized the principle of non-discrimination in Tanzania's Constitution. The High Court has provided other landmark judgments that improved women's access to land (Ikdahl et al. 2005: 40). These views are reflected in the 1999 Land Acts' abolition of discriminatory practices. In general, written law is superior to customary law (Shivji et al. 2004: 19).

Second, the reform lacked a definition of customary authorities. Customary authorities are allowed to participate in dispute settlement under the auspices of the state-backed village government, but who are they? Furthermore, with the prohibition of discriminatory practices and the streamlining of administrative and dispute settlement structures, the laws paradoxically 'lean towards homogeneity of customary laws' (Gastorn 2008: 217; Knight 2010: 187). Scholars differ on whether this homogenization should be welcomed or not.

Some scholars focus on the need for the recognition of customary institutions, in particular in protecting the rights of vulnerable groups. Odgaard (2006: 34) suggests that recognition would be more in line with the wishes of local people, who 'want conflicts solved as close as possible to the arena where the conflicts occur'. In the same vein, the chairman of the Presidential Commission of Inquiry into Land Matters, Issa Shivji (1998: 102), was disappointed that the Land Acts had not followed the Commission's advice to place greater emphasis on the role of elders and criticized the reform for not having changed anything at all.

Conversely, other scholars stress the changing character of land conflicts. Statutory law, they say, is increasingly being used to enhance the rights of women (Isinika and Mutabazi 2010: 142; Pedersen 2015). Dzodzi Tsikata (2003: 179) is highly critical of Shivji's glorification of customary institutions and states that 'to ask women to wait until customary practices have themselves evolved through contest within their societies is to deny them a level playing field'.

These positions point to the complexity of reforming land dispute settlement at the local level. Land reform should not be expected to revolu-

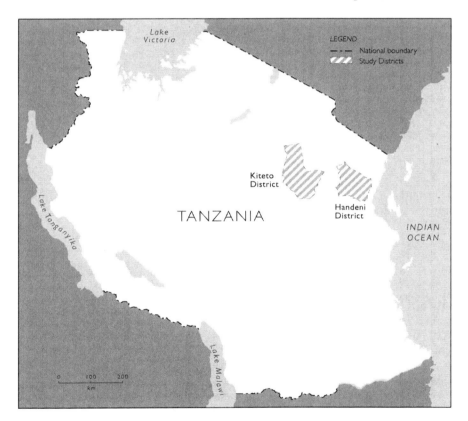

Map 7.1 Study districts.

Source: Map illustration prepared by Allan Lind Jørgensen based on official map by Surveys and Mapping Division, Ministry of Lands, Housing and Human Settlements Development, United Republic of Tanzania, Dar es salaam, Tanzania, 2012

tionize practices overnight. Previous research has described the failure to recognize customary rights, the overlapping jurisdiction between the formal and informal institutions, and the arbitrariness of state courts prior to reform (Tenga and Kakoti 1993; Donge 1993: 434). More recently, post-reform research has presented similar findings (Maganga 2002; Diehl 2009: 190).

Still, the debates do not answer the important question raised by Jan Kees van Donge in his case-study article about pre-reform land dispute settlement in Tanzania, namely why people at the local level keep opening cases in the formal courts if they are likely to be disadvantaged due to corruption, irregular procedures and prohibitive costs (Donge 1993: 432). They also do not provide any clear answers to the related question raised by this chapter, namely whether the Tanzanian land reform has had any systemic impact on local-level dispute settlement. The presentation of evidence from two case-study villages helps shed some light on these questions.

Land conflicts and dispute settlement in Kimana village, Kiteto district

Kiteto district is situated in an arid to semi-arid landscape on the fringes of the Maasai steppe in the northern part of Tanzania. The case-study village in Kiteto, Kimana, borders the district's main town, Kibaya. The majority of the population is Maasai, but one of the four sub-villages, Napilukunya, is inhabited by a hunter-gatherer people, the Akiye, who have started growing maize and living in permanent huts, just as the Maasai increasingly did from the 1980s.

Kimana is known to be fertile, thus attracting immigrants searching for farmland. In another sub-village, Mbeli, the majority is now non-Maasai. Especially from the 1990s onwards, the pressure on land has been on the increase and has given rise to conflicts between residents and newcomers, ultimately leading to arson attacks and killings.

The increasingly mixed population has posed a challenge to village governance, which, traditionally, has been dominated by customary institutions, namely the Maasai elders. As a response, Kimana has managed to establish the state-prescribed institutions for settling land disputes quite firmly. A pastoralist NGO, CORDS, has been present in the village from the early 2000s, assisting it in making land use plans and disseminating information about land rights and land laws.

One of the significant changes in the local governance of land, the making of a land use plan, has changed conflict patterns in the villages. Not only did it lay out the ideal pattern for future development in the village, it also turned what previously would have been defined as civil conflicts over ownership or boundaries into different types of criminal cases. If, for instance, a pastoralist grazes his cattle on land designated for farming, the owner can demand compensation or take the perpetrator to court for 'criminal trespass'.

However, the land use plan mainly targeted another problem in the village, namely the decade-long influx of poor immigrants and agribusiness investors from elsewhere in Tanzania, who come to Kiteto to find 'vacant' land for farming. Evidence from the Presidential Commission of Inquiry into Land Matters had pointed to contradicting national policies, which had led to widespread irregularities in land allocations in Kiteto district in the 1980s, involving the district, regional and national level authorities, often in cooperation with corrupt village chairmen and elders (GOT 1992a, 1992b).

This development posed a threat to the Maasai majority's traditional grazing patterns, and the land use plans were an attempt to control the development. Consequently, the Kimana village chairman had taken immigrant farmers, who had settled without formal permission and thus violated the land use plan, to court for environmental destruction, or 'maliciously damaged property', as the District Court called it (interview, 16 May 2010). Furthermore, in 2012 the Tanzanian Court of Appeal ordered the eviction of a large number of farmers who had cleared a large area that Kimana and other villages had set aside as a game reserve (see also Askew et al. 2013).

Increasingly, therefore, the Maasai village leaders saw the state-prescribed institutions as their best defence against losing their land. Regularized allocations of land in Kimana were introduced in the 1990s and strengthened in the 2000s. Before 1990, land was mostly allocated by elders in the village or converted to farming use by clearing virgin land with the elders' permission. For instance, one man received his first two plots of land from the elders in the 1970s, but received his third plot through a village allocation in 1991 (interview with old man, Kimana Village, 7 April 2010). Though the continued influx of immigrants and their unauthorized clearing of bush land set aside for grazing show that the village institutions did not have the situation under control, the more formal village allocations have now become the norm:

> In the present, the village council insists that all applications [for land allocations] should be sent to the village council, so later they can be provided with village titles. It has not been like this before. Now if you want to get the right to own, then it requires you to list your name, so that they know how many acres you have.
> (Interview with chairman of elders, Kimana Village, 17 May 2010)

This change in how land was allocated also affected the way land conflicts were handled. For instance, a male Maasai who had lost access to the land he had been allocated by the village and district authorities in the late 1990s explained that, because of the new allocation procedures, he preferred the state-backed institutions to settle the conflict rather than the customary ones: 'I did not use the Maasai elders, because I was given the land based on national laws. So I decided to follow that channel' (interview with older man, Kimana Village, 18 March 2010).

Thus, the state-backed land dispute settlement institutions were gradually strengthened in Kimana village. The Maasai, who are often described as anarchistic, unruly and the victims of formal development planning (see, for instance, Benjaminsen, Maganga and Abdallah 2009; Hodgson 2004: 238), had, in other words, turned the formal law and institutions into weapons of their own, much in line with Julie Eckert's findings from urban India, where she describes how the poor can use state laws to address their grievances in acts of legalism from below, as described in the article 'From subjects to citizens: legalism from below and the homogenisation of the legal sphere' (Eckert 2006).

Currently, Kimana village continues along these same lines and issues individual title deeds, the Certificates of Customary Ownership (CCROs). The village chairman (interview, 16 May 2010) and the main representative of the elders in Kimana were both unequivocal about the need to use these tools. The chairman of the elders explained: 'I see it is good, because the country is being stolen by the smart ones. It is like the cows. They are many, but we put marks on them so that we can recognize them if they get mixed with others' cows' (interview with chairman of elders, Kimana Village, 17 May 2010).

Not only does the development signify a certain pressure from below on the state-backed land administration and land dispute settlement system, it also contradicts a widespread view among land rights activists who tend to see individual certificates as threats to the Maasai lifestyle, with its communal grazing (interviews with NGO representatives, 18 January and 19 May 2010).

Land conflicts and dispute settlement in Mzeri village, Handeni district

Handeni District is situated in a semi-arid landscape in Tanga Region in the north-east of Tanzania and has a mixed population. In the case-study village, Mzeri, situated thirty kilometres to the east of Handeni town, the majority are Zigua, but pastoralist Maasai are dominant in one of the ten sub-villages.

Handeni has also witnessed an increase in the competition for land and in land conflicts in the last couple of decades (Oppen 1996: 208; Ylhäisi 2007: 32), and Mzeri had seen some immigration due to Tanzanian ministers having announced that there was 'free land' in Handeni District (interview with district official, 13 May 2010). However, generally the pressure on land is not comparable to the pressure felt in Kiteto District.

A titling pilot project in Mzeri and six other villages in Handeni District in 2006–2007 has had a major impact on land administration and dispute settlement. It has reinforced the strengthening of the state-backed village government that had been going on since the village became an Ujamaa village in the mid-1970s. The project was implemented in a three-month period. In each pilot village, a number of activities were carried out to prepare for the issuing of CCROs. Village boundaries were surveyed, land-use plans were made, a village land council was established to handle disputes, and people were trained in formal land allocation and land administration procedures.

The initial activities were coordinated by MKURABITA (Mpango wa Kurasimisha Rasilimali na Biashara Tanzaniam, or in English, the Property and Business Formalization Programme) in partnership with Handeni District. Previously, clan leaders had had a bigger role in allocating land, but this changed with the project:

> Everybody had to have a certificate that recognizes you as the owner of this place. Because if you do not reserve the areas, everybody would just go and do whatever. So we specified that you can stay here, bury here, go to school here ... After specifying this, it brings respect to a place.
> (Interview with former village chairman in Mzeri Village, 17 August 2010)

The titling project approach also strengthened the role of the state-backed, more formal village institutions. Prior to the issuing of CCROs, neighbours had collaborated in establishing their common boundaries – something which had often not previously been done because land was plentiful and boundaries therefore fluid. Now, in contrast, most people knew the boundaries of their plots, and this reduced the number of conflicts. Since the village leaders had been involved in the demarcation processes during the project, they became more important in settling land conflicts. The elders were still involved, but primarily as witnesses, as one man explained who had had a conflict over the ownership of a plot:

> His dad said: 'I cannot involve myself in this because now there is MKURABITA [the villagers call the village office MKURABITA]. So, you can use it [the village office].' He had nothing important to tell.
> (Interview with 61-year-old man, Mzeri Village, 23 April 2010)

Subsequently the case went to the village leaders, then to the ward tribunal, and finally to the district land and housing tribunal in Tanga town.

Access to the state-prescribed land dispute settlement institutions in the village was, at the same time, both more and less well established compared to the case-study village in Kiteto district. Though the titling project had established a village land council for dispute settlement, it had not been a priority of the project. The village land council had received no support, its members had been given no training, and it had stopped functioning immediately after being set up (interview with former village chairman, 17 August 2010). Subsequently, the Village Executive Officer, the village chairman and chairmen of the sub-village sought to settle conflicts. Otherwise, however, they followed the same laws and procedures for land dispute settlement as in

Kimana. Therefore, in Mzeri too, state law was becoming more important, and the role of the state-backed, more formal institutions was increasing.

The increase in the number of land conflicts

Though the situation in the case-study villages and districts was not uniform, a general, large increase in the number of land conflicts handled by the state-backed land dispute settlement institutions could be observed when comparing 2000 – that is, before the enactment of the Land Acts in 2001 and the Land Court Act in 2004 – with 2009.

In Kiteto, in 2000, the primary court covering Kimana village was the court in the district's main town, Kibaya (one of three primary courts in the district), and it had eight land-related cases in its civil registry that year. In 2009, the new village land council in Kimana village alone (one of 58 villages in the district) had nineteen cases, the new Partimbo Ward Tribunal (one out of fifteen wards in the district), covering Kimana and five other villages, had 51 cases, and the new District Land and Housing Tribunal, covering the entire Kiteto District, though situated in neighbouring Simanjiro District, had 56 new cases or appeal cases from Kiteto district that year (interview with Simanjiro District Land and Housing Tribunal chairman, 15 March 2010).

Because there was a less rigorous paper trail, the picture in Handeni district was less clear, but it also pointed in the direction of a large increase in the number of land conflicts. The main land dispute settlement institution for Mzeri village in 2000 was Chanika Primary Court (one of three primary courts in the district), situated in Handeni town, which handled twenty land-related conflicts. In the new Mzeri village office (one of 112 villages in the district), I found only two or three land conflict files from 2009, but the figure is highly insecure and unusually low, not least because it was a year of hunger in the village, and therefore people had stopped pursuing justice and were looking for food instead (interviews, 2 May 2010 and 7 May 2010). The new Misima Ward Tribunal (one of 23 wards in the district), covering Mzeri and four other villages, on the other hand, handled 28 land conflict cases in 2009 (interview with ward tribunal secretary, 10 April 2010) and the new Tanga District Land and Housing Tribunal, five hours' drive away, handled 38 new cases and appeal cases in 2009 (interview with District Land and Housing Tribunal chairman, 26 September 2012).

In sum, the number of conflicts being settled at state-prescribed land dispute settlement institutions exploded in both districts from 2000 to 2009. Does this merely reflect a general increase in the number of land conflicts, or does it also signify a change in the proportion being dealt with at the more state-prescribed institutions? As part of their nature, the informal and customary institutions produce less written evidence, and statistical comparisons are therefore hard to make. However, a combination of interviews, reports and articles gives us an idea about the proportion of change.

Village leaders are like elders

Tanzania's new-wave land reform does not herald a revolution. Rather, it reinforces the strengthening of the more formal land dispute settlement institutions that have been in place for decades. At the national level, the strengthening of the more formal institutions started with the abolition of the office of the chiefs in 1962.

In Handeni District, the strengthening of the formal village authorities gained speed with the Ujamaa villagization programme in the first half of the 1970s, which weakened the customary authorities. A former chairman in Mzeri Village explains how land dispute settlement changed:

> Before Ujamaa, the people lived in their different places and they used their elders. Back then, the chairman was maybe far from that sub-village where the conflict occurred. So the elders could solve it. After Ujamaa started, we just stopped following this system. Now, the system of government started. So the village council now started solving conflicts.
> (Interview with former chairman, 21 August 2010)

However, the development was probably less smooth than the former chairman describes. Oppen, in his analysis of land conflicts in Western Handeni – today probably Kilindi District – describes the way the new village institutions were contested, their ability to handle land conflicts being 'hampered by a constant lack of legitimacy in the eyes of the villagers' (Oppen 1996: 101). This lack of legitimacy was caused by their establishment during the deeply unpopular period of forced Ujamaa villagization (Schneider 2003: 428; Oppen 1996).

Today, the role of the state-backed village institutions in settling land conflicts is stronger. For instance, one man who had had a dispute over the ownership of one of his plots of land described how he had first gone to the sub-village chairman, who is also a member of the village council, and to the village leaders, because they were the ones who had been involved during the titling project:

> You go to the sub-village office because you know the sub-village chairman was among the witnesses for your field. Each field has four witnesses. There are three neighbours. They are the ones who accept your application. And your sub-village chairman also has to be present during the survey [...] You know there are laws these days, and the sub-village chairman is like an elder. And if it [the settlement of the dispute] fails there, then we go to the village government chairman.
> (Interview with old man, Mzeri village, 4 May 2010)

Whereas the changes in Mzeri started under Ujamaa, the development in Kimana village, which was not an Ujamaa village, is of more recent date.

Gradually, the village council became more important in allocating land during the 1990s and therefore, because it registered the boundaries or the number of acres, it is increasingly being called upon in case of land conflicts. With the making of a land-use plan and the establishment of land court institutions in the 2000s, the role of the more formal institutions in dispute settlement was further strengthened. This was conspicuously demonstrated in a case from Kiteto district between the Maasai, represented by Kiteto District Council, and farmers who had acquired – or grabbed – land in the district using irregular means and not respecting existing plans, which was also the reason why the latter lost the case (Tenga and Mramba 2014: 69–71; Pedersen 2016). In this respect, the case-study villages and districts are more similar than they are different.

State-orchestrated land dispute settlement

The gradual strengthening of the state-backed, more formal village institutions does not imply that everything follows the letter of the law. As described above, the dispute settlement procedures in Mzeri were less rigorous and the production of written evidence patchier than in Kimana. Still, the reconfiguration of land dispute settlement institutions in both villages is happening on such a scale that it would be misleading merely to call it 'increased competition'. The co-existence of institutions should not disguise the fact that the state-backed institutions are becoming more important in settling land disputes. Typically, they also have the upper hand in defining where to settle land disputes.

For instance, the local chairman of the Maasai elders still claimed to be playing a significant role in settling land conflicts in the village. He told me about a case where he had gone to the District Land and Housing Tribunal in neighbouring Simanjiro District to get a land dispute between two Maasais – not previously heard by the elders – transferred to the elders' council. He succeeded, but only after promising to return the case to the District Land and Housing Tribunal if it remained unresolved (interview, 17 May 2010). Similarly, the ward tribunal for Kimana referred cases back to the lower village-level institutions or elders' councils, but it saw this as a division of labour rather than as competition (interview with Ward Tribunal secretary, 4 March 2010).

How applicable are these findings to other parts of Tanzania? In 2005, only 40 per cent of villages in Tanzania had village land councils, and the same problem plagued the ward tribunals (Bruce and Knox 2008: 1364). From the same period, a study of the pastoralist Simanjiro District showed similar mixed evidence, whereas in the more densely populated Bariadi District all villages had village land councils (Gastorn 2008: 112, 127). This was a year after the enactment of the Land Court Act in 2004.

My own, more recent figures show more positive findings. According to the Kiteto District Land Office, 51 of 58 villages in the district had village land councils (interview with acting district land officer, Kiteto district, 5 February 2010). In Handeni District, all 112 villages and 19 wards were supposed to have the prescribed institutions for land dispute settlement. This does not mean that the councils are functioning, as was demonstrated in this chapter. A recent evaluation similarly assesses that whereas the required dispute settlement institutions have been established across the country challenges in terms of capacity persist (Massay 2016). Still, the state-backed village institutions seem to be strengthened even when they do not follow the state-prescribed procedures.

Though the situation is not uniform across the country, it points to a demand from below for state-backed land dispute settlement services. When a new-wave land reform can accommodate this demand, its impact is likely to be significant at the local level.

In her book *Informal institutions and citizenship in rural Africa*, Lauren M. Maclean (2010: 238) concludes that it is better to focus on processes of mutual transformation in which the state plays a key role than merely to focus on institutional competition as a zero-sum relationship between the state and communities. I would argue that the Tanzanian new-wave land reform, with its decentralized land court system, is a prime example of such a transformation, involving a general strengthening of the state-backed land dispute settlement institutions.

In-between land conflicts 1: intra-ethnic conflicts

The increase in the number of cases at the state-backed, more formal land dispute settlement institutions and the reconfiguration of the institutions for land dispute settlement are not only signs of increased pressure on land. They also reflect changing practices due to the emergence of an ethnically more mixed population. As people from different ethnic groups have to live together through migration, it becomes harder to settle land disputes using the customary authorities. In the case-study villages analysed in this chapter, conflicting parties rarely trusted the elders of other ethnic groups, resorting instead to the state-prescribed land dispute settlement institutions.

Intra-ethnic conflicts, on the other hand, were still often settled using the customary institutions. Particularly among the Maasai in Kimana village in Kiteto District, conflicts between persons from the same ethnic group were most often settled by their own elders. A sub-village chairman in the village, a non-Maasai, told me that similar preferences could be found among all ethnic groups, but they were stronger among the Maasai, who 'respect their traditional ways more than they respect the normal laws' (interview, 2 April 2010). Conflicting parties from the Maasai typically only went to the state-prescribed institutions *after* the elders, as a male Maasi who had done so explained:

The village chairman by that time was a Maasai elder, and he should be able to settle that dispute. But when I went to him he said he would not be able to settle it. He advised me to look for another solution. Then, I decided to go to the village land council.

(Interview with younger man, Kimana village, 5 April 2010)

In Mzeri village, where the change in dispute settlement had been under way for many years, people also sought to settle conflicts by using the elders, but it seemed less of a taboo to seek justice from the village leaders or ward tribunal in case of intra-ethnic conflicts. The sub-village chairmen, who are part of the village council, were even described as being similar to the elders of the past.

In-between land conflicts 2: women and family conflicts

Another exception to the strengthened role of the state-backed, more formal land dispute settlement institutions is provided by the settling of the specific land conflicts that women may encounter. Both case-study villages provided strong evidence of this aspect.

In Kimana village in Kiteto district, only a few women had gone to the village land council, and women typically denied having conflicts over land. However, when I rephrased the question and asked about women's problems related to divorce and inheritance, women told different stories of a loss of access to land, though they described it differently. Such conflicts, they said, were not about land, but about the relationship between a woman and her family:

> When there is no ownership [i.e. when it has not yet been decided to whom the land belongs and it has not been registered in one person's name] it becomes a question of the relationship between a wife and the husband. Because the wife needs a piece of land to own, but the man says that you did not come to my family with land ... or when it comes to the point of dividing that piece of land, for instance ten acres, the woman may take one acre only and the man may take the remaining nine acres.
>
> (Woman during Kimana village focus-group interview, Kiteto district, 19 March 2010)

The situation was similar in Mzeri village in Handeni district. There, several women had been divorced, leaving their marriages with no property at all. One woman explained that she had chosen to do so herself 'because there was nothing important to take' (interview with younger woman, Mzeri village, 24 August 2010). Her choice not to claim anything reflects a typical practice in the area, where rights to land typically follow the husband. Therefore, from a customary perspective, her choice reflects the fact that she felt she had no rights to keep land and property. She now lives from the land of her relatives.

However, it was becoming more common for women to involve the formal leaders when partners from different ethnic groups divorced. Similarly, women who had been formally registered as the owner of a plot seemed more likely and better able to access the state-prescribed land dispute settlement institutions and fight for their rights, even in disputes with relatives. One woman, who had had a conflict with a neighbour – a cousin – over the ownership of the land she had registered as her own, insisted that the registration programme had helped her defend her rights to the land:

> MKURABITA used to say: 'this woman has stayed here for so long so she must be the owner of this land'. And since they saw on my papers that I am the neighbour of [the other party], they knew that the land was mine.
> (Interview with middle-aged woman, Mzeri village, 4 May 2010)

Indeed, Tanzania's new-wave land reform makes it clear that the responsibility for protecting women's rights is vested in the formal village authorities, not in the women and vulnerable groups themselves (see Ikdahl et al. 2005: 42). However, some studies have also pointed out that access to land and land dispute settlement may become more socially uneven; their use is rarely free (Peters 2007; Pedersen 2015).

Conclusion

Though often overlooked, land dispute settlement has been an important element in the new wave of land reforms that have been introduced in a number of Sub-Saharan African countries in the last couple of decades. These reforms, with their decentralized institutions and recognition of customary rights and institutions, differ from previous state-led reforms. Nonetheless, they still tend to be evaluated in similar terms.

Based on empirical field studies of access to land dispute settlement in rural areas in mainland Tanzania, this chapter has argued that the introduction of a new-wave land reform is likely to herald a reconfiguration of institutions at the local level. Tanzania's reform provided a new, decentralized land court system, which, when implemented, strengthened the more formal land dispute settlement institutions operating with the backing of the state.

Furthermore, various forms of written registration of rights to land, land titling and the making of village land-use plans have become more common and have reinforced the importance of the more formal institutions in settling land disputes. In Tanzania, the number of conflicts settled by these institutions is on the increase. So is their share, seemingly, of the total number of land conflict cases.

The implementation of Tanzania's new-wave land reform has been slow and uneven. Customary, informal and downright irregular practices are likely to persist, as demonstrated in this chapter. Indeed, the customary institutions for land dispute settlement continue to play a role in settling certain types of land conflict, particularly in intra-ethnic conflicts and in the land conflicts that women may encounter that are related to divorce and inheritance. As such, Rie Odgaard (2006) is right when she stresses the need to work with these customary institutions to ensure better protection for vulnerable groups. However, with an increasingly ethnically mixed population and the increased involvement of state-backed land administration authorities in the allocation and registration of rights to land, the state-backed land dispute settlement institutions are growing proportionately more important. Ensuring vulnerable groups better access to them is therefore equally important.

The reform reinforces trends that have been going on for decades. A general reconfiguration of institutions is taking place at the local level. The customary and less formal institutions are increasingly being incorporated into the state-prescribed land court system and are adhering to the rules and regulations provided by state law. Overall, this should be analysed as a series of gradual changes, instead of merely being diagnosed as competition between institutions, as both formalization proponents and access scholars tend to do. In Tanzania, the state-backed and customary institutions for land dispute settlement cooperate more than they compete. Rather than constituting a paradox, these trends denote a mutual transformation of institutions that is only being speeded up by the current reform.

References

Askew, K., et al. 2013. Of land legitimacy: a tale of two lawsuits. *Africa* 83(1), 120–141.

Benda-Beckmann, K. v. 1981. Forum shopping and shopping forums: dispute processing in a Minangkabau village in west Sumatra. *Journal of Legal Pluralism* 19, 117–159.

Benjaminsen, T.A., Maganga, F.P. and Abdallah, J.M. 2009. The Kilosa killings: political ecology of a farmer-herder conflict in Tanzania. *Development and Change* 40(3), 423–445.

Berry, S. 1993. *No condition is permanent: the social dynamics of agrarian change in Sub-Saharan Africa*. Madison, WI: The University of Wisconsin Press.

Berry, S. 1994. Resource access and management as historical processes. *Occasional Papers at International Development Studies, Roskilde University* 13, 23–44.

Berry, S. 2009. Property, authority and citizenship: land claims, politics and the dynamics of social division in West Africa, In *The politics of possession: property, authority, and access to natural resources*, edited by T. Sikor and C. Lund. Chichester: Blackwell Publishing, 23–45.

Boone, C. 2007. Property and constitutional order: land tenure reform and the future of the African state. *African Affairs* 106(425), 557–586.

Boone, C. 2014. *Property and political order in Africa: land rights and the structure of politics*. New York: Cambridge University Press.

Bruce, J.W. and Knox, A. 2008. Structures and stratagems: making decentralisation of authority over land in Africa cost-effective. *World Development* 37(8), 1360–1369.
Carey, J.M. 2000. Parchment, equilibria, and institutions. *Comparative Political Studies* 33, 735–761.
Comaroff, J. and Roberts, S. 1981. *Rules and processes: the cultural logic of dispute in an African context.* Chicago, IL: University of Chicago Press.
De Soto, H. 2000. *The mystery of capital: why capitalism triumphs in the West and fails everywhere else.* New York: Basic Books.
Deininger, K. 2003. *Land policies for growth and poverty reduction.* Washington, DC: World Bank and Oxford University Press.
Derman, B., Odgaard, R. and Sjaastad, E. 2007. *Conflicts over land and water in Africa.* Oxford: James Currey.
Diehl, E. 2009. Can paralegals enhance access to justice? The example of Morogoro paralegal centre in Tanzania. *Verfassung und Recht in Übersee* 42, 187–211.
Donge, J.K. van. 1993. The arbitrary state in the Uluguru Mountains: legal arenas and land disputes in Tanzania. *Journal of Modern African Studies* 31(3), 431–448.
Eckert, J. 2006. From subjects to citizens: legalism from below and the homogenisation of the legal sphere. *Journal of Legal Pluralism* 53–54, 45–75.
Evers, S., Spierenbur, M. and Wels, H. 2005. Introduction: competing jurisdictions: settling land claims in Africa, including Madagascar, in *Competing jurisdictions*, edited by S. Evers, M. Spierenbur and H. Wels. Leiden: Brill Academic Publishers, 1–20.
Fimbo, G.M. 2004. *Land law reforms in Tanzania.* Dar es Salaam: Dar es Salaam University Press.
Gastorn, K. 2008. *The impact of Tanzania's new land laws on the customary land rights of pastoralists: a case study of the Simanjiro and Bariadi districts.* Berlin: LIT Verlag.
GOT. 1985. *The Ward Tribunals Act, 1985. No. 7.* Dar es Salaam: Government of the United Republic of Tanzania.
GOT. 1992a. *The Presidential Commission of Inquiry into Land Matters: evidence, volume I A: Arusha region, Kiteto and Monduli districts.* Available at the University Library in University of Dar es Salaam, Tanzania.
GOT. 1992b. *The Presidential Commission of Inquiry into Land Matters: evidence, volume XXVI A: analysis of evidence.* Available at the University Library at University of Dar es Salaam, Tanzania.
GOT. 1994. *Report of the Presidential Commission of Inquiry into Land Matters, volume 1: land policy and land tenure structure.* Uppsala: The Ministry of Land, Housing and Urban Development and the Scandinavian Institute of African Studies.
GOT. 2002. *The Courts (Land Disputes Settlements) Act, 2002.* Dar es Salaam: Government of the United Republic of Tanzania.
Hart, K. 2008. *Between bureaucracy and the people: a political history of informality.* Working paper 2008(27). Copenhagen: DIIS.
Hodgson, D.L. 2004. *Once intrepid warriors: gender, ethnicity, and the cultural politics of Maasai development.* Bloomington, IN: Indiana University Press.
Ikdahl, I. et al. 2005. *Human rights, formalisation and women's land rights in southern and eastern Africa.* Studies in Women's Law no. 57. Oslo: University of Oslo.

Isinika, A.C. and Mutabazi K. 2010. Gender dimensions of land conflicts: examples from Njombe and Maswa districts in Tanzania, in *Tanzania in transition: from Nyerere to Mkapa*, edited by K. Havnevik and A.C. Isinika. Dar es Salaam: Mkuki na Nyota, 131–158.

Joireman, S.F. 2011. *Where there is no government: enforcing property rights in common law Africa*. New York: Oxford University Press.

Knight, R.S. 2010. *Statuary recognition of customary land rights in Africa: an investigation into best practices for lawmaking and implementation*. FAO Legislative Studies. Rome: FAO.

Leftwich, A. and Sen, K. 2011. 'Don't mourn; organise': institutions and organisations in the politics and economics of growth and poverty-reduction. *Journal of International Development* 23(3), 319–337.

Lipton, M. 2009. *Land reform in developing countries: property rights and property wrongs*. New York: Routledge.

Lund, C. 2008. *Local politics and the dynamics of property in Africa*. New York: Cambridge University Press.

Maclean, L.M. 2010. *Informal institutions and citizenship in rural Africa: risk and reciprocity in Ghana and Côte d'Ivoire*. New York: Cambridge University Press.

Maganga, F. 2002. The interplay between formal and informal systems of managing resource conflicts: some evidence from south-western Tanzania. *European Journal of Development Research* 14(2), 51–70.

Massay, G.E. 2016. Tanzania's Village Land Act 15 years on. *Rural* 21, 18–19.

Moore, S.F. (2000). *Law as process: an anthropological approach*. Münster: LIT Verlag.

Mwangi, E. 2010. Bumbling bureaucrats, sluggish courts and forum-shopping elites: unending conflict and competition in the transition to private property. *European Journal of Development Research* 22(5), 715–732.

North, D.C. 1990. *Institutions, institutional change and economic performance*. Cambridge: Cambridge University Press.

Nyamu-Musembi, C. 2007. De Soto and land relations in rural Africa: breathing life into dead theories about property rights. *Third World Quarterly* 28(8), 1457–1478.

Odgaard, R. 2005. The struggle for land rights in the context of multiple normative orders in Tanzania, in *Competing jurisdictions*, edited by S. Evers, M. Spierenbur and H. Wels. Leiden: Brill Academic Publishers, 243–264.

Odgaard, R. 2006. *Land rights and land conflicts in Africa: the Tanzania case*. Copenhagen: DIIS.

Oppen, A. von. 1996. Villages beyond Ujamaa: land conflicts and ecology in western Handeni, in *Changing rural structures in Tanzania*, edited by D. Schmied. Münster: LIT Verlag, 85–106.

Ostrom, E. 2001. The puzzle of counterproductive property rights reforms: a conceptual analysis, in *Access to land, rural poverty, and public action*, edited by A. de Janvry et al. Oxford: Oxford University Press, 129–150.

Pedersen, R.H. 2012. Decoupled implementation of new-wave land reforms: decentralisation and local governance of land in Tanzania. *Journal of Development Studies* 48(2), 268–281.

Pedersen, R.H. 2015. A less gendered access to land? The impact of Tanzania's new wave land reform. *Development Policy Review* 33(4), 415–432.

Pedersen, R.H. 2016. Access to land reconsidered: the land grab, polycentric governance and Tanzania's new wave land reform. *Geoforum* 72, 104–113.

Peters, P.E. 2004. Inequality and social conflict over land in Africa. *Journal of Agrarian Change* 4(3), 269-314.

Peters, P.E. 2007. Whose security? Deepening social conflict over 'customary' land in the shadow of land tenure reform in Malawi. *Journal of Modern African Studies* 45(3), 447–472.

Platteau, J. 1993. *Formalization and privatization of land rights in Sub-Saharan Africa: a critique of current orthodoxies and structural adjustment programmes.* London: London School of Economics.

Quan, J. 2000. Land tenure, economic growth and poverty in Sub-Saharan Africa, in *Evolving land rights, policy and tenure in Africa*, edited by C. Toulmin and J. Quan. London: DFID/IIED/NRI, 31–50.

Ribot, J.C. and Peluso, N.L. 2003. A theory of access. *Rural Sociology* 68(2), 153–181.

Schneider, L. 2003. Developmentalism and its failings: why rural development went wrong in 1960s and 1970s Tanzania, PhD thesis, Columbia University, New York.

Shivji, I. 1998. *Not yet democracy: reforming land tenure in Tanzania.* Dar es Salaam: HAKIARDI and IIED.

Shivji, I. et al. 2004. *Constitutional and legal system of Tanzania: a civics sourcebook.* Dar es Salaam: Mkuki na Nyota Publishers.

Sikor, T. and Müller, D. 2009. The limits of state-led land reform: an introduction. *World Development* 37(8), 1307–1316.

Sundet, G. 1997. The politics of land in Tanzania. PhD dissertation, University of Oxford, UK.

Tenga, R. and Kakoti, G. 1993. The Barabaig land case. In '... *Never drink from the same cup': Proceedings of the Conference on Indigenous Peoples in Africa. Tune, Denmark, 1993*, IWGIA Document no. 74, edited by Veber et al. Copenhagen: IWGIA and the Centre for Development Research, 39–58.

Tenga, R. and Mramba, S.J. 2014. *Theoretical foundations of land law in Tanzania.* Dar es Salaam: LawAfrica.

Tsikata, D. 2003. Securing women's interests within land tenure reforms: recent debates in Tanzania. *Journal of Agrarian Change* 3(1–2), 149–183.

Wily, L.A. 2003. *Governance and land relations: a review of decentralisation of land administration and management in Africa.* London: IIED.

Ylhäisi, J. 2007. Changes in traditionally protected forests and leadership in the village of Mkata in northeastern Tanzania, in *Contextualising natural resource management in the south*, edited by H. Vihemäki. Helsinki: University of Helsinki, 32–61.

Yngstrom, I. 2002. Women, wives and land rights in Africa: situating gender beyond the household in the debate over land policy and changing tenure systems. *Oxford Development Studies* 30(1), 21–40.

8 One country, two systems

Hybrid political orders and legal and political friction in Somaliland

Markus Virgil Hoehne

Introduction

In the wake of the civil war, Somaliland (formerly north-western Somalia) seceded unilaterally from the collapsing Somali Republic in 1991. In the past two decades, it advanced from a war-ravaged place void of substantial resources to an in many regards flourishing de *facto state* (Pegg 1998). Characteristic of this progress are massive investments by the diaspora and other actors (including, since around the year 2000, some international NGOs, private companies and foreign governments, albeit short of political recognition) in key towns like Hargeysa (the capital), Berbera and Burco.[1] These investments build schools, universities, hospitals and businesses, infrastructure like roads or the harbour in Berbera, and let the telecommunication and media sector flourish. A multi-party system is in place and elections are held periodically (Kent et al. 2004; Lindley 2008; Bradbury 2008; Ibraahim 2010; Hoehne and Ibraahim 2014). Somaliland therefore is highlighted as a story of successful state-formation. One key-element of its success, it is argued by several specialists (Walls 2009: 383–389; Pham 2012: 21, 28, 31), is the integration of traditional authorities (who administer customary law) into the state apparatus. This chapter investigates the dynamic relationships between state and non-state actors in Somaliland with regard to national politics and the provision of security and justice in various parts of the country.

Politically, Somaliland exhibits a hybrid political order (HPO) combining 'traditional' with 'modern' features of governance (Boege et al. 2008). In the case of Somaliland, this meant that elders representing patrilineal descent groups gained general recognition and sometimes official representation at various levels of governance (Renders 2007; Hoehne 2007). In this way, 'clan' (as shorthand for various forms of patrilineal descent groups) was 'brought back in' after it had been suppressed for decades during the post-

---

1 Somali place and personal names in this text follow the Somali orthography (with the exception of Somali authors who adopted an anglicized version of their names). The Latin 'c' stands for a sound close to the Arabic 'ع' (ayn); 'x' denotes 'ح' (ha).

colony, which had resulted in 'behind-the-scenes'-manipulations and, finally, the complete undermining of the state apparatus (Samatar 1992; Compagnon 1992).[2] The established literature on Somaliland's statehood agrees that the involvement of elders in government provides the necessary space for 'culture' and 'custom' to stabilize the country's statehood (Walls 2009, 2014; Renders 2012; Richards 2015; APD 2015). Additionally, it creates a link between 'state' and 'society' that has been missing before in postcolonial Somalia.[3] Particularly the Upper House of Parliament, the *Guurti* (House of Elders), can be understood as 'a permanent representation of the Somaliland clans in the government' (Richards 2015: 15). The *Guurti* is therefore at the centre of the HPO of Somaliland. Decisions within this political system are taken partly by vote and partly – particularly when crisis emerges, which happens regularly – by complex negotiations and consensus building, which often involves clan representatives and traditional mediation strategies.

In this way, Somaliland has overcome numerous deadlocks, such as the lack of transparency surrounding voter registration (2008–2009) and the postponement of the presidential elections (2008–2010, and again 2015–2017). Richards (2015) calls the political system of Somaliland a 'dual hybrid'. It combines 'traditional' and 'modern' forms of statehood and 'within this it also balances external demands and internal necessities' (ibid.: 3). External demands refer to what is deemed necessary to be an 'acceptable' state in the eyes of the international community (peacefulness, representative government, democratic elections); internal necessities comprise power sharing between clans, respecting Somali culture and traditions, and mediating conflicts. Richards emphasizes that state building in Somaliland is an ongoing process during which the placement and purpose of the *Guurti* will change. So far, the most important tasks of the House of Elders were related to domestic leadership and the legitimation of the political process (ibid.: 18).

Walls (2009, 2014), like Richards, takes a deep look into the concrete working of politics in Somaliland. He stresses that, '[t]he consensus-based style is very different from the adversarial representative approach practiced in many of established European-style democracies' (Walls 2014: 26). He characterizes Somali consensus-based decision-making as slow, and reasons that 'the fierce sense of individual and clan pride that works so well in the harsh environment in which the hardiness of individuals and the support of close kin is critical, militates against the *detached representation* required of nation-state politics' (ibid.: 24, emphasis added). Walls uses the term

---

2   For instance, in the first half of 1971, the Somali Revolutionary Council (SRC) under General Maxamed Siyaad Barre staged the 'burial of tribalism' in major urban centres of Somalia; see Mohammed Abdullahi Artan (2015).
3   Others believe that, with regard to Somalia as a whole, a political order based on reformist Islam could provide such a link (Abdurahman M. Abdullahi 2007).

'detached representation' here arguably to emphasize that in the political order of Somaliland, the involvement of traditional authorities provides for closer representation of ordinary people. Below I show that this is not necessarily the case. Moreover, in Walls's eyes, it is a key achievement of the HPO in Somaliland to nurture the hope that an 'accommodation is possible between the discursive politics of tradition and a representative system more suited to the Westphalian state' (ibid.: 27). I also disagree with that.

In my view, Walls makes a static and almost essentialist argument here.[4] Regarding HPOs, he does not consider what Richards correctly emphasized in her article: the constant evolution of such orders (not in a sense of unilineal, teleological political evolution, but in the sense of evolution as an open, dynamic and non-teleological process); this can, theoretically, also lead to a reversal of certain achievements, or to the 'going astray' of institutions. Both Walls and Richards are united in overlooking the increasing incompatibility between the 'traditional' and the 'modern' aspects of the HPO in Somaliland. I have argued elsewhere (Hoehne 2013) that the HPO in Somaliland's centre has become a 'crippled' hybrid in which traditional legitimacy and democratic processes suffer. This leads increasingly to political conflicts and instabilities (see also ICG 2015a).

Admittedly, Walls and Richards exhibit some ambiguity concerning their assessment of the HPO of Somaliland. Walls (2014: 30) cautions that 'the nation-state structure is not one that lends itself to accommodation of the egalitarian and consensus-based traditions that are the strength of Somali democracy.' Still, he adds that Somaliland has made 'great strides in negotiating a difficult path' (ibid.). Richards mentions that the *Guurti* has been politicized and that its role is increasingly criticized from within Somaliland (Richards 2015: 17–20). At the end, however, she argues that '[c]ertainly there are areas where there are gaps between the state and societal expectations. However, because the state is a relationship rather than an imposition, there is not only the flexibility, but also the capability, to lessen the gap' (ibid.: 21).

I argue that Richards and Walls can only come to their conciliatory conclusions concerning the ongoing process of state formation in Somaliland because of their strong focus on 'high politics' (e.g. concerning national elections) in the centre (mainly: the area between Hargeysa, Berbera and Burco which constitutes what I would call the central-state-triangle). There, one can see how complicated problems of governance have indeed been overcome repeatedly by finding *ad hoc* solutions that involved 'traditional' or 'customary' ways of conflict settlement within the 'modern' state. However, if one focuses on 'everyday life' political and legal issues, especially politics of employment and the dealing with petty crime, even within the central-state-triangle, and particularly if one looks at politics in the eastern margins of

---

4 As if Somalis would be 'forever' bound by certain environmental conditions and not be in a position to develop different political systems.

Somaliland, one can see that Somaliland exhibits not only one HPO, but actually several different HPOs. The HPO in the centre that is concerned with 'high politics' is clearly dominated by the 'modern' state authorities (mainly, the executive). I call this in Somali *habka dawladeed* (the government system). Besides, everyday life matters – concerning, for example, who gets which position in mid- to lower-level of administration, who is employed as driver, secretary, or guard in public or private businesses, how, for example, the theft of a mobile phone or an injury during a street football match are dealt with, etc. – are often dealt with by ordinary elders (and sometimes sheikhs) who in such matters can pressure state officials (e.g. policemen or judges) or even side-line the state completely. More important for the argument of the chapter is, however, that at the considerable margins of Somaliland, a HPO is in place at the highest level of politics (concerning issues of war and peace and infrastructural development) as well as at the level of 'everyday governance' (regarding security and justice) in which mainly the traditional authorities (and sometimes the religious authorities) call the shots. In Somali, this could be called *habka dhaqameed* (the traditional system). I argue that this HPO at the margins resembles the HPO that existed in the early 1990s throughout Somaliland, when the *Guurti* was really powerful and guaranteed peace and political order in the emerging polity as a whole. Ever since the late 1990s, however, the HPO in the centre, concerned with 'national issues', has developed differently from the one persisting at the margins. These different developments have led to a disconnect between both HPOs. In the past decade or so (since roughly 2005) representatives of *habka dawladeed* fail to conduct their work in areas where *habka dhaqameed* is prevalent. On the other hand, traditional and religious authorities have some more room for manoeuvre in the realm of *habka dawladeed*; but, in the centre, 'high politics' are controlled by state officials who are not bound by traditional modes of legitimacy in the Weberian sense. Contrary to the conciliatory position of Richards and Walls mentioned above, these hybrid arrangements do not lead to more state-society integration and stabilization of statehood, but to instabilities and political rifts. This is in line with recent critical reflections on hybrid governance in general, stressing that the outcome of hybridization processes is difficult to predict and often not beneficial for local people (nor even legitimate in their eyes) (Meagher et al. 2014; Mac Ginty and Richmond 2015).

At a generic level, the just mentioned multiplicity of HPOs in Somaliland and the disconnect between them underscores the need to scrutinize the concept of HPO. Kraushaar and Lambach (2009: 1) argue that 'hybrid orders are better able to tap into local knowledge, to mobilize citizens and to generate legitimacy than "top-down" arrangements of governance'. Clements et al. (2007) provide a more critical evaluation of the concept and point to the potential for conflict within HPOs. Still, they perceive hybridity 'as a starting point' that may lead to 'new forms of the state' in which 'strong social relationships, high social resilience and effective and legitimate institutions are combined' (ibid.: 54). What is missing here, however, is an understanding of HPOs as constantly evolving and multiplying. In Somaliland, one has, at the 'top-level' of governance, a HPO dominated by government officials in the centre and one dominated by traditional authorities at the margins.[5] If one understands HPOs as operating along a spectrum, one can say that *habka dawladeed* and *habka dhaqameed* in Somaliland constitute two extremes. It is assumed that also beyond the specific case of Somaliland, different HPOs or degrees of HPOs exist next to each other. The frictions and incompatibility produced by this simultaneous existence of different HPOs in the country is the focus of the chapter.

The text proceeds by briefly discussing the role of the *Guurti* concerning state-building in Somaliland. This helps to understand the starting point for the development of the original HPO in Somaliland in the 1990s. Subsequently, I present two case studies that substantiate the argument that Somaliland constitutes one country with two systems[6] – meaning: with (at least) two different HPOs – which are inharmonious and therefore cause

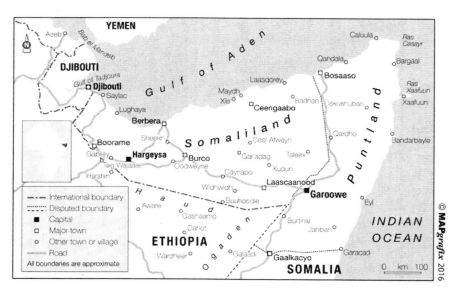

Map 8.1 Northern Somalia.

5 As mentioned above, even in the centre two different HPOs are operating simultaneously, depending if on looks at 'high politics' or everyday political and legal matters. But for reasons of space, this chapter does not go further into the different forms of HPOs in the centre.
6 This terminology has been inspired by the constitutional principle formulated by Deng Xiaoping for the reunification of China during the early 1980s. The idea was that there was only one China, but within it Hong Kong and Macau could retain their own capitalist economic and political systems, while the rest of China uses the socialist system.

legal and political friction. The first example deals with the provision of justice and security in the regions Saraar and Sanaag (focusing on the towns Caynabo, Ceerigaabo and Gar'adag). It shows how, at the level of 'everyday politics', local state officials at the margins endorse 'customary' practices to ensure the delivery of basic services, and thereby sideline the state. The second case study comprises attempts to deal with armed conflict in the clan-borderlands between Isaaq and Darood groups around Kalshaale (between Caynabo and Buuhoodle). It concerns 'high politics' and illustrates the failure of representatives of the centre to fulfil their peace missions at the margins, where the state enjoys little legitimacy and both HPOs are essentially clashing.

The imbalanced HPO in the centre of Somaliland: the role of the Guurti

In pre-colonial time, leaders among the predominantly pastoral-nomadic Somalis enjoyed only nominal authority. They had to continuously proof their skills as negotiators, war-leaders or peace-makers not to be deposed by their own followers. During the colonial period, Somali elders were integrated into the system of 'indirect rule'. The British in the northwest and the Italians in the northeast and south of the Somali Peninsula partly co-opted and partly repressed traditional authorities. After the independence of the Somali Republic in 1960, nationalist officials rejected any form of 'tribalism'. They developed policies designed to eclipse the role of the traditional authorities. These politics culminated under the regime of General Maxamed Siyaad Barre, who came to power in a *coup d'état* in 1969. Combining pan-Somalism with socialism, the new government launched a number of social and economic reform programs. In this context, 'tribal label leaders were officially abolished, or at any rate re-christened "peace-seekers" (s. *nabad-doon*), and became theoretically bureaucrats capable of being posted to any part of the country' (Lewis 1994: 157). The situation changed in the late 1980s, when the guerrillas of the Somali National Movement (SNM) in their struggle against the Somali regime relied on traditional authorities for financial and logistical support.[7] They collected money or food for the rebels among the local population and in the diaspora, recruited fighters and settled conflicts in the liberated areas (Reno 2003: 24–26; Walls 2014: 150). In January 1991, the Somali government crumbled in the south and the SNM took control of much of north-western Somalia. It called upon the people and their elders to come together and negotiate between those who had

---

7   There are different types of traditional elders: *suldaan* or *garaad* is the title of the highest-ranking clan leaders; *caaqil* is the name of the mid-range group-leader who, in the past, served also as intermediary between colonial powers and people; *ooday* is the 'ordinary' elder who enjoys the confidence of his (patrilineal) relatives and is respected among his peers.

supported the Somali regime and those on the side of the guerrillas. Many small-scale conferences at the village-level provided the ground for national reconciliation (Terlinden and Ibraahim 2008). In May 1991, representatives of all groups met in the city of Burco and agreed on peace. At this conference, the secession from the rest of collapsing Somalia was also declared. Consequently, the SNM leadership took over the state.

The administration, however, was inexperienced and conflicts within the SNM erupted. Elders had to step in frequently to prevent or end fighting. At the Boorama conference in 1993, the next step towards building a new political system for Somaliland was taken. There, the clans agreed upon the following division of power: each clan was 'allocated quotas of delegates prior to commencement, reflective of their [estimated] numeric and political strength, and broadly based on previous formulae adopted by the SNM and in the constituency system used in the last colonial elections [under British rule] in 1960' (Walls 2014: 178).[8] Delegates met for about four months; a slow process of consensus-building in small committees was characteristic for this conference. Cabdi Waraabe, one of Somaliland's preeminent elders, is cited by Walls with the words: 'Voting is fighting; let's opt for consensus' (ibid.: 178). The two key outcomes of the Boorama conference were that, first, a civilian government was selected, led by former Somali prime-minister and ambassador, Maxamed Xaaji Ibraahim Cigaal. Second, a transitional constitution was agreed upon. It introduced a bicameral parliament with the *Guurti*, the House of Elders (who essentially represented patrilineal descent groups) as Upper House. The main task of this house was keeping the peace in the nascent polity. It was also tasked with safeguarding religion, culture and tradition. The Lower House was called the House of Representatives. It was the main legislative body that also controlled the government's finances.

The members of both houses were selected among the 150 elders presiding over the conference. Of these, half became members of the upper and half of the lower house. The established literature on the matter is silent about the criteria according to which delegates were selected as *Guurti*-members or as members of parliament (Cabdiraxmaan Jimcaale 2005; Bradbury 2008: 98–100; Renders 2012: 101–102; Walls 2014: 176–178). It is noteworthy that the original SNM-*Guurti* in the 1980s had consisted only of around 40 Isaaq elders.[9] When the national *Guurti* was established in Boorama, it was joined by those willing to represent their clans (including non-Isaaq). Some of them were members of the urbanized elite and not necessarily 'elders' in the traditional sense (who would have to be well-versed

---

8   North-western Somalia was a British protectorate; north-eastern and southern Somalia was under Italian control until 1960.
9   The SNM was an Isaaq-dominated movement; Isaaq inhabit central Somaliland. The clans who in the north fought on the side of the government against the guerrillas mainly belonged to the Daarood and the Dir clan families residing in the east and the far west of the region.

in Somali culture, traditions and Islam).¹⁰ In 1997, a third big conference was held in Hargeysa to elect a new president. While the previous conferences were hosted by the local communities in Burco and Boorama, the conference in 1997 was hosted by the government. This gave the incumbent, President Cigaal, some advantage over competitors. Cigaal was re-elected. His success was partly due to the (low) calibre of the contending candidates and problems related to inter-clan fighting preceding the conference;¹¹ Cigaal could position himself as peacemaker whereas other candidates, such as Saleebaan Gaal and Maxamed Xaashi Cilmi, were considered 'war-mongers' (interview with Cabdulqadir Jirdeh, Hargeysa, 2 November 2015). But allegations of corruption and undue influence over the conference were also made against Maxamed Xaaji Ibraahim Cigaal (Bradbury 2008: 126). After his election, President Cigaal granted some oppositional clans additional seats in the *Guurti* and the House of Representatives (ibid.).

A new constitution was adopted by a referendum in 2001. This step was preceded by wrangling over the character of the constitution (strengthening the president, or rather the parliament). The referendum also took place against the background of a peace conference for Somalia in Arta, Djibouti, held in 2000. This conference and the Transitional National Government (TNG) for Somalia established there was perceived by the government in Hargeysa as a threat to its independence (Hoehne 2002: 116–117; Walls 2014: 209). The first article of the new constitution reaffirmed the independence of the country. The referendum was therefore taken as a vote on the claim of Somaliland for international recognition. Putting its result (official sources mention that 97 per cent of the voters accepted the constitution) into context, it has to be noted that the referendum was not held in the eastern territories of the country inhabited by Dhulbahante and Warsangeli. These groups had distanced themselves from the secessionist project of Somaliland over the years and were eager to 're-unite' with the larger Darood group, which had a bigger stake in Somali affairs in general (Hoehne 2015: 40–61). Yet, most members of the Isaaq clan-family, who at least constitute two thirds of the population of Somaliland, accepted the constitution. This means that the 97 per cent of all voters constitute around two-thirds of the total electorate (Bryden 2004: 178). This is still a comfortable majority, but worrying concerning 'clan consensus' in the region. Moreover, for many people, the vote expressed their aspiration to gain recognition for their state; it hardly concerned the details of the constitution.

---

10 The Daarood clans in the east that had not been part of the SNM, mainly Warsangeli and Dhulbahante, were split concerning their participation at the Boorama conference. The delegates who went to Boorama did not have the full backing of their patrilineal relatives (Hoehne 2015: 51, 54).

11 Armed conflict between various Isaaq strongmen and their followers in Hargeysa and Burco had destabilized Somaliland between 1993 and 1996. Cigaal used the conflict to get rid of competitors and consolidate his authority (Balthasar 2013).

The new constitution cemented a presidential system and prescribed the introduction of a multi-party democracy. The first multi-party elections took place in 2005. In these elections only the members of the House of Representatives were elected. While many Isaaq (and also Dir in the far west of Somaliland) participated in them, most Daarood did not (and up until today, subsequent elections have not taken place or have only partly taken place in the east). In this way, elections undermined the power sharing agreement established with the help of the elders at Boorama in 1993, which actually went back to the quota system established under the British in the late 1950s (Hansen and Bradbury 2007: 470–471). In the 2005 election, the Dhulbahante and Warsangeli clans lost four seats; the number of their representatives dropped from 14 to 10. Additionally, the Ciise and Gadabuursi in the west, who are part of the Dir clan-family, lost 2 seats in total (going from 16 seats to 14). Isaaq candidates won ten additional seats and eventually had 57 representatives in parliament (Walls 2014: 251; Abdirahman Omar Hussein 2015).[12] Yet, clan-representation in the *Guurti* remained the same as before. The *Guurti* was not elected.

Looking back at the 1990s, one can see that negotiations between descent groups headed by traditional authorities provided the basis for peace and order in nascent Somaliland. Traditional authorities, who, despite the modernist orientations of the post-colonial governments, never had ceased to be of relevance in the (northern) Somali hinterlands, filled the void left by the collapsing state.[13] In a second step, some of them were elevated to new powers and positions at the national level (Hoehne 2006). The national *Guurti* in the capital became the emblem of these hybrid arrangements that institutionalized 'tradition' and clan-representation within the newly established 'modern' state. In this way, Somaliland's first HPO was established between 1991 and 1993. It was comprehensive and effective.

But soon things began to change. To understand the growing imbalance within this HPO, one needs to ask: what was actually institutionalized in the *Guurti*? While some *Guurti*-members arguably were genuine elders in the sense that they enjoyed legitimacy in the eyes of their constituency (members of lineages, sub-clans or clans), others were, as already mentioned above, candidates of convenience chosen on the spot in 1993 or added by the president in 1997. Some lacked credentials as 'elders' among the groups they were supposed to represent (interview with Axmed Bando, Ceerigaabo, 5

---

12   Despite the introduction of political parties in 2002, clan politics and clannism remained a vital factor in politics in Somaliland (including the Lower House) (Ciabarri 2008; APD 2015: 21–22).

13   Prunier (2010) convincingly outlines the different colonial traditions in the Somali territories that facilitated the prevalence of traditional authority in north-western Somalia, which was under British indirect rule and had little resources to be exploited, whereas the Italian dominated northeast and south of Somalia was subject to more direct colonial rule and economic exploitation.

August 2002; interview with Cabdulqadir Jirdeh, Hargeysa, 2 November 2015). For instance, when a *Guurti*-member died, his seat was usually inherited by a close relative, in some cases by a brother, son, cousin or even his widow. 'This has not been legalized; but it became customary' (interview with Cabdulqadir Jirdeh, Hargeysa, 2 November 2015). Often, these new members did not have credentials as elders. They simply took over the position as it provided their immediate family with considerable income (ibid.).[14] This is contrary to the 'customary' way of selecting a group representative, who should enjoy widespread legitimacy as wise person with extensive social capital.[15] Moreover, the longer the members of the *Guurti* remained in the capital, the more they became dependent on the executive, particularly the president. A Somali analyst captured this as early as 2005 by stating that the *Guurti*-members 'have become more and more linked both formally and informally to the government structures' (Ahmed Mohamed Hashi 2005: 22). He continued:

> It can be claimed by now that there is no more traditional *Guurti* in the classical sense in control of societal and clan constituency affairs as such. Over the years of transformations, they were joined in their roles, and often overpowered, by the military, political and economic elite with whom they constitute a new social and elite class. The peace-making and reconciliation meetings were convened, organized and implemented by this class spearheaded by the SNM political and military elite and later by President Egal's [*sic*] administration. The idealistic and romantic traditional *Guurti* of which researchers on Somaliland reconciliation processes talk a lot about would not have the political and power assets to guide and implement such processes.
> (Ahmed Mohamed Hashi 2005: 22; emphasis in the original)

Until the mid-2000s, the *Guurti* as an institution enjoyed respect mostly for its past role – dating back to the days of the SNM and the early 1990s. Things changed in the 2000s. Between 2002 and 2005, a series of elections were held in Somaliland. The *Guurti*'s term originally ended in 2003 (six years after the Hargeysa conference had ended, at which the number of its seats had been increased from 75 to 82). It was then extended three times for a year

> through a one clause law passed by the House of Representatives and the Guurti and a law that linked the term of office of the Guurti to the

---

14 A member of the *Guurti* earns, with salary and bonuses, around US$2300 per month, compared to the circa US$100 per month that an ordinary soldier or policeman receives.
15 Furthermore, traditional positions of authority were originally not inherited, but candidates were selected by consensus. This, however, partly changed during the colonial and postcolonial periods when state officials sought to establish control over elders (Hoehne 2006).

> previous House of Representatives so that the Guurti can benefit indirectly from any extension of the term of the Representatives under Article 42(3) of the Constitution which allows extension of the Representatives' term of office in situations when 'dire circumstances' make the election impossible to hold.
>
> (Somaliland Forum 2006)

In May 2006, the then president of Somaliland, Daahir Rayaale Kaahin, issued a decree extending the term of the *Guurti* by four years. This move was heavily criticized by the opposition and those voices in the country and abroad that demanded the continuation of a 'real' democratic transition.[16] An even more critical discussion began when the members of the *Guurti* extended the term of the president between 2008 and 2010 no less than four times. They did so by referring to article 83(5) of the constitution citing 'security considerations'. Here, the 'unholy' alliance between the president and the House of Elders, that abused if not undermined the constitution, became clearly visible. The opposition parties, many civil society actors and some activists in the diaspora regarded these extensions as unconstitutional. They staged demonstrations in Hargeysa and Burco that, however, were restrained by the government deploying armed forces in the streets of the main cities of the country.[17]

The crisis surrounding the prolongation of the president's term was accompanied by problems with the voters' registration. While here is not the place to go into details concerning the registration process between late 2008 and early 2009, it is noteworthy that despite the ambitious plan to prevent multiple registrations through photograph and fingerprint taking, '[s]ampling suggested that between 25 and 30% of registrations were likely to be false' (Walls 2014: 270).

Presidential elections finally happened in June 2010. Axmed Maxamuud Maxamed Siilaanyo, the opposition leader, won and a peaceful transition of power took place. In 2011, a local Somaliland think tank published a study on these affairs, particularly the prolongation by the presidential term by the *Guurti*. According to this report,[18]

> Most respondents believe that though the Guurti has played a crucial positive role both during the SNM struggle and the early years of the

---

16 See, for instance, the elaborate legal criticism provided by the Somaliland Forum in its position paper, posted on the reputable website specialized on Somaliland law, available at www.somalilandlaw.com/tiltleelders__term_extension.html.

17 Author's own observations during a research visit to Somaliland between December 2008 and May 2009; see also SomalilandTimes (2008).

18 The report is based on qualitative research. The respondents were politicians, lawyers and judges, civil society activists and members of local think tanks. A total of 80 people were interviewed in Hargeysa (SONSAF 2011: 16–17).

establishment of Somaliland, their political impartiality is under question particularly relating to the process of extending the term of the incumbent President. Critics maintain that the Guurti is no longer relevant in managing conflict between the competing political actors, because it has itself become a party in ongoing political disputes. This politicization has begun to undermine the Guurti's credibility as an honest neutral broker in managing the conflicts between competing political actors. [...] Some respondents argue that these extension powers have safeguarded the national political system by legitimizing institutions and avoiding political and legal vacuums, when needed. However, most participants argue that they [the Guurti members] have failed to even attempt to develop their own election law (preferring to stay in the House forever), have continually caused national political discord by extending the term of the sitting president and have seriously undermined the powers of the elected legislature.

(SONSAF 2011: 31)

More recently, the periodic crisis of the imbalanced HPO in the centre of Somaliland has continued. According to the constitution, the next presidential elections should have happened in May 2015. But preparations were not made in time, as in the years before. Again, pressured by the executive, the *Guurti* decided to prolong the term of the government, this time for two years (up to November 2017).

From the 'high politics' in the centre, let's now switch our attention to the political dynamics at the margins of Somaliland. In what follows, I will focus on the provision of basic state services, like security and justice, and on conflict and conflict settlement in eastern Somaliland. These case studies underpin the argument that Somaliland not only features an imbalanced HPO in the centre, but also a quite different HPO in the peripheries.

A different kind of HPO at the margins

Case study 1: Security and justice in the regions Saraar and Sanaag

Caynabo is the capital of Saraar region.[19] It is a relatively small place along the tarmac road to the east of Somaliland. It has 30,000 to 50,000 inhabitants.[20] The area is mostly inhabited by Isaaq/Habar Jeclo. The region has been established relatively recently as administrative entity, in 2008, and, five

---

19 This section is based on three weeks of field research I did as consultant for DFID as part of a study on security and justice in Somaliland between February and March 2013.
20 All population numbers in this chapter are very rough estimates based on the author's subjective assessments. Numbers are only presented to give the reader a basic idea about differences in size of the places mentioned.

years later, at the time of fieldwork, the regional government was still struggling to increase its own capacity and develop the infrastructure of the region. The main security problems were related to land conflicts, conflicts over enclosures in the countryside, charcoal burning and revenge killings (interview with former governor Ibraahim, mayor Faysal and head of regional court Xasan, Caynabo, 19 February 2013). When asked about the enclosures, which produced frequent conflicts among pastoral nomads, Ibraahim, the former governor of the region (who in early 2013 was about to be transferred to a new region as governor), argued that the police could not effectively deal with this issue since they lacked resources. They needed the support of the local elders, particularly to prevent armed resistance from the nomads.

In 2013, the court system in Caynabo was underdeveloped. There was one regional and one district court. These were the only courts in the Saraar region. When necessary, judges or courts (e.g. a court of appeal, which did not exist in Saraar) from other regions were supposed to help out. Lawyers, too, had to come from elsewhere. The problems with administering security and justice in the countryside were even bigger than those in the town. If something happened in an area where there were few roads or cars, state officials could hardly reach there and, even if they could, they had little influence. Traditional authorities were the most relevant actors there. Only when a conflict could not be settled through the use of customary law (Somali: *xeer*) would nomads sometimes come to the court in Caynabo. When the security of the whole region was threatened (e.g. related to ongoing oil exploration around Caynabo), the national army was called in (interview with former governor Ibraahim, mayor Faysal and head of regional court Xasan, Caynabo, 19 February 2013).

A common problem, unfortunately, was cases of rape. There were two traditional ways of dealing with rape. One was to marry the raped girl to the rapist. In this way, a 'legitimate' relationship could be established.[21] The family of the rapist would have to pay all the necessary marriage payments, plus an extra fine. The other way was to fine the rapist, who had to pay around 40 goats and a number of camels, or a monetary equivalent. The fine was paid collectively by the rapist and his close relatives. It was received by the victim's close male relatives. The victim herself would not see much of the 'compensation' payment. In this way, rape was 'cheap'. There were attempts by the new head of the regional court to bundle the dealing with rape cases under his authority (interview with former governor Ibraahim, mayor Faysal and head of regional court Xasan, Caynabo, 19 February

---

21 Things would be different if the rape victim would be married already. In practice, however, married women are usually not raped. In the countryside, people know each other and to rape the wife of another man would most probably provoke an armed attack by the husband and his male relatives on the rapist.

2013). But the results of this initiative were not yet clear when field research was conducted on this matter in Caynabo in early 2013.

In addition to the elders, religious authorities also had a role to play in administrating local justice and security. Sheikh Adan explained that he and a colleague had an office in Caynabo that offered judgements according to shari'a.

> When we take on a complicated case, we are five to seven sheikhs. While a single kadi can rule according to Shari'a, it is better to have several. Here [in Caynabo/Somaliland], people are concerned about clan. To satisfy each party, we make sure that every clan/lineage has its sheikh involved.
> (Interview with Sheikh Aadan, Caynabo, 23 February 2013)

Sheikh Aadan outlined aspects of typical legal procedures: First, the parties before the Islamic court had to agree to trust the court and follow its decisions. This needed to be signed. Additionally, a lineage head (in Somali: *caaqil*) or another respected elder from each party's side was contacted and asked to make sure that the decision of the court would be implemented. Sheikh Aadan emphasized that 'the elders and the sheikhs work together'. shari'a courts usually worked expediently and did not charge huge amounts of money. State courts were said to work slowly and often had problems with corruption. Sheikh Aadan mentioned that, for instance, in land-related cases, a fee needed to be paid to the shari'a court that was related to the size of the land in question. The fee could vary from 50 to 500 USD. He added that he and his colleagues would not take on cases involving corporal punishment or death sentences. The latter would be exclusively negotiated before state courts. The sheikh mentioned that he and his colleagues would settle three to four cases per month (interview with Sheikh Aadan, Caynabo, 23 February 2013).

The capital of the Sanaag region, Ceerigaabo, is located some 300 kilometres northeast of Caynabo. In contrast to Saraar, Sanaag has a well-established administrative structure. Until recently, it was the largest region of Somaliland (before eastern Sanaag has been declared a separate region called Badhan, in 2008). Ceerigaabo has approximately 80,000 to 100,000 inhabitants. It is the only truly 'multi-clan' town in Somaliland. It is inhabited roughly to the same extent by members of various Isaaq and Daarood clans, between whom long-standing traditions of intermarriage exist. But when the locals started fighting on different sides during the northern Somali civil war 1988–1991 – and most Daarood sided with the Somali government, while most Isaaq supported the guerrillas – social ties were severed. In the aftermath of the fighting, it took several years to negotiate peace and establish trust again. From the mid-1990s onward, people returned to Ceerigaabo to rebuild their lives. Despite or probably because of this horrific past, Ceerigaabo seems very calm today and people are extremely conscious about anything that could disturb their peace.

There is a well-established peace committee (Somali: *guddiga nabadgeliyada*) in town. It consists of male representatives of each of the dominant clans in the region. This committee is a home-grown institution (it has not been founded by a NGO or by the government in Hargeysa). It falls under the local government. The vice-mayor functions as chairman of the committee. The members are concerned with keeping the peace in Ceerigaabo and Sanaag region. Whenever a security issue arises, they discuss and advise the local and regional government. Members of this committee stressed that, on the one hand, security and justice are managed by the police, courts, and the custodial corps responsible for the jails. On the other hand, the civilian population led by traditional and religious authorities is concerned with these matters. The latter work quite effectively, while much remains to be done regarding the formal state institutions (interview with Ibraahim Axmed Faarax, Maxamed Warsame Xirsi, Axmed Ismaaciil Cali, Axmed Yuusuf Maxamed, and Siciid Mire Jaamac, Ceerigaabo, 3 March 2013).

Two police commanders mentioned that revenge killings and land conflicts were the biggest problems in town. In the countryside, rape was a key issue. In their operations, the policemen worked with the judiciary as well as with elders and sheikhs. Since many civilians had firearms in their houses, police work was risky. One needed to cooperate with a reliable elder of the family to be able to arrest a suspect without too much risk of armed resistance (interviews with Maxamed Cali Faarax and Siciid Ciise Ducaale, Ceerigaabo, 4 March 2013). In some cases, suspects escape to Puntland, an autonomous administration in north-eastern Somalia. Then, through negotiations between elders on both sides, one could try to arrange the return of the suspect to Ceerigaabo; among state officials, such negotiations would be more complicated and take longer (interview with Ibraahim Axmed Faarax, Maxamed Warsame Xirsi, Axmed Ismaaciil Cali, Axmed Yuusuf Maxamed, and Siciid Mire Jaamac, Ceerigaabo, 3 March 2013).

In 2013, District, regional and appeal courts were in place in Ceerigaabo and well-staffed. Still, Xuseen Aw Diriiye, the head of the appeal court and possibly the most experienced judge in town, emphasized that there was a 'war over legal codes,' by which he meant that there was some confusion between statutory law and shari'a law. In some cases, judges would not know when and how to use which codex (interview with Xuseen Aw Diriiye, Ceerigaabo, 3 March 2013). This was confirmed by members of the peace committee. Simultaneously, and somewhat in contradiction to the general concern about legal pluralism in the local setting, the chairmen of all three courts in town added that traditional authorities were playing an important role in settling legal issues in the community.[22] Adan, the head of the regional

---

22 From a formal legal perspective it needs to be noted that, while shari'a was officially the foundation of the legal system of Somaliland, according to Article 4(2) of the country's constitution, it remained unclear what the official legal foundation for the use of customary law in Somaliland was.

court, stressed: 'many people finalize their cases outside of the courts. Only 50 per cent [of all cases] go before court' (interview with Aaden Jaamac Seleebaan, Ceerigaabo, 3 March 2013). Homicide cases in particular were dealt with by elders (in contrast to what the sheikh in Caynabo had said). But rape cases were usually taken on by the courts. According to Aadan, this was because the traditional settlement of rape cases would not satisfy women. Family matters and cases involving injuries were often negotiated by religious authorities under shari'a. Aadan added that the courts frequently had problems with the implementation of their decisions. People were armed and this, as well as clanism, would hinder the police from ensuring obedience to court sentences. In contrast, the elders' decisions were frequently implemented without much resistance due to the fact that elders always sought to establish consensus (interview with Aaden Jaamac Seleebaan, Ceerigaabo, 3 March 2013).

Members of the peace committee in Ceerigaabo mentioned that people in Ceerigaabo and in many other parts of Somaliland complained about the corrupt court system. It was said: 'In the whole country, if you bring a case before [state] court, you check your finances and the finances of the other party' (interview with Ibraahim Axmed Faarax, Maxamed Warsame Xirsi, Axmed Ismaaciil Cali, Axmed Yuusuf Maxamed, and Siciid Mire Jaamac, Ceerigaabo, 3 March 2013). This means that the financially better-off party had much better chances to win before the court. Judges responded differently to these accusations. The head of the appeal court stressed that some judges are corrupt, others are not. He also added that, 'there is a huge discrepancy between our work and our salary. We receive 120 to 130 US dollars [per month]. This actually is the reason for corruption' (interview with Xuseen Aw Diriiye, Ceerigaabo, 3 March 2013). The head of the regional court emphasized that people themselves came with an offer to pay bribes (interview with Aaden Jaamac Seleebaan, Ceerigaabo, 3 March 2013).

Religious judges, administering shari'a, also played a role in Ceerigaabo. In March 2013 they did not have an office anymore. But there were several sheikhs in town who were well-known as legal specialists. One of them, Sheikh Xasan Yuusuf Ismaciil, stressed that mostly injuries, family issues and property conflicts were settled under shari'a law. One needed a minimum of one sheikh, but ideally two or three sheikhs for that. A normal case would take three days, a complicated one a week. People would pay a small fee to the shari'a court. The state officials accepted the rulings of the sheikhs. But homicide and rape cases were usually not negotiated under shari'a law.

Gar'adag is a district town in Sanaag region, half way between Ceerigaabo and Caynabo. The town has approximately 10,000 inhabitants, mainly from the Habar Jeclo and Habar Yunis clans (both belonging to the Isaaq clan-family). The male officials interviewed stressed that there were not many problems in the area. The police commander for the district mentioned that he commanded around 30 men; they had one car. If more than one matter occurred at a time in a place further away, the police needed the support of civilians. The local elders frequently assisted the police (interview with Maxamuud Cawad Diriiye, Gar'adag, 5 March 2013). There were bullet holes in one side of the police car. The commander mentioned that they had been shot at by pastoral-nomads when on a recent operation in the countryside.

The head of the district court was a teacher by training. He explained that he had studied several law books, but he had never received any formal legal training. The task of the public prosecutor was taken over by the police commander. There was no further staff for the district court. The judge stressed that there were not many criminal cases per year, and in more complicated cases, the courts in Ceerigaabo were asked to send a mobile court team (which received moderate support by UNDP). There was no lawyer in Gar'adag, and the judge never heard of anybody demanding one. According to him, the elders and religious authorities of the place would assist the court and the police in their work (interview with Jaamac Awil Aadan, Gar'adag, 5 March 2013). Later, a female civil society activist mentioned that contrary to the statements by the male officials, rape was a major issue in Gar'adag district.

> They [the authorities] do nothing about rape. The elders of the two sides [the rapist and the victim] negotiate. Nobody cares about the victim. Nobody prevents rape. Nobody speaks for the rights of women. Women in the countryside cannot find any professional medical help after rape or during childbirth. Those who do not make it to Gar'adag [to get some assistance] sometimes just die.
> (Interview with Fulki Cabdi Xaaji Xirsi, Gar'adag, 5 March 2013)

There were no groups in town that would defend women and raise awareness about the issue of rape. 'We would need a car, fuel, loudspeakers to go around and educate people.' The civil society activist said that, among the nomads, rape was frequently not perceived as a very serious matter (interview with Fulki Cabdi Xaaji Xirsi, Gar'adag, 5 March 2013).

Clearly, 'everyday governance' concerning justice and security in Somaliland's considerable margins is characterized by plural arrangements (Benda Beckmann and Benda Beckmann 2006). Traditional (and religious) actors are central to the guarantee of 'law and order'. State officials in the judiciary and the security sectors 'accept' their limitations regarding staff, funding and local legitimacy and willingly concede the superior position to the traditional (and religious) authorities. Even in urban spaces such as Ceerigaabo, with its well-established state administration, elders are always involved as advisors, and judges and policemen know that one needs the assistance of the elders to implement a sentence or to capture a suspect. Only with regard to rape cases, were customary solutions not satisfactory; some state officials stressed rapists should generally be sentenced by courts. The situation in Gar'adag showed, however, that ignoring the issue was one way male state officials could also deal with it.

The approach of elders to delivering justice and security at the margins was related to consensus formation.[23] This required time and the careful consideration of power differences as well as (historical) grievances of the parties involved (Schlee 2013). Customary settlements are generally restorative, not retributive. The aim is to restore peaceful living conditions within or between groups. The difference between this HPO at the margins and the one in the centre (regarding 'everyday governance') is a matter of degree. Even in Hargeysa (and other places in the central-state-triangle) 'everyday governance' is frequently in the hands of elders and sheikhs. However, the potential of state interference is much higher in the centre than at the margins. In the centre, the police and the courts are much better equipped and officials are much better trained. People there have a real choice, for example, to settle a legal dispute before court or with the help of elders or sheikhs, which is a case of 'forum shopping' (Benda Beckmann 1981). Some cases are also successfully monopolized by the state upon its own initiative. At the margins, the choice of the locals (ordinary people and state representatives) is limited (e.g. in Ceerigaabo) or there is (almost) none (e.g. in Gar'adag).

The following case study shows how the interference of state officials from the centre in a local conflict mediation process at the margins not only undermined conflict settlement, but actually escalated the situation. Indeed, it resulted in dozens of people killed and many more wounded and/or temporarily displaced. For years, a considerable part of Somaliland's (claimed) territory became inaccessible for any official coming from Hargeysa.

Case study 2: The Kalshaale conflict

Kalshaale is a grazing area south of Burco. It is a buffer zone between two clans, the Dhulbahante and the Habar Jeclo. Megaagle, some kilometres south-east of Kalshaale, is Dhulbahante territory, while Qorulugud, a few kilometres to the north-west, is Habar Jeclo territory.

This clan-borderland has long been wrought with conflict. Once, the Dhulbahante provoked the Habar Jeclo by building a *berked* (cistern) or a house or even a mosque in one place that was considered Habar Jeclo land or a neutral space; once, the Habar Jeclo did the same in a space that made Dhulbahante nervous. Kalshaale itself was jointly used by Habar Jeclo and Dhulbahante nomads for grazing. It had one big *balli*, or clay reservoir, for watering the animals. Tensions began to grow in October 2010, when Habar Jeclo men started to build several cisterns there. In the pastoral-nomadic setting of northern Somalia, building a house or a cistern in a previously uninhabited place stakes your claim to it, and in this way descent groups can

---

23 Religious authorities built on the respect for Islam; in order to implement their rulings, however, they also cooperated with elders.

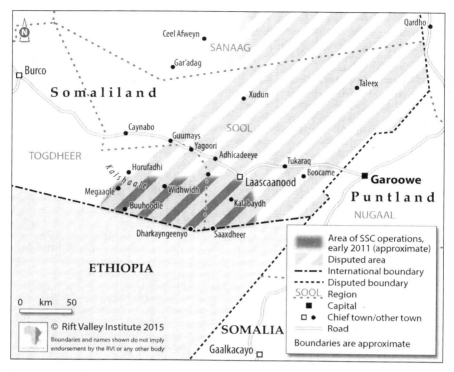

Map 8.2 Conflict in the Hawd, 2010–2012.

expand and secure important resources for themselves, including pasture and water.[24]

The reasons for attempts by nomads to control resources more permanently include environmental degradation, population growth, and state politics. As a result, groups have been clashing more frequently over pasture and water. The state politics impinging negatively on the area were, on the one hand, Ethiopia's tightening of the border control, monitoring Somali movement from the area into Region 5 (the Somali Region of Ethiopia, bordering Somaliland), and, on the other hand, Somaliland's military expansion into Laascaanood and surroundings. Laascaanood had been a hot-spot of conflict between Somaliland and Puntland for many years, from around 2000 onward. Both state-like entities claimed the area. From December 2003 to October 2007 Laascaanood had been occupied by Puntland forces. For genealogical reasons (Puntland is ruled by Darood/Harti, among them Dhulbahante from Lassacaanood and surroundings) these forces were mainly

---

24 All the important settlements in the interior of northern Somalia developed around a permanent source of water.

accepted by the locals. In November 2007 a violent change of power took place, and henceforth, Somaliland troops ruled in Laascaanood. Many locals rejected this as 'Isaaq-domination' (Hoehne 2015: 62–74).

When the conflict around Kalshaale escalated in the second half of 2010, Axmed Maxamuud Maxamed Siilaanyo had just been elected president of Somaliland. By clan he was Habar Jeclo from the area south of Burco. Many Dhulbahante argued that their Habar Jeclo neighbours and long-term rivals around Kalshaale would use their chance of 'being the government' to gain more power.[25] In a way, this continues the 'trauma' experienced by the Dhulbahante under the British in the aftermath of the Dervish wars (1899–1920), when the Habar Jeclo, many of whom had been allies of the British against the Dervishes (who often had been Dhulbahante), expanded into their areas and took over much of the grazing lands and wells. Even if this was just a paranoid fantasy of many Dhulbahante, it remained practically relevant as it shaped their perception of what was going on in the buffer zone around Kalshaale in the years between 2010 and today (late 2017). Facing Habar Jeclo encroachment from the north and standing with their backs against the strongly controlled Ethio-Somali border in the south, the Dhulbahante between Kalshaale and Buuhoodle felt 'squeezed'.

When the Habar Jeclo had started building cisterns at Kalshaale, the Dhulbahante from Buuhoodle asked them to stop. But the Habar Jeclo refused. Elders from both sides agreed to postpone discussions on the issue until the end of Ramadan (2010), but shortly before the Holy Month ended, an elderly Dhulbahante man passing by the area on his way to the port of Berbera, where he wanted to sell his animals, was shot dead by Habar Jeclo men at Kalshaale. Local nomads had accused him of being one of those who wanted to prevent the building of their cisterns (interviews with Axmed Daakir, Laascaanood, 11 December 2010, and Siciid Xaaji Nuur, Hargeysa, 27 February 2011). On 15 November 2010, during the Eid prayer that concluded the Ramadan fast, a group of Dhulbahante attacked the Habar Jeclo in the area, killing seven men and wounding six. Three Dhulbahante were killed and three others wounded in the attack.

Somaliland troops in the vicinity went straight to Kalshaale to position themselves between the two conflict parties. Subsequently, traditional leaders from other Dhulbahante and Habar Jeclo lineages rushed to the scene, and a few days later religious and traditional leaders, intellectuals, and politicians came from as far as Hargeysa and Garoowe (the capital of Puntland). The politicians' arrival indicated that the conflict was more than an ordinary

---

25 This is typical for the 'clan logic' that still plays a major role in Somaliland politics, even though the official system is based on political parties and elections (APD 2015: 61). Locals assess the government frequently according to the clan identities of the key-leaders; certain positions in the government and the wider administration are also 'inherited' by clan relatives.

shootout between nomads. The two governments in northern Somalia, Somaliland and Puntland, that were competing for control of the Dhulbahante and Warsangeli lands, tried to use the conflict to increase their influence in the region. In addition, a local Dhulbahante militia called Sool, Sanaag iyo Cayn (SSC) operated in the area. It was founded with the help of Dhulbahante in the diaspora (a typical case of 'long-distance clanism') in 2009 and sought to bring stability and development to the Dhulbahante lands independent of Somaliland and Puntland. The impetus for this was the long-standing marginalization of the Dhulbahante lands by both centres, the Somaliland administration in Hargeysa and the Puntland administration in Garoowe (Hoehne 2015: 78–81).

In line with the Somali tradition of conflict settlement, a large mediation committee was established near Kalshaale, comprising traditional authorities from various groups who were not directly involved in the conflict. While this third-party mediation was under way, the government in Hargeysa decided to hand over responsibility for adjudicating this case to nine religious leaders, who would pass a judgement on the basis of the shari'a. Although the religious leaders were thought of as being above clan-politics, some Dhulbahante complained that they were mostly Isaaq. Moreover, they were urban elites from the political centre of Somaliland.

After several weeks, the sheikhs came to a decision and formally ordered both sides to pay *mag* (Somali for 'compensation') for those who had been killed: the Dhulbahante for the seven dead Habar Jeclo men, and the Habar Jeclo for the three dead Dhulbahante attackers and the elderly man. They were also ordered to care for each other's wounded until they recovered.[26] The Habar Jeclo were allowed to keep their three cisterns, while the Dhulbahante were allowed to build three for themselves. Both sides were to be permitted to use the area, but without any further construction.

This decision was accepted by the Habar Jeclo but rejected by the Dhulbahante, who argued that the area should be used for grazing animals and there should be no permanent dwellings or cisterns. Following the fighting they no longer were comfortable living with the Habar Jeclo, who, they felt, could rely on the Somaliland army and were 'close' to President Siilaanyo. After the decision of the sheikhs, the Dhulbahante delegation retreated in anger (interview with Maxamed Qoryooley, Laascaanood, 12 December 2010). The settlement engineered by the Somaliland government

---

26 The *mag* for a dead man is normally 100 camels, payable in cash or kind. Two groups can also agree on a reduced *mag*, if that suits their interests, for example when the parties in conflict are actually two lineages within one sub-clan who do not want to 'overburden' each other. In exceptional cases, the *mag* can be raised up to 120 or even 150 camels, if the killing was particularly gruesome or if the person killed was a senior figure such as an *caaqil*. Besides these general rules, power differences influence customary legal proceedings and decisions. For an in-depth treatment of these matters, see Schlee (2013).

had failed, and in the following weeks many Dhulbahante and other members of the Darood clan-family accused Hargeysa of having sided with the Habar Jeclo in deploying the 'national' army in a clan dispute, essentially using the army as an Issaq clan militia.[27]

On 9 January 2011, President Siilaanyo declared all local clan militias had to leave and that Kalshaale was, for the time being, a military zone controlled by the Somaliland national army (Boocame Media 2011). For the vast majority of Dhulbahante, this amounted to another illegal occupation of their territory. By then, the Kalshaale issue had become a matter of concern for basically all clan members in the area, from around Buuhoodle to the Sanaag region, and even in the diaspora. This provided a strong basis for the SSC, which so far had refrained from open involvement, to become active and coordinate the armed resistance. On 30 January 2011, the first clashes between Dhulbahante/SSC units and Somaliland troops occurred around Hagoogane, a village near Kalshaale. The next day there were anti-Somaliland demonstrations in Laascaanood. On 7 February, the SSC and Somaliland's troops engaged in a substantial battle in the Kalshaale area that left several dozen people dead and up to a hundred wounded (Somaliland-Press 2011).

Clashes between SSC/Dhulbahante militias and the Somaliland army continued until about 20 February 2011. Demonstrations for and against military engagement by Puntland happened in Garoowe. Eventually, the Ethiopian government used its diplomatic channels to ensure that Puntland, which officially claimed to 'protect' Dhulbahante, would refrain from military engagement in order to not destabilize an area that was vital to Ethiopia's security interests. The conflict zone between Kalshaale and Buuhoodle was close to the Ogadeen region, also known as Region 5 of Ethiopia, where insurgents of the Ogadeen National Liberation Front (ONLF) were active. The Ethiopian government feared that the ONLF could use the insecurity in eastern Somaliland for its own purposes (e.g. to establish bases there and increase arms trafficking).

Somaliland's President Axmed Siilaanyo, for his part, published an appeal for peace on 23 February 2011, stating that his government was ready to engage in further conciliation efforts. In Somali, this was referred to as rolling out the 'mattress of peace' (*gogosha nabadeed*), where one could 'sit and talk'. The president had reportedly already ordered the destruction of the cisterns built by the Habar Jeclo, an order carried out on 27 February, opening the door to more dialogue between the Habar Jeclo and the Dhulbahante. But the Dhulbahante elders now demanded that *mag* (compensation) was paid for dozens more people killed in January and February 2011, a demand rejected by the government in Hargeysa and by the Habar Jeclo, who wished to start

---

27 In fact, the Somaliland army, also those troops stationed in Kalshaale, included members of various Isaaq and non-Isaaq clans. However, the Darood were less strongly represented in the army compared to other groups.

afresh from where the settlement of the religious leaders had failed the previous December (Hoehne 2015: 96–97). As of late 2017, the issue has not yet been settled.

The Kalshaale conflict essentially concerned 'high politics' (questions of war and peace in a large area). This case study shows how a localized dispute over water, dry season pasture and a clan buffer-zone could become a major political conflict involving a national army, delegates from two rival state administrations, and increasingly well-equipped, well-organized clan militias, backed by diasporic actors. It underlined both the instability of the contested borderlands and the distance, at least in political terms, of many Dhulbahante from Hargeysa. The conflict massively increased Dhulbahante concerns over being a minority in Somaliland under what they saw as an Isaaq-dominated government.

The affair also underscored Hargeysa's poor conflict management skills. The then new President of Somaliland, Axmed Siilaanyo, came from an eastern branch of the Isaaq – and thus must have had some understanding of the concerns of Dhulbahante around Buuhoodle – but was unable to keep the situation under control. In my view, the reason behind this failure was that the state actors were blinded by the power they exercise in the centre, where 'the government system' (*habka dawladeed*) prevails. They did not realize the limitations of their influence in the realm of 'the traditional system' (*habka dhaqameed*) that continues to dominate at the margins. Also differences in 'political culture' (i.e. how to settle an issue, how to negotiate) played a role. An effective communication between both sides (representing two different HPOs) was impossible because their intentions and concerns were incompatible. The one side saw itself as acting in the name of the state, using the national army and state officials or envoys sent from the capital as 'tools' to settle the conflict. The aim was top-down control. The other side, however, consisted of concerned locals (elders as well as ordinary people) and clan members in the diaspora who saw their livelihood and resources at stake. They defended their land against what they perceived as a continuous, decades-long encroachment by rivals in the pastoral buffer zone; only this time, their rivals (Habar Jeclo) were drawing also on the power of the state. What most Dhulbahante wanted was a negotiation 'at eye level' between local traditional authorities from both sides (Darood and Isaaq), focusing on pastoral matters, not state politics, and eventually guaranteeing peaceful coexistence.

Conclusion: different forms of HPOs and ongoing state-formation

Somaliland is widely perceived as an emerging polity featuring an HPO *par excellence*, successfully combing 'traditional' and 'modern' elements of statehood. This has significance beyond the particular case. Some argued that 'hybridising political systems in these ways may well represent a positive step toward deepening democracy in Africa' (Logan 2009: 123–124). In Somaliland, integrating traditional authorities in the political process certainly contributed to peacebuilding in the early 1990s (Boege 2006: 11, 14; Menkhaus 2016: 16). Two decades later, this hybrid formula still is considered as one of the factors stabilizing statehood and enhancing positive state-society relations (Walls 2014; Richards 2015). As one of the key exponents of this view, Walls (2014: 306) stressed that 'Somaliland has made remarkable progress in instituting a system of multi-party, electoral democracy that draws both on customary practice and on external systems.' However, despite this seeming success in hybrid state formation, a discussion in Somaliland and abroad has begun (as early as 2005) that focuses on the House of Elders/the *Guurti*. This institution lies at the heart of the HPO in the centre. But it is increasingly seen as problematic (Ahmed Mohamed Hashi 2005; SONSAF 2011; IRIN 2013; APD 2015). Its members are not elected, their credentials as 'clan representatives' are weak and, for the past decade, several *Guurti*-decisions have sparked major conflicts. The most recent of these conflicts, in May 2015, concerned the two-year extension of the current government's term, including a further postponement of the presidential and parliamentary elections (ICG 2015b). Reform is not easy: Some suggest abolishing the *Guurti* (which, however, remains a symbol of Somaliland's impressive peacebuilding process, and therefore the thought of abolishing it is not acceptable to many). Others propose to transform it from a selected into an elected body, possibly also including women, which, however, would put an end to the *Guurti*'s seemingly 'traditional' credentials. This would also eliminate the distinction between the *Guurti* and the House of Representatives, whose members are elected (IRIN 2013).

Richards argued that the debate over the future of the *Guurti* 'serves as an indicator of the arising tensions between "old" Somali society and governance, and "new" democratic practices and principles' (Richards 2008: n.p.). In my view, this statement is based on a misinterpretation of traditional relations of authority in Somali society. Those relations were characterized by the absence of institutionalized authority. Traditional authorities were heavily dependent on their followers and did not constitute any permanent governing body. The formalization of the *Guurti* as a House of Elders in the Somaliland political system can be understood as an 'invented tradition' (Hobsbawm and Ranger 1983). It inserted a seemingly traditional element into the newly emerging political order. Once established, the *Guurti* forced other government bodies and those involved in fostering Somaliland's democratic transition to deal with this element. One central aspect of the *Guurti*'s 'traditional' character was that its members were not elected. They presented themselves as selected by their clansmen (and women, but only indirectly, as women do not have much voice on clan-conferences). In reality, however, while some were genuine elders, many were urban elites who were out of touch with their constituencies. Over the years, the dependence of the *Guurti* members on protection by the president against critics in the House of Parliament and the civil society has increased. This, and the wish of *Guurti* members and their families to hold on to their powerful and lucrative position (all of which is not in accordance with pastoral-nomadic traditions of authority, according to which an elder can also lose his influence if he does not satisfy his constituency), led to the 'unholy' alliance between the elders and the president to mutually extend one another's terms between 2006 and 2010 and again between 2015 and 2017. This has nothing to with 'tensions between "old" Somali society and governance, and "new" democratic practices and principles', as Richards has it, but is an effect of the corruption of traditional authority and democracy produced by the imbalanced and 'crippled' HPO existing in the centre of Somaliland. A general lesson to be drawn from this case is that HPOs are constantly evolving and hardly ever in balance. How the state-society relation and the mode of political order in a HPO plays out cannot be predicted (Meagher et al. 2014: 4).

This chapter also showed that besides this one HPO in the centre, a second HPO exists at the broad margins Somaliland. While most people in Hargeysa (and other places in the central-state-triangle) have come to accept the state as quasi-independent actor (despite it continuing to work partly according to clan and other related logics), people at the margins experience the state as rather powerless actor, and less effective than local traditional (and religious) authorities. One reason for this is that the financial and human resources of state institutions at the margins are extremely limited. This means there still exists a void of governance by state institutions at the margins (as was the case throughout Somaliland in the early 1990s), which is filled by local non-state actors (mainly traditional authorities).[28]

Consequently, security and justice are provided less by state agents than by clan representatives, sometimes in cooperation with religious authorities. But the traditional system (*habka dhaqameed*) operates *ad hoc*. It does not provide any long-term security. It also does not foster transparency and equality in the justice sector. It works better for stronger groups than for weaker ones. Moreover, the situation of women seems to be unfortunate. They have quite limited access to justice and security. Their voices are heard before courts, and even in front of elders or religious authorities, but their positions are always mediated by men.

Looking at 'high politics' in the centre of Somaliland, and particularly at the actions of the *Guurti*, it become obvious that the 'customary practices' mentioned by Walls with regard to political developments in Somaliland from

---

28 Menkhaus (2016) recently provided an 'inventory' of (mostly armed) non-state actors providing security (and sometimes justice) in southern Somalia. Elders were featuring there only as relatively weak actors. Due to the ongoing violence there, the most relevant non-state actors filling the void left by weak state are clan militias, paramilitaries, private security firms and Al Shabaab.

the late 1990s up until today do not correspond with the traditional system that used to be in place in Somaliland in the early 1990s and that, arguably, constitutes the 'real' tradition of northern Somalis. Walls mentioned:

> For people so firmly rooted in a patriarchal, egalitarian and consensus-based customary regime governed by principles relating to conflict and peace, this attempt [of post-colonial governments, particularly under Maxamed Siyaad Barre] of a centralized state to claim a monopoly on violence and the co-optation of clan into the state structure proved wholly unacceptable to those excluded.
> (Walls 2014: 160)

Considering what has happened in Somaliland since the Hargeysa conference 1997, and more so since the mid-2000s, one can see the co-optation of men (elders or not) who claim to represent clans into the state structure. Many of them are out of touch with their alleged constituencies (whose members often reside in the countryside) and have become part of the urban elite. Moreover, given the non-participation of most people in the east in the democratic process from 2001 onward, a considerable part of the population of the country was excluded or, to put it differently, opted out. Against this backdrop, the argument by Walls (2014) about the 'positive' integration of 'traditional' and 'modern' forms of governance in Somaliland as a basis for (nation-)state formation proves unconvincing.

The case study of Somaliland illustrates the multiplicity of simultaneously existing HPOs in an emerging polity. It also points out the dynamics and 'degrees' of HPOs and the complex and difficult to predict evolution of such orders. This defies 'quick and easy' conclusions about the benefit of hybrid arrangements for government in Africa and elsewhere.

References

Abdirahman Omar Hussein. 2015. Underrepresented clans in the parliament. Retrieved 7 September 2016 from http://hadhwanaag.ca/detail.aspx?id=162460.

Abdurahman M. Abdullahi. 2007. Recovering the Somali state: the Islamist factor, in *Somalia: diaspora and state reconstitution in the Horn of Africa*, edited by A. O. Farah, M. Mushie, and J. Gundel. London: Adonis & Abby Publishers, 196–221.

Ahmed Mohamed Hashi. 2005. *The implication of traditional leadership, 'Guurti' and other non-state actors in local governance in Somaliland*. Study Report for the Traditional Structures and Local Governance (TSLG) Project of the Community Empowerment and Social Inclusion Program (CESI) of the World Bank Institute. Retrieved 7 September 2016 from http://info.worldbank.org/etools/docs/library/153068/somaliafinal.pdf.

APD. 2015. Confronting the future of Somaliland's democracy: lessons from a decade of multi-partyism and the way forward. Retrieved 7 September 2016 from http://apd-somaliland.org/wp-content/uploads/2015/06/Report-website-version.pdf.

Balthasar, D. 2013. Somaliland's best kept secret: shrewd politics and war projects as means of state-making. *Journal of Eastern African Studies* 7(2), 218–238.

Benda Beckmann, K. von. 1981. Forum shopping and shopping forums: dispute processing in a Minangkabau village. *Journal of Legal Pluralism* 19, 177–159.

Benda Beckmann, F. von and Benda Beckmann, K. von. 2006. The dynamics of change and continuity in plural legal orders. *Journal of Legal Pluralism*, 53 and 54, 1–44.

Boege, V. 2006. *Traditional approaches to conflict transformation: potentials and limits*. Retrieved 7 September 2016 from http://edoc.vifapol.de/opus/volltexte/2011/2565/pdf/boege_handbook.pdf.

Boege, V., Brown, A., Clements K. and Nolan, A. 2008. *On hybrid political orders and emerging states: state formation in the context of 'fragility'*. Berlin: Berghof Conflict Research Centre. Retrieved 7 September 2016 from www.berghof-handbook.net/documents/publications/boege_etal_handbook.pdf.

Boocame Media. 2011. Axmed Maxamed Siilaanyo oo Go'aan Ka soo saaray Arinta Kalshaale. 9 January. Retrieved 17 October 2016 from www.somaliaonline.com/community/topic/president-siilaanyo-makes-decision-on-kalshaale-issue.

Bradbury, M. 2008. *Becoming Somaliland*. Oxford: James Currey.

Bryden, M. 2004. A State-within-a-failed-state: is Somaliland headed for recognition or reunification?, in *States-within-states: incipient political entities in the post-Cold War era*, edited by P. Kingston and I.S. Spears. New York: Palgrave Macmillan, 167–188.

Cabdiraxmaan Jimcaale 2005. Consolidation and decentralization of government institutions, in *Rebuilding Somaliland: issues and possibilities*, edited by War-Torn Societies Project. Lawrenceville NJ and Asmara: Red Sea Press, 49–121.

Ciabarri, L. 2008. No representation without redistribution: Somaliland plural authorities, the search for a state and the 2005 parliamentary elections, in *Beside the state: emergent powers in contemporary Africa*, edited by A. Bellagamba and G. Klute. Köln: Köppe, 55–73.

Clements, K.P., Boege, V., Brown, A., Foley, W. and Nolan, A. 2007. State building reconsidered: the role of hybridity in the formation of political order. *Political Science* 59(1), 45–56.

Compagnon, D. 1992. Political decay in Somalia: from personal rule to warlordism. *Refuge* 12(5), 8–13.

Hansen, S.J. and Bradbury, M. 2007. Somaliland: a new democracy in the Horn of Africa? *Review of African Political Economy* 34(113), 461–476.

Hobsbawm, E. and Ranger, T. (eds). 1983. *The invention of tradition*. Cambridge: Cambridge University Press.

Hoehne, M.V. 2002. *Somalia zwischen Krieg und Frieden: Strategien der friedlichen Konfliktaustragung auf internationaler und lokaler Ebene*. Hamburg: Institut für Afrika-Kunde.

Hoehne, M.V. 2006. *Traditional authorities in northern Somalia: transformation of powers and positions*. Working paper no. 82. Halle/Saale: Max Planck Institute for Social Anthropology. Avialable at: www.eth.mpg.de/pubs/wps/pdf/mpi-eth-working-paper-0082.pdf.

Hoehne, M.V. 2007. From pastoral to state politics: traditional authorities in northern Somalia, in *State Recognition and Democratisation in Sub-Saharan Africa: A New Dawn for Traditional Authorities?*, edited by L. Buur and H.M. Kyed. New York: Palgrave Macmillan, 155–182.

Hoehne, M.V. 2013. Limits of hybrid political orders: the case of Somaliland. *Journal of Eastern African Studies* 7(2), 199–217.

Hoehne, M.V. 2015. *Between Somaliland and Puntland: marginalization, militarization and conflicting political visions*. London: Rift Valley Institute.

Hoehne, M.V. and Ibraahim, M.X.. 2014. Rebuilding Somaliland through economic and educational engagement, in *Diasporas, development and peacemaking in the Horn of Africa*, edited by L. Laakso and P. Hautaniemi. London: Zed Books, 53–76.

Ibraahim, M. X. 2010: *Somaliland's investment in peace: analysing the diaspora's economic engagement in peace building*. Diaspeace Working Paper 4. Retrieved 7 September 2016 from https://jyx.jyu.fi/dspace/handle/123456789/36878.

ICG. 2015a. *Somaliland: The strains of success*. Crisis Group Africa Briefing no. 113. Retrieved 7 September 2016 from https://d2071andvip0wj.cloudfront.net/b113-somaliland-the-strains-of-success.pdf.

ICG. 2015b. *Somaliland's Guurti sparks a crisis*. Retrieved 7 September 2016 from http://blog.crisisgroup.org/africa/somalia/2015/05/21/somalilands-guurti-sparks-a-crisis.

IRIN 13 July 2013. *Debating reform of Somaliland's House of Elders*. Retrieved 7 September 2016 from www.irinnews.org/news/2013/07/18/debating-reform-somaliland%E2%80%99s-house-elders.

Kent, R., Hippel, K. von and Bradbury, M. 2004. *Social facilitation, development and the diaspora: support for sustainable health services in Somalia*. London: International Policy Institute

Kraushaar, M and Lambach, D. 2009. *Hybrid political orders: the added value of a new concept*. Occasional Paper No. 14. Brisbane: Australian Centre for Peace and Conflict Studies.

Lewis, I.M. 1994. *Blood and bone: the call of kinship in Somali society*. Lawrenceville, NJ: Red Sea Press.

Lindley, A. 2008. Transnational connections and education in the Somali context. *Journal of Eastern African Studies* 2(3), 401–414.

Logan, C. 2009. Selected chiefs, elected councillors and hybrid democrats: popular perspectives on the co-existence of democracy and traditional authority. *Journal of Modern African Studies* 47(1), 101–128.

Mac Ginty, R. and Richmond, O. 2015. The fallacy of constructing hybrid political orders: a reappraisal of the hybrid turn in peacebuilding. *International Peacekeeping* 23(2), 219–239.

Meagher, K., de Herdt, T. and Titeca, K. 2014. *Unravelling public authority: paths of hybrid governance in Africa*. IS Academy, Research Brief No. 10. Retrieved 7 September 2016 from www.kpsrl.org/browse/browse-item/t/research-brief-unravelling-public-authority-paths-of-hybrid-governance-in-africa.

Menkhaus, K. 2016. *Non state security providers and political formation in Somalia*. Centre for Security Governance Paper No. 5. Retrieved 7 September 2016 from www.secgovcentre.org/files/www/NSSPs_in_Somalia_April2016.pdf.

Mohammed Abdullahi Artan. 2015. *Rewinding revolution: rhetoric in reliving the past: the Kacaan era*. Retrieved 7 September 2016 from www.garanuug.com/taariikh/rewinding-revolution-rhetoric-in-reliving-the-past-the-kacaan-era/.

Pegg, S.1998. *International society and the de facto state*. Aldershot: Ashgate.

Pham, J.P. 2012. The Somaliland exception: lessons on postconflict state building from the part of the former Somalia that works. *Marine Corps University Journal* 3(1), 1–33.

Prunier, G. 2010. Benign neglect versus La Grande Somalia: the colonial legacy and the post-colonial state, in *Milk and peace, drought and war: Somali culture, society and politics*, edited by M.V. Hoehne, Markus and V. Luling. London: Hurst, 35–49.

Renders, M. 2007. Appropriate 'Governance-Technology'? Somali clan elders and institutions in the making of the Republic of Somaliland, *Africa Spectrum* 42(3), 439–459.

Renders, M. 2012. *Consider Somaliland: state-building with traditional leaders and institutions*. Leiden: Brill.

Reno, W. 2003. *Somalia and survival in the shadow of the global economy*. Queen Elisabeth House Working Paper No. 100. Oxford: University of Oxford.

Richards, R. 2008. Democratisation in the Horn of Africa: contestation between the 'old' and 'new' in Somaliland. Paper presented at the annual meeting of the ISA's 49th Annual Convention, Bridging Multiple Divides, Hilton San Francisco, San Francisco, CA, USA, 26 March 2008. Retrieved 7 September 2016 from www.mbali.info/doc555.htm.

Richards, R. 2015. Bringing the outside in: Somaliland, statebuilding and dual hybridity. *Journal of Intervention and Statebuilding* 9(1), 4–25.

Samatar, A.I. 1992. Destruction of state and society in Somalia: beyond the tribal convention. *Journal of Modern African Studies* 30(4), 625–641.

Schlee, G. 2013. Customary law and the joys of statelessness: idealised traditions versus Somali realities. *Journal of Eastern African Studies* 7(2), 258–271.

Somaliland Forum. 2006. A term extension too far: Guurti resolution is unconstitutional and unacceptable. Retrieved 7 September 2016 from www.somaliland law.com/elders__term_extension.html.

SomalilandPress. 2011. Somaliland: fighting erupts in Kalshale between troops and clan militia. *SomalilandPress*, 7 February.

SomalilandTimes. 2008. Somaliland expatriates deplore Guurti's decision to extend Riyale's term in office. *Somaliland Times*, 12 April. Retrieved from www.somali landtimes.net/sl/2008/326/78.shtml.

SONSAF. 2011. *Somaliland elections review report*. Retrieved 7 September 2016 from www.somalilandlaw.com/SOMALILAND_ELECTIONS_REVIEW_2011.pdf.

Terlinden, U. and Maxamed Xasan Ibraahim. 2008. Somaliland – a success story of peace-making, state-building and democratisation? In *Hot spot Horn of Africa revisited*, edited by E.-M. Bruchhaus and M. M. Sommer. Hamburg: LIT Verlag, 68–85.

Walls, M. 2009. The emergence of a Somali state: building peace from civil war in Somaliland. *African Affairs* 108(432), 371–389.

Walls, M. 2014. *A Somali nation state: history, culture and Somaliland's political transition*. Pisa: Ponte Invisible.

9 The complexity of legal pluralist settings
An afterword

Janine Ubink

This book advances from the question how states deal with the alternative normative orders present in their territories. In other words, how they regulate the pluralistic character of their legal order. Pluri-legal settings pose serious governance challenges to sovereign states. How to effectively govern a country where many localities have their own normative orders, leadership structures and dispute settlement institutions; where many relations and rights are regulated by non-state law? Governance choices regarding these issues impact not only on the economy, peace and security, and general well-being of the country, but also on the sovereignty of states, their administrative efficiency, and their reach into the rural and more remote areas of the country.

The term legal pluralism, generally defined as the presence in a social field of more than one legal order (Griffiths 1986: 1; Merry 1988: 870), was originally established as a sensitizing concept. It was a response to the ideology of legal centralism, which holds that law is and should be the law of the state and that other, lesser normative orderings are hierarchically subordinate to state law (Benda-Beckmann 2002: 37; Griffiths 1986: 3). In contrast, legal pluralists find that the key to the legality of normative orders does not depend on their relation to the state, but lies in their authority to direct people's behaviour and generate feelings about what ought to be done (Griffiths 1986: 14; Himonga et al. 2014: 45). It builds on the thinking of Eugene Ehrlich, who coined the term 'living law' in his writings about the common law in the eighteenth century to explain how legal norms may arise outside or independently of the state:

> The living law is the law which dominates life itself even though it has not been posited in legal propositions. The source of our knowledge of this law is, first, the modern legal document; secondly, direct observation of life, of commerce, of customs and usages, and of all associations, not only of those that the law has recognized but also of those that it has overlooked and passed by, indeed even of those it has disapproved.
> (Ehrlich, Pound and Ziegert 2002: 493)

Studies in legal pluralism focus on 'the dialectic, mutually constitutive relationship between state law and other normative orders' and on 'the dynamics of change and transformation' in pluri-legal settings (Merry 1988: 879–880). Much research in this field 'emphasizes the way state law penetrates and restructures other normative orders through symbols and through direct coercion and, at the same time, the way non-state normative orders resist and circumvent penetration or even capture and use the symbolic capital of state law' (ibid.: 881). Much less studied – as mentioned by Merry (ibid.: 884) and which still holds true – is the way non-state normative orders constitute state law.

This book transcends the common approach of studying the impact of state law on non-state law by analysing the impact of the interaction of state and non-state normative orders *on the state*. The book outlines three 'moments of paradoxy', three occurrences where state entities and public officials need to navigate conflicting notions and ideas about other normative orders. The first paradox, that of liberal statecraft, sees to the question whether to accommodate customary law or not, and the paradox lies in the fact that such state accommodation has simultaneously inclusionary as well as exclusionary aspects: it is thus demanded by some and dismissed by others. The paradox of jurispathic state recognition denotes the catch-22 that even when the state displays a genuine desire to recognize and preserve living customary law, the act of recognition itself will change its form and reconstruct the living customary law into the next version of official customary law. The third paradox, the paradox of policultural states at work, focuses on the lived reality of public servants in their state work. Whether these public servants want to or not, and however official state policy tells them to act vis-à-vis customary law, public servants do not only encounter customary law and traditional authorities in their work, but will need to engage with them to get their state work done, even if this involves transcending, in practice, the official rules of the state. These three paradoxes together make up what the book terms 'the paradox of customary law'.

To study the paradox of customary law the book enters into a broad analysis of 'normative orders'. It goes beyond the more commonplace study of norms and courts to include the role of other institutions and actors of both state and non-state normative orders. These include, among others, 'bush-level bureaucrats' involved in South Africa's land restitution (Olaf Zenker, Chapter 2, this volume); the newly established local police in rural Mozambique (Helene Kyed, Chapter 3, this volume); traditional authority and modern decentralized leadership in Guinea (Anita Schroven, Chapter 6, this volume); and traditional elders and state judges and politicians in Somaliland (Markus Hoehne, Chapter 8, this volume).

Several chapters furthermore explore how the strength or weakness of a state and its institutions impact on legal pluralism choices and regulation. The relationship between state and non-state normative orders is particularly poignant in the context of failing or post-conflict states as it is often only by working with traditional institutions that the state is able to reconstitute itself, at least in certain parts of the country. As state-building is an ongoing process in general, and particularly in post-conflict states, the pluri-legal configurations are constantly in flux and the relationships between state and non-state institutions are continually evolving. According to Katrin Seidel (Chapter 5, this volume), addressing questions of the governance of legal pluralism may positively impact on national unity, when the 'negotiation spaces' that exist due to norm conflicts between different normative orders can be used to identify and formulate mutual values in light of respect for different moralities. She adds, however, that in contexts of weak states such as South Sudan, where state actors are not able to impose their rules on other local actors, the real question may be how much scope non-state legal orders leave for the recognition of other legal orders and governance authorities, including those of the state.

Anita Schroven and Markus Hoehne (Chapters 6 and 8, this volume) both question to what extent the non-state and the state normative orders can be accommodated and integrated. In her chapter on decentralization in Guinea, Schroven finds that including traditional authorities or elders into governance processes does not necessarily increase the authenticity and legitimacy of these processes. Nor does it lead to the transformation, or 'domestication', of traditional leaders into more democratic institutions. In fact, even references to shared history and traditions, meant to ensure solidarity, may be counterproductive. Colonial and postcolonial interactions between state and 'traditional' actors have rather led to intricately interwoven institutions, where state actors and elders fuse discourses from different historical periods. Hoehne (Chapter 8, this volume) in his case study on Somaliland is similarly critical about the accommodation of state and non-state normative orders. Outlining the corruption of elders who have been integrated into the government and the limited influence state officials exercise in the extensive margins of the country, he voices reservations about the success of hybrid institutions and political orders.

Pedersen (Chapter 7, this volume), describing recent land reforms in Tanzania, has a more positive assessment of the ability of the state to impose its rules and policies on non-state institutions. With two case studies he shows that state-backed land dispute settlement institutions in Tanzania are growing proportionally more important while customary institutions gradually lose relevance. In Tanzania customary and less formal institutions have been significantly weakened for a long time. The current land reforms thus reinforce trends that have been going on for decades, and started with the abolition of the office of chiefs in 1962 and the introduction of new village councils during the *Ujamaa* villagization programme in the 1970s. Customary institutions are not fully ignored, though, and continue to play a role in settling certain types of land conflicts, which is recognized by the state.

State recognition of 'traditional' institutions never implies a full or unconditional embrace of the customary, a move that would be seen as threatening state sovereignty (Kyed, Chapter 3, this volume, cf. Ubink 2008a: 16). Due to the partial recognition of customary normative orders, lower-level state institutions and street-level bureaucrats find themselves having to operate state law and state recognized customary law in arenas where rights are still predominantly determined by 'lived' customary law, which may differ substantially from the recognized official customary law and may include non-recognized parts of customary law that have strong social relevance. Land reforms are a prominent example of such a field, as becomes clear in both Rasmus Pedersen's and Olaf Zenker's chapters. The latter presents a case study of South African bureaucrats and their processing of a communal land claim for the restitution of 17 farms in Limpopo province. He shows that while legislation of the 1990s did not provide for a formal role of chiefs in the restitution process, chiefly authority in daily life operated as an extrinsic challenge to the work of the 'bush-level bureaucrats'. This challenge became more formidable over time, when the political environment changed from ambivalence and hesitancy towards traditional authority after independence, to a clear political momentum in favour of chiefs. Recent laws and proposed legislation aim to centralize the power of senior traditional leaders within the contested tribal boundaries inherited from the apartheid era and ignore and undermine the participatory features of customary systems (Claassens 2005: 73 and 95). Zenker shows how this changed context altered the rules of the game and the game of the rules regarding restitution claims. The chapters of Helene Kyed and Cherry Leonardi both address witchcraft as an example of 'illegal tradition' state actors need to engage with despite the state's attempts to outlaw the practice.

The chapters of this edited volume display several interconnected themes that have wider resonance outside of the studied countries, each connected to one of the paradoxes mentioned in this book: the recognition of non-state normative orders (the paradox of liberal statecraft); attempts to make customary law legible and understandable for outsiders (the paradox of jurispathic state recognition); and the challenges for actors and institutions operating between the various normative orders (the paradox of policultural states at work). I will discuss these three themes below.

Recognition of non-state normative orders

Recent scholarship increasingly highlights the political and governance aspects of legal pluralism (Benda-Beckmann et al. 2009). The regulation of non-state normative systems is intertwined with questions of political power, control, subjugation, integration and exclusion. Policies of recognition of customary norms and institutions are informed by political interests to consolidate local power and mobilize votes, to form or strengthen alliances with strategic local actors, and to increase relevance and popularity through linkages with the customary justice system. Traditional actors in their turn hope to use state alliances and recognition to consolidate and expand their power. Close association with the state can also work to their detriment, though, in cases where limited legitimacy of the state impacts negatively on their own local standing. State and non-state actors thus both have an interest in policies of recognition, although they do not necessarily hope for the same results. This ties in with Pedersen's assertion (Chapter 7, this volume) that changes in the pluri-legal setting can better be analysed by focusing on processes of mutual transformation in which the state plays a key role than by analysing institutional competition as a zero-sum game between the state and local actors.

As said above, state recognition of non-state normative orderings never entails a wholesale acceptance of these systems without conditions or exceptions. It is usually partial, conditional, and meant to make the customary order governable and in line with certain normative values of the state. The embrace of 'tradition' is connected to an urge to claim state sovereignty, by making the customary realm dependent on, and regulated by, the state. Kyed (2009), in a study of post-war Mozambique, points out that official discourses of simple, benign recognition of existing customary norms and structures mask aspects of state intervention, regulation and reform. Seidel (Chapter 5, this volume) similarly highlights that in South Sudan the term harmonization masks the hegemonic project of legal and judicial control by the state (cf. Leonardi et al. 2011: 117). This is in line with research that shows that the customary law that was recognized by colonial governments was in fact a new hybrid, a product of struggles between the colonizer and the colonized (Chanock 1985; Merry 1991: 897–906; Moore 1986; Ranger 1983). Several restrictions were placed on recognized customary law by colonial powers, the best-known of which is the 'repugnancy clause', which prescribed that the courts shall not enforce any customary law rule if it is repugnant to natural justice, equity and good conscience. Chris Mojekwu (1978) highlights several other restrictions on customary law in colonial Igboland. These include statutory limitations that customary norms could not be incompatible with colonial legislation nor contrary to public policy; extraordinary powers of the colonial senior administrative officer over the procedural operation of the native courts, including to appoint, suspend and dismiss judges; negating the final authority of the elders by creating an appeal to a colonial court; and statutory penalties on exercising judicial powers outside of the recognized native courts.

Mojekwu (1978) also points out that, despite the various far-reaching restrictions on paper, the lived customary law is resilient and the state deals creatively with people's circumventions of the state's regulations. In a case study of 'the Honourable Chief Gregory Agbasiere and His Traditional Court', he highlights how elders largely continue their dispute settlement in their traditional areas despite the statutory prohibition on exercising judicial powers outside of the recognized native courts. When one such elder, Chief Gregory, is taken to a colonial court for violating this prohibition, the appeal court distinguished between mediation and exercising judicial powers and thus allowed Chief Gregory's – and many other elders' – dispute settlement to continue. Another scholar who has highlighted the resilience of local normative orders is Sally Falk Moore. In her seminal study on 'Law and Social Change' (Moore 1973), she explains the limited impact of state legislation as instrument of social change by approaching research fields as 'semi-autonomous social fields', which she describes as follows: 'The semi-autonomous social field has rule-making capacities, and the means to induce or coerce compliance; but it is simultaneously set in a larger social matrix, which can, and does, affect and invade it, sometimes at the invitation of persons inside it, sometimes at its own instance' (ibid.: 720, 722). This approach emphasizes that individual behaviour and processes of interaction, struggle and negotiation within and between semi-autonomous social fields determine what the law effectively is at a particular time and location (Griffiths 1986: 36). Introducing new state legislation into a semi-autonomous social field often has different outcomes than expected or intended, as it may rather add a new layer of normativity to the existing plural normative structure than replace it. Laws and norms emanating from the state can be mobilized by institutional actors and justice seekers as resources in the negotiation of local law and social relations and for challenging or consolidating power relations (Corradi 2012: 93–96; Oomen 2005: 211–212). As such, '[m]uch that is new co-exists with and modifies the old, rather than replacing it entirely' (Moore 1973: 742).

Recognition of customary justice systems in contemporary settings will inevitably entail a reordering of authority and power (Weilenmann 2005: 5; Kyed 2009: 89). In keeping with the above, the impact of state regulation of the relationship between state and non-state normative systems is an empirical question, both as to the impact on the non-state normative order, as on the state itself. However, what is clear is that the 'natural' domination of the statutory order cannot be taken for granted.

Legibility through recording

This book echoes the widespread pre-occupation with making customary law 'legible'. From the colonial era onwards, administrators and judges have struggled to understand customary law. In the 1960s and 1970s, this resulted in the large 'Restatement of African Law' project undertaken in several newly independent African countries, including Tanzania, something Pedersen refers to in his chapter. Current interest in the matter is evidenced for instance by South Sudan's exploration of self-statements, which are partly due to an advisor who was heavily involved in the self-statements that have taken place in Namibia (Hinz 1997; Ubink 2011a).

Anthropologists have criticized any attempt to find and record 'the' customary law as a futile venture, an idea that 'can only come up in the confinement of legalistic doctrines' (Benda-Beckmann 1984: 30). They rather advise to 'shift the analytical focus from rules and outcomes to ongoing negotiation and debate' (Berry 1997: 1229). While this is sound advice for researchers, it is not helpful – as this book shows in much detail – for judges who need to decide a case on the basis of customary law or administrators who need to recognize customary rights to land. Seidel (Chapter 5, this volume) points to the inevitability of appellate bodies applying different law or being left to second-guess the interpretation and application of (lived) customary law. Resulting from the need of administrators, judges and legislators, over the years, several 'recording devices' have been developed to assist external users of customary law in understanding its content, viz. codifications and restatements.[1] These devices have met with various objections.[2]

A first objection follows from the diversity of customary law. Most African countries have so many variations in customary law, both within and between communities, that it will be nearly impossible to record them all. Attempts to somehow record one unified customary law, consisting of the main shared norms or of norms of the largest population group, would lead to grave problems of legitimacy and acceptability, and might be ignored by all those groups who do not recognize the new customary norms as their own. Tanzania in the 1960s more or less adopted the customary law practiced by a majority group to the exclusion of others. In practice, the groups whose customary laws were not represented in the codified version largely ignored the new law and continued to follow their own customary norms in their dealings with each other (Cotran 1962; Osinbajo 1991: 265; Azinge 1991: 287). Bennett and Vermeulen (1980: 219) point out that recording devices created by outsiders will anyhow suffer from a lack of credibility and acceptability because they can be seen of an imposition by outsiders instead of a natural evolution of the system in its local environment, by the local populace.

Another objection, which also has been outlined in detail in the introduction to this volume, perceives that the fluid nature of customary law would necessarily be frozen at its current stage in any type of recording, which would hinder future developments (Shadle 1999: 416; Ajayi 1971: 124; Osinbajo 1991: 261; Pogucki 1954: 193). Even recording devices that are not binding might over time in practice be used as such, as has happened to the restatement of civil customary laws in Kenya (Shadle 1999: 430).

A last prominent criticism of these recording devices is that members of restatement panels, local experts in codification programs and other informants may not give reliable accounts of the existing customary law.

---

1 A codification lays down customary law in a binding code; a restatement leads to an authoritative non-binding instrument.
2 For a more elaborate discussion of the objections to recording devices and how this impact on a judge's task to apply customary law, see Ubink (2011b). For the analysis of the impact of a self-statement on the functioning of local customary law, see Ubink (2011a).

Informants tend to present customary law in their favour. Shadle (1999: 424) shows how in colonial Kenya, information provided by elders on expert panels led to the institution of rules that permanently favoured elders to the disadvantage of junior men and women. Even when an informant's presentation of customary law is not influenced by self-interest, corruption or ignorance, there may be other causes for a variation between the actual lived customary law and the expert's statement. Allott (1957: 248) points to a tendency to idealize the law, to present what ought to be instead of what is, and, related to that, present an earlier version of customary law while it has evolved in practice. The task of an informant to translate a flexible, negotiable norm into clear-cut rules almost inevitably leads to an invention of rules or to inaccurate statements or subjective interpretations (Verhelst 1970: 42)

More recently, self-statements have entered the scene, which can have both internal and external uses.[3] As these recordings of customary law are undertaken by the communities themselves, at a local level, they ought not be hindered by the diversity of customary law. The second and the third objection may, however, remain relevant. The exercise of recording a flexible, negotiable norm that operates as starting point for a discussion, may lead to its more rigid application. This is particularly to be expected when these self-stated rules are used by outsiders such as state court judges, administrators or legislators. While these processes are undertaken at the local level, this does not guarantee that every voice is heard. Local elites, prominently among them male elders, may be able to co-opt the process and represent their interests as customary law, to the detriment of interests and rights of less powerful groups such as women and youth. This is not to say that self-statements and the resultant reduction of flexibility are necessarily negative for the communities. Research in the Uukwambi Traditional Authority in northern Namibia shows that the recording of fixed fines for certain types of crimes and offences was regarded as a positive change by a large majority of respondents. Disputants and villagers in general felt it reduced the discretion of traditional leaders and dispute settlers and as such gave less opportunity for corruption and nepotism. Traditional leaders and dispute settlers felt penalties were regarded as more legitimate now that they were recorded and standardized, which led to higher acceptance of and compliance with the imposed sanctions (Ubink 2011a).

Operating the pluri-legal setting

In pluri-legal settings, people have to operate the complexity of state law, including recognized customary law and possibly recorded versions of

---

3   A self-statement is a recording of customary laws by the community itself. The latter terminology is borrowed from Hinz (1997). A possible internal use a self-statement can have is to unify the punishments that go with several crimes and violations (see Ubink 2011a).

customary law, and the lived customary law – which may include non-recognized parts of customary law that have strong social relevance. This provides justice seekers with a choice of normative systems and of related fora, although within the restrictions of the social, cultural and political contexts in which justice seekers operate (cf. Thomas 2017: 20–46). As legal fora compete for authority and income deriving from the provision of justice, the threat of forum shopping and the cumulative effect of litigant choice affect fora and press them to accommodate justice seekers preferences and demands (Hoekema 2004: 21–22; Merry 1988: 883). When they do not accommodate, they risk losing potential litigants. A good example of this is found in Namibia, where rape cases are in large numbers withdrawn from state courts once the guilt of the rapist has been established, because the victim's family prefers a customary solution that includes the payment of compensation (Legal Assistance Centre 2009). In Somaliland, as Hoehne (Chapter 8, this volume) outlines, most legal professionals and women's rights activists demand rape cases to be withdrawn from customary (ad hoc) courts, since according to Somali tradition, compensation would be mainly paid to the male relatives of the victim and the rapist could, according to collective responsibility, get away with literally no fine on him personally. In this way, rape is very 'cheap' which increasingly becomes a societal problem. Keebet von Benda-Beckmann details how situations of legal pluralism not only provide opportunities for justice seekers to shop for fora, but also for fora to be selective in which cases they want to hear, in order to pursue their local political ends (Benda-Beckmann 1981: 117).

The literature on forum shopping and shopping fora highlights that not only justice seekers, but also institutions and their representatives operate in this pluri-legal arena, with several normative orders and institutions interacting with and constituting each other. While this literature originally focused on legal fora, there is no need to restrict it to courts and dispute settlement institutions. One can think of lower-level state institutions and street-level bureaucrats, such as the police or land agencies tasked to recognize or protect customary land rights, but also of lawmakers who wish to build on customary justice systems, or development actors involved in rule of law building. These institutions and actors similarly actively navigate the pluri-legal setting, responding to local preferences and demands, while pursuing their political ends. Kyed (Chapter 3, this volume) writing on the police in Mozambique, highlights the paradox that the officers embrace tradition and thereby violate state law to increase the relevance of the state and establish its sovereignty. This includes the outsourcing of certain police tasks to traditional elders as well as the police recognizing parts of tradition that are illegal according to statutory laws of Mozambique, particularly witchcraft, with the aim to establish 'state police monopoly over the use of force and over defining and prosecuting crimes'. The prominence of witchcraft to the local communities makes it imperative for the police to have an answer to witchcraft accusations, and not to leave such an important field of conflict resolution exclusively to the customary realm.[4] This also comes to the fore in Leonardi's description (Chapter 4, this volume) of witchcraft cases in southern Sudan during the colonial period. She sees these cases as exposing fault lines and contradictions within legally pluralistic systems, and revealing how the state justice system in practice overcomes or circumvents legal contradictions. Leonardi shows that the solutions found by the colonial judges represent compromise and pragmatism rather than the fusion or actual commensurability of state and non-state laws. She explains this from a concern to meet popular demand for government protection from witchcraft and poisoning and to prevent extrajudicial local responses to alleged witches. This again points to a preoccupation with establishing the state's monopoly over criminal law and the use of force. Popular demand for state involvement in witchcraft cases, while a challenge, thus also presents an opportunity to establish the primacy of state justice and protection. Parallel to the Mozambican police dependency on traditional authority, Hoehne (Chapter 8, this volume) describes the strong reliance of Somaliland state officials and judges on customary law and elders, for instance for arrests of suspects and implementation of court decisions. In his opinion, however, the intensity of this reliance in Somaliland due to the weakness and low legitimacy of the state can in fact sideline the state and make it irrelevant instead of boost its relevance. As such, Hoehne perhaps shows the limits and risks of the outsourcing of state functions, in a context where state sovereignty is under severe pressure.

Besides having to operate in social fields where multiple versions of customary law exist – recognized, recorded and lived customary law – street and bush-level bureaucrats also need to realize that there are competing versions of lived customary law *within communities*. Various people and groups within communities may have different ideas about customary norms, and these ideas are expressed not only in normative, ideal statements of what the law ought to be, but also in their lived practices (Chanock 1989). This is especially so in societies where profound economic and social transformations have changed the control over labour, land and capital, and have altered the social fabric and the role of gender and age groups.[5] Zenker's chapter in this volume displays the different normative ideas and claims traditional leaders and common citizens express regarding ownership and administrative powers over land. Even where norms are clear or uncontested, they serve rather as starting points for discussions in customary dispute settlement than to be directly applied, determining the winners and losers of

---

4   There is ample literature that makes clear that courts and police in many other African countries similarly struggle to operate between a state prohibition on making witchcraft accusations and local realities of belief in witchcraft and violent local responses to alleged witches when the state does not come in. See for instance Marsland (2015), Forsyth and Eves (2015) and Allen and Reid (2015).
5   See for instance Amanor (1999, 2001), Becker (2006) and Ubink (2008c).

the dispute. Combined with the unwritten character of (lived) customary law, the mediation style of most traditional dispute settlement imbeds a high level of flexibility and negotiability in customary justice systems. Some see this as a positive aspect of these systems, opening up possibilities and access to justice for all, while others highlight the limits to negotiability and that some are in a better position to negotiate than others (Peters 2002: 46–47; Ubink 2008b: 264–265; Woodhouse 2003: 1705–1706).

Street- and bush-level bureaucrats often lack in-depth knowledge of the functioning of customary justice systems; of the various versions or contestations of norms found in lived customary law; of the negotiable, relational nature of customary justice; and of existing power relations at local levels. Whom they engage with, whom they listen to, whom they give the power to define customary norms is of critical importance. Relying on elite representatives, such as (male) traditional leaders and elders, may easily lead to a representation of customary law that serves the interests of the elite, to the detriment of other groups. Where public servants approach customary law as homogeneous and generally accepted by and acceptable to all community members, the balance of power may tilt further towards the traditional elite that is often seen as the mouthpiece of customary law.[6]

The paradox of customary law

This book makes an important contribution to the thinking on all three themes discussed above. The chapters provide in-depth country case-studies that highlight the three paradoxical moments that together constitute the paradox of customary law. Regarding the paradox of liberal statecraft, it analyses the state's stance regarding accommodation, or lack thereof, of non-state normative systems – via ignorance, awareness, recognition and rejection – and its impact not only on these systems but particularly also on the functioning, relevance and legitimacy of the state itself. The paradox of jurispathic state recognition underscores the drive to make customary law legible, workable for external actors, how this informs the thinking of state actors regarding the regulation of non-state normative orders, and how recognition, particularly when it leads to a recorded version of customary law, impacts on the nature of customary norms and processes. Lastly, the analysis of the paradox of policultural states at work examines in-depth how state actors operate within the pluri-legal setting. It asks how the official rules of the game interact with the practical norms, which together inform the game of the rules. Together, these three paradoxical moments clearly bring to the fore the ultimate paradox of customary law that state officials, in order to effectively execute their state work, need to engage with the customary

---

6 See Ubink and Rooij (2011) for a more elaborate discussion how this plays out in the field of legal development cooperation.

realm and accomplish a certain extent of cooperation with customary actors such as traditional authorities. How state officials manage to do this in practice, attempting to translate and mediate between state and customary normative orders, and thereby process this paradox, which at least in theory appears hard if not impossible to overcome, is at the heart of this volume.

References

Ajayi, F.A. 1971. The judicial development of customary law in Nigeria, in *Integration of customary and modern legal systems in Africa: a conference held at Ibadan on 24th–29th August 1964*, edited by A.N. Allott. Ile-Ife: University of Ife Press, 116–131.

Allen, T. and Reid, K. 2015. Justice at the margins: witches, poisoners, and social accountability in northern Uganda. *Medical Anthropology* 34(2), 106–123.

Allott, A.N. 1957. The judicial ascertainment of customary law in Africa. *Modern Law Review* 20, 244–263.

Amanor, K.S. 1999. *Global restructuring and land rights in Ghana forest: food chains, timber and rural livelihoods*. Uppsala: Nordiska Afrikainstitutet.

Amanor, K.S. 2001. *Land, labour and the family in southern Ghana: a critique of land policy under neo-liberalisation*. Uppsala: Nordiska Afrikainstitutet.

Azinge, E.C.J. 1991. Codification of customary law: a mission impossible?, in *Towards a restatement of customary law in Nigeria*, edited by Y. Osinbajo and A.U. Kalu. Lagos: Federal Ministry of Justice.

Becker, H. 2006. 'New things after independence': gender and traditional authorities in postcolonial Namibia. *Journal of Southern African Studies* 32(1), 29–48.

Benda-Beckmann, F. von. 1984. Law out of context: a comment on the creation of traditional law discussion. *Journal of African Law* 28(1–2), 28–33.

Benda-Beckmann, F. von. 2002. Who's afraid of legal pluralism? *The Journal of Legal Pluralism and Unofficial Law* 34(47), 37–82.

Benda-Beckmann, F. von, Benda-Beckmann, K. von and Eckert, J. 2009. Rules of law and laws of ruling: law and governance between past and future, in *Rules of law and laws of ruling: on the governance of law*, edited by F. von Benda-Beckmann, K. von Benda-Beckmann and J. Eckert. Farnham: Ashgate, 1–30.

Benda-Beckmann, K. von. 1981. Forum shopping and shopping forums: dispute processing in a Minangkabau village in West Sumatra. *The Journal of Legal Pluralism and Unofficial Law* 13(19), 117–159.

Bennett, T.W. and Vermeulen, T. 1980. Codification of customary law. *Journal of African Law* 24(2), 206–219.

Berry, S. 1997. Tomatoes, land and hearsay: property and history in Asante in the time of structural adjustment. *World Development* 25(8), 1225–1241.

Chanock, M. 1985. *Law, custom and social order. The colonial experience in Malawi and Zambia*. Cambridge: Cambridge University Press.

Chanock, M. 1989. Neither customary nor legal: African customary law in an era of family law reform. *International Journal of Law and the Family* 3, 172–187.

Claassens, A. 2005. Women, customary law and discrimination: the impact of the Communal Land Rights Act. *Acta Juridica* 2005(1), 42–81.

Corradi, G. 2012. Advancing human rights in legally plural Africa: the role of development actors in the justice sector. Dissertation, Ghent University, Belgium.

Cotran, E. 1962. Some recent developments in the Tanganyika judicial system. *Journal of African Law* 6(1), 19–28.
Ehrlich, E., Pound, R. and Ziegert, K.A. 2002. *Fundamental principles of the sociology of law*. New Brunswick, NJ: Transaction Publishers.
Forsyth, M. and Eves, R. 2015. *Talking it through. responses to sorcery and witchcraft beliefs and practices in Melanesia*. Canberra: Australian National University Press.
Griffiths, J. 1986. What is legal pluralism? *Journal of Legal Pluralism* 24, 1–55.
Himonga, C., Nhlapo, T., Maithufi, I.P., Weeks, S.M., Lesala, M. and Ndima, D. 2014. *African customary law in South Africa: post-apartheid and living law perspectives*. Cape Town: Oxford University Press.
Hinz, M.O. 1997. Law reform from within: improving the legal status of women in northern Namibia. *Journal of Legal Pluralism* 39, 69–79.
Hoekema, A.J. 2004. *Rechtspluralisme en Interlegaliteit*. Amsterdam: Vossiuspers University of Amsterdam.
Kyed, H.M. 2009. The politics of legal pluralism: state policies on legal pluralism and their local dynamics in Mozambique. *Journal of Legal Pluralism and Unofficial Law* 41(59), 87–120.
Legal Assistance Centre. 2009. *Withdrawn: why complainants withdraw rape cases in Namibia*. Windhoek: Legal Assistance Centre.
Leonardi, C., Isser, D., Moro, L. and Santschi, M. 2011. The politics of customary law ascertainment in South Sudan. *Journal of Legal Pluralism and Unofficial Law* 43(63), 109–140.
Marsland, R. 2015. Keeping magical harm invisible: public health, witchcraft and the law in Kyela, Tanzania, in *The clinic and the court: law, medicine and anthropology*, edited by T. Kelly, I. Harper and A. Khanna. Cambridge: Cambridge University Press, 27–48.
Merry, S.E. 1988. Legal pluralism. *Law and Society Review* 22(5), 869–896.
Merry, S.E. 1991. Law and colonialism (book review). *Law and Society Review* 25(4), 889–922.
Mojekwu, C.C. 1978. Law in African culture and society, in *African society, culture and politics: an introduction to African studies*, edited by C.C. Mojekwu, V.C. Uchendu and L.F van Hoey. Washington: University Press of America.
Moore, S.F. 1973. Law and social change: the semi-autonomous social field as an appropriate subject of study. *Law and Society Review* 7(4), 719–746.
Moore, S.F. 1986. *Social facts and fabrications: 'customary' law on Kilimanjaro, 1880–1980*. Cambridge: Cambridge University Press.
Oomen, B. 2005. *Chiefs in South Africa: law, power and culture in the post-apartheid era*. Oxford: James Currey.
Osinbajo, Y. 1991. Proof of customary law in non-customary courts, in *Towards a restatement of customary law in Nigeria*, edited by Y. Osinbajo and A.U. Kalu. Lagos: Federal Ministry of Justice, 255–269.
Peters, P.E. 2002. The limits of negotiability: security, equity and class formation in Africa's legal systems, in *Negotiating property in Africa*, edited by K. Juul and C. Lund. Portsmouth: Heinemann, 45–66.
Pogucki, R.J.H. 1954. A note on the codification of customary law on the Gold Coast. *Journal of African Administration* 8(4), 192–196.
Ranger, T. 1983. The invention of tradition in colonial Africa, in *The invention of tradition*, edited by E. Hobsbawm and T. Ranger. Cambridge: Cambridge University Press, 211–262.

Shadle, B.L. 1999. 'Changing traditions to meet current altering conditions': customary law, African courts and the rejection of codification in Kenya, 1930–60. *Journal of African History* 40(3), 411–431.

Thomas, M.S. 2017. *The challenge of legal pluralism: local dispute settlement and the Indian–State relationship in Ecuador*. Abingdon: Routledge.

Ubink, J.M. 2008a. *Traditional authorities in Africa: resurgence in an era of democratisation*. Leiden: Leiden University Press.

Ubink, J.M. 2008b. Negotiated or negated? The rhetoric and reality of customary tenure in an Ashanti village in Ghana. *Africa* 78(2), 264–287.

Ubink, J.M. 2008c. *In the land of the chiefs: customary law, land conflicts, and the role of the state in peri-urban Ghana*. Leiden: Leiden University Press.

Ubink, J.M. 2011a. Stating the customary: an innovative approach to the locally legitimate recording of customary law in Namibia, in *Customary justice: perspectives on legal empowerment*, edited by J.M. Ubink. Rome: International Development Law Organization, 131–150.

Ubink, J.M. 2011b. The quest for customary law in African state courts, in *The future of African customary law*, edited by J. Fenrich, P. Galizzi and T.E. Higgins. Cambridge: Cambridge University Press, 83–102.

Ubink, J.M. and Rooij, B. van. 2011. Towards customary legal empowerment: an introduction, in *Customary justice: perspectives on legal empowerment*, edited by J.M. Ubink. Rome: International Development Law Organisation, 7–27.

Verhelst, T. 1970. *Safeguarding African customary law: judicial and legislative processes for its adaptation and integration*. Occasional Papers Series. Los Angeles, CA: UCLA International Institute, James C. Coleman African Studies Center.

Weilenmann, M. 2005. The primary justice project of Malawi. an assessment of selected problem fields from a legal pluralistic viewpoint. Unpublished report commissioned by GTZ.

Woodhouse, P. 2003. African enclosures: a default mode of development. *World Development* 31(10), 1705–1720.

Index

acknowledgement of customary law 17, 22
administration. *see* state officials
Africa: land reform in 163; legal pluralism in 14, 164; liberal states in 19; policulturalism in 19
Allott, Antony N. 23, 220
Anderson, Benedict 8, 111
awareness of customary law: de facto awareness 26, 27; as normative response 5, 22, 24, 25, 27, 28, 31, 32, 223; shift from rejection to 26

Baldwin, Kate 13, 21
Banjal Diola 6
Barre, Maxamed Siyaad 185, 189
Benda-Beckmann, Keebet von 221
Bennett, C. H. A., Chief Justice of Sudan 87, 93
Benton, Lauren 15
British colonial administration. *see* Somaliland; South Africa; South Sudan; Tanzania
bureaucrats. *see* state officials
bush-level bureaucrats. *see* South Africa
Buur, Lars 9

centralism, legal. *see* legal centralism
Chanock, Martin 6, 7
chiefly authorities: in African political cultures 10, 33; chiefly families, role of. *see* 28, 32, 34, 158; colonialism and 6, 9; democracy and 12, 21; in Hybrid Political Orders (HPOs) 12; 28, 32, 34, 158; persons acknowledged as 34

choice of law. *see* private international law
Cigaal, Maxamed Xaaji Ibraahim 190, 191
civil servants. *see* state officials
Clements, Kevin P. 187
codification (colonial 'invention') of customary law 8, 112
Collier, Jane 2
colonialism: and chiefly authorities 6, 9; and customary law 1, 4, 5, 6, 14, 17, 18, 19, 20, 24, 26, 27, 28, 30, 32, 33, 215, 217, 220, 222; 'decentralized despotism' 10; dispossession of native peoples' land 45; and 'invention' of customary law 8, 112; law as 'cutting edge' of 7; and legal pluralism 14, 23, 87; postcolonial continuity with colonial law 105; postcolonialism. *see* postcolonialism; precolonial era. *see* precolonial era; and witchcraft accusations. *see* South Sudan; and women's rights 6
Comaroff, Jean 14, 19
Comaroff, John 14, 19
conflict of laws. *see* private international law
constitutional recognition of customary law. *see* South Sudan
Cover, Robert 18
customary authorities. *see* chiefly authorities
customary law: colonialism and 'invention' of 8, 112; constitutional recognition of. *see* South Sudan;

content and structure of current study 25; historiography of 5; introduction to 1; 'living customary law' 18; 'official customary law' 18; paradox of. *see* paradox of customary law; recognition of. *see* recognition of customary law; role in African political cultures 9; 'tradition', meaning of 8; typology of state responses to 22

Das, Veena 82
Davidson, L. S. 91
de facto responses to customary law: awareness 26, 27; ignorance 33; rejection 26
de Herdt, Tom 24
De Soto, Hernando 163
decentralization programme. *see* Guinea
decolonisation. *see* postcolonialism
deference method of legal recognition 17, 23
delegation method of legal recognition 17, 23
democracy/democratization, chiefly authorities and 12, 21
Deng, Francis M. 114, 132
Deng Xiaoping 188
Diala, Anthony 2
Didiza, Thoko 56
Dijk, Rijk van 12
Diriiye, Xuseen Aw 198, 199
dispossession of land 45
dispute settlement. *see* Tanzania
Diwan, Mohammed 87
Donge, Jan Kees van 170

Ehrlich, Eugene 213
Ekhaya, Sibuyela 50, 51, 52, 53
El Yuzbashi Negib Yunis 98
elders. *see* chiefly authorities
Elias, Norbert 142, 151
Equatoria Province. *see* South Sudan
Eriksen, Thomas Hylland 20
Ethiopia: legal pluralism in 110
Evans, Tony 25
evidence requirement in witchcraft cases 95, 105

forum shopping: and legal pluralism 164, 221; literature on 221; in Somaliland 201
French colonial administration. *see* Guinea

Galanter, Marc 16
Geschiere, Peter 80
Gilfillan, Durkje 47, 48, 49, 50, 51, 56
government officers. *see* state officials
Griffiths, John 15, 16
Guinea: chiefly families, role of 28, 32, 34, 158; continuity and change in local governance 141, 159; decentralization programme 140, 143, 159; historical precedents for local development 155; institutional development and reform 146; legal pluralism in 140; local elders 139, 146, 148, 149, 151, 159; political participation 144; responses to customary law 28, 31, 34; state officials 139, 140, 145, 150, 151, 155, 159
Guurti (House of Elders) (Somaliland) 190

Hanekom, Derek 56
Hashi, Ahmed Mohamed 193
Hinz, Manfred O. 220
historical precedents for local development in Guinea 155
Hobsbawm, Eric 115
Hoehne, Markus Virgil 29, 31, 32, 33, 215, 221, 222
Hooker, Michael Barry 15
hybrid political systems: chiefly authorities as 64; creation of 12; Hybrid Political Orders (HPOs). *see* Somaliland; and private international law 22

ignorance of customary law: de facto ignorance 33; legal centralism and 22; as normative response 5, 22, 24, 25, 26, 27, 28, 29, 31, 32, 33, 220, 223
impregnated women or girls, rejection of. *see* South Sudan

incorporation method of legal recognition 17, 23
independence. *see* postcolonialism
'invention' of customary law 8, 112
Islamic religious authorities (shari'a) in Somaliland 197

Jellinek, Georg 109
Johnson, Douglas H. 118
judgment recognition, doctrine of 16
jurispathic state: legal pluralism and 18; operation and practice of 18; paradoxical recognition of customary law 5, 19, 20, 24, 31, 34, 214, 216, 223

Kaahin, Daahir Rayaale 194
Khalil, M. I. 114
Kiir, Salva 129, 130
'killing' of law. *see* jurispathic state
Krämer, Mario 13
Kraushaar, Maren 187
Kyed, Helene 9, 26, 30, 31, 32, 33, 216, 217, 221

Lambach, Daniel 187
land disputes settlement. *see* Tanzania
land reform in Africa 163
land restitution. *see* South Africa
legal centralism: and ignorance of customary law 22; and legal pluralism 3, 4, 15, 17, 213
legal pluralism: in Africa 14, 164; 'classical' view of 15; colonialism and 14, 23, 87; conceptions of 16; and customary law 18, 87; 'deep' version of 16, 55; definition of 14, 213; discussion of 4; in Ethiopia 110; forum shopping and 164, 221; 'global' 16; governance of 215, 216; in Guinea 140; and jurispathic state 18; and legal centralism 3, 4, 15, 17; legislation in support of 69; in Mozambique 64, 68, 69; 'new' view of 15; 'non-essentialist concept of 16; and paradox of customary law 5, 31; and private international law 16; recognition of 64, 68, 110; and recognition of non-state laws 17;

social-scientific concept of 15, 16; in Somaliland 198; sovereignty and plurality in relation 84; 'state law' version of 16, 23; 'strong' versions of 15, 16, 17, 19, 214; studies in 214, 216; 'weak' versions of 16, 17, 18, 19, 23, 214
legislation in support of legal pluralism 69
Leonardi, Cherry 27, 32, 33, 216, 222
liberal states: in Africa 19; paradox of liberal statecraft 5, 19, 21, 31, 214, 216, 223; policulturalism 19; recognition of non-state laws 30
Lipsky, Michael 24, 43, 59
'living customary law' 18
local law and governance: constitutional recognition of local laws and authorities 110, 116, 131; continuity and change 141, 159; 'harmonization' of local laws with state and international laws 122; historical precedents for local development 155; hybrid local state authority 64, 83; local elders. *see* chiefly authorities; local 'microstates' within the State 82; local state authorities and chiefly authorities in relation 69; women's rights and 28, 123, 124, 130
Logan, Caroline 12
Lugard, Frederick John Dealtry Lugard, 1st Baron 10

Mabhoko, King of Ndzundza Ndebele 46
Machar, Riek 129
Maclean, Lauren M. 177
Mahlangu, Maphepha I Poni Jafta, Chief of Ndzundza Ndebele 46
Mahlangu, Maphepha II Poni Jafta, Chief of Ndzundza Ndebele 51, 52, 53
Mahlangu, Mphezulu Jack, Chief of Ndzundza Ndebele 48, 51, 52
Mahlangu, Sipho 53
Makec, John W. 121
Mamdani, Mahmood 4, 8, 10, 11, 12

Mandela, Nelson 44, 56
Matsitsi, Chief of Ndzundza Ndebele 46
Max Planck Institute for Social Anthropology 140
Mayitjha III ka Mabhoko, King of Ndzundza Ndebele 52
Mbeki, Thabo 44, 56, 57
Merry, Sally Engle 15
Michaels, Ralf 16, 17, 23
Middleton, John 99
Migdal, Joel 3
Mojekwu, Chris 217
Moore, Sally Falk 7, 218
Mozambique: chiefly authorities 26; extension of state law enforcement 72; hybrid local state authority 64, 83; legal pluralism in 64, 68, 69; local 'microstates' within the State 82; local state authorities and chiefly authorities in relation 69; non-official police resolution of non-criminal cases 73; recognition of traditional leaders 64, 66, 70, 82; responses to customary law 26, 31; state formation processes 66; state officials 64, 65, 66, 68, 69, 70, 82, 83, 221, 222; witchcraft accusations 26, 78
Muller, Nicholaas 50, 51, 52
multliculturalism. *see* policulturalism

Ndzundza Ndebele people. *see* South Africa
normative responses to customary law, typology of 22
Ntshoe, Peter 47, 49, 50, 51, 52, 56, 57, 58
Nyabela, King of Ndzundza Ndebele 46

Odgaard, Rie 180
'official customary law' 18
officials. *see* state officials
Olivier de Sardan, Jean-Pierre 24
Oluwa, Ajuko 99
Owen, Howell, Chief Justice of Sudan 93, 94, 95, 97

paradox of customary law: analytical approach to 214; appearance of 3, 4, 19, 20, 21, 31; legal pluralism and 5, 31; levels of abstraction ('moments' of paradox) 5, 214, 223; processing of. *see* state officials
paradox of liberal statecraft 5, 19, 21, 31, 214, 216, 223
paradox of policultural states at work 5, 19, 21, 214, 216, 223
paradox of recognition by jurispathic state 5, 19, 20, 24, 31, 34, 214, 216, 223
Parr, Martin Willoughby, Governor of Equatoria province (Sudan) 97, 100, 102
Pedersen, Rasmus Hundsbæk 29, 31, 32, 33, 216, 217
Pels, Peter 12
pluralism, legal. *see* legal pluralism
poisoning, accusations of. *see* South Sudan
policulturalism: in Africa 19; and paradox of customary law 19; policultural states at work 5, 19, 21, 29, 31, 214, 216, 223
Poole, Deborah 82
Popitz, Heinrich 13
Portuguese colonial administration. *see* Mozambique
postcolonialism: continuity with colonial law 105; and customary law 2, 4, 7, 9, 11, 18, 19, 20, 31, 33, 215
precolonial era: customary law in 5, 6, 7, 10
private international law: background of 4, 17; function of 16; hybrid political systems and 22; legal pluralism and 16; and recognition of non-state laws 17, 20
public servants. *see* state officials

Randeria, Shalini 60
Ranger, Terrence 7, 8
rape cases in Somaliland 196
recognition of customary law: conditional 32; forms of 31; 'jurispathic' nature of 2n2; legal

pluralism and 87; legislation in support of 29; mode of 5, 22, 23, 24, 25, 26, 27, 28, 30, 31; paradoxical recognition by jurispathic state 5, 19, 20, 24, 31, 34, 214, 216, 223; practice of 33
recognition of foreign judgments, doctrine of 16
recognition of foreign law, process of 17
recognition of legal pluralism. *see* legal pluralism
recognition of non-state laws: customary law. *see* recognition of customary law; legal pluralism and 17; private international law and 17, 20; theme of 216; ways of 17
rejection of customary law: de facto rejection 26; extent of 31; as normative response 5, 22, 24, 25, 28, 31, 33, 223; shift to awareness from 26
restitution of land. *see* South Africa
Richards, Rebecca 185, 186, 208
rights. *see* women's rights

Santos, Boaventura de Sousa 66, 82
Schlee, Günther 8
Schlichte, Klaus 3
Schroven, Anita 28, 31, 32, 34, 215
Seidel, Katrin 27, 32, 215, 217, 219
Senwana, Makhanana 54, 58
Shabangu, Simon 47, 48, 49, 50, 51, 53, 54
Shadle, Brett L. 220
shari'a authorities in Somaliland 197
Siilaanyo, Axmed Maxamuud Maxamed 194, 205, 206
Simeon, Richard 116
Snyder, Francis 5, 6
Somaliland: clan disputes 197, 201; forum shopping in 201; House of Elders (*Guurti*) 190; Hybrid Political Orders (HPOs) 29, 33, 184, 189, 195, 201, 206; Islamic religious authorities (shari'a) 197; legal pluralism in 198; local elders 184, 185, 187, 189; new state formation 206; rape cases 196; responses to customary law 29, 31, 33; state officials 187, 189, 193n15, 196, 198, 199, 200, 201, 206, 222
South Africa: bush-level bureaucrats 25, 26, 43, 45, 48, 49, 50, 51, 52, 54, 55, 57, 58; chiefly authorities 13, 25, 33, 43, 44, 45, 46, 51, 55, 58, 59; land restitution, process of 25, 33, 41, 45, 46, 55, 59; Ndzundza Ndebele people, colonial dispossession of 45; responses to customary law 25, 33; state officials 43, 59
South Sudan: chiefly authorities 27, 28; colonial and customary law in relation 89; constitution drafting process 110, 126, 131; constitutional recognition of local laws and authorities 110, 116, 131; 'cultural' approach to witchcraft murder prosecutions 91; customary law and colonial rule 112; customary law and colonial statutory recognition 113; evidence requirement in witchcraft cases 95, 105; 'harmonization' of local laws with state and international laws 122; hybrid legal systems 109; judicial institutions 117; new state formation 109; 'poisoning', accusations of 97, 103; postcolonial continuity in witchcraft prosecutions 105; rejection of impregnated women or girls 120; responses to customary law 27, 32, 33; state officials 110, 123, 222; 'unity in diversity' approach 111; witchcraft accusations 27, 33, 87, 91, 95; women's human rights and local law 28; women's right to local political participation 123, 124, 130
sovereignty and plurality in relation 84
Spear, Thomas 8
Starr, June 2
'state law pluralism'. *see* legal pluralism
state officials: bush-level bureaucrats in South Africa 25, 26, 43, 45, 48, 49, 50, 51, 52, 54, 55, 57, 58; daily work of 3; Guinea 139, 140, 145,

150, 151, 155, 159; Mozambique 64, 65, 66, 68, 69, 70, 82, 83, 221, 222; processing of paradox of customary law 2, 14, 21, 31, 215, 223; Somaliland 187, 189, 193n15, 196, 198, 199, 200, 201, 206, 222; South Africa 43, 59; South Sudan 110, 123, 222; Tanzania 166, 172

Tamanaha, Brian 16
Tanzania: chiefly authorities 175; increase in land conflicts 174; intra-ethnic land conflicts 177; 'land conflicts', meaning of 166; land disputes settlement 29, 165, 167, 170, 172, 179; land reform 165, 167, 179; local elders 166, 169, 170, 171, 172, 173, 175, 176, 177; responses to customary law 29, 31, 33; state officials 166, 172; state-backed land dispute settlement 176; village leaders' role in dispute settlement 175; women's land conflicts 166, 178
Teubner, Gunther 16
Thiik, Ambrose Riiny 111
Touré, Sékou 28, 149, 154
Tracey, D. C. 88
traditional authorities. *see* chiefly authorities
traditional law. *see* customary law
Tshabangu, Jacob 53, 54, 58

Ubink, Janine 30
United Kingdom, colonial administration. *see* Somaliland; South Africa; South Sudan; Tanzania

van Rouveroy van Nieuwaal, Adrian 12
van Vuuren, Chris J. 52

Waller, Richard D. 96
Walls, Michael 186, 190, 209
Waraabe, Cabdi 190
Weber, Max 3, 8, 13, 14
witchcraft. *see* Mozambique; South Sudan
women's rights: colonialism and 6; human rights and local law 28; land conflicts 166, 178; local political participation 123, 124, 130; poisoning, accusations of 97, 106; rape cases 196; rejection of impregnated women or girls 120
Woodman, Gordon 16, 117
World Bank Group 143, 144

Zambia, role of chiefly authorities 12
Zenker, Olaf 25, 32, 33, 44, 216, 222
Zuma, Jacob 41, 44